CLAYTON OF TOC H

Clayton of Toc H

TRESHAM LEVER

'He was a Lamp that burned and shined;
and ye were willing for a season to reioice
in his light.'

JOHN MURRAY

Printed in Great Britain by
Cox & Wyman Ltd.,
London, Fakenham and Reading.

0 7195 2426 1

TO MY WIFE

Contents

Illustrations

*The author wishes to thank the authorities at Toc H for their help in providing
the illustrations.*

Preface

When it was arranged that I should write his authorised biography Dr Clayton gave me access to the whole of his correspondence. It was unfortunate that many of the letters had been destroyed in the blitz. Nevertheless, a very large portion remained, and this has proved of great assistance in writing his life story. Without the use of those intimate and often revealing letters this account of his work would inevitably have been incomplete. To Dr Clayton himself and to many others I am grateful for help and encouragement as my work progressed.

My warm thanks are due to Her Majesty Queen Elizabeth the Queen Mother, who placed at my disposal the relative portions of her papers at Clarence House. I am also grateful to the late Sir Godfrey Thomas, formerly Private Secretary to the Prince of Wales, for making available to me His Royal Highness the Duke of Windsor's Toc H papers at Windsor Castle.

In North America many of Clayton's friends lightened my task. The late General Eisenhower received my wife and me at Gettysburg, talked to us at length of the padre, and subsequently wrote an appreciation which appears in the biography. In New York, General Cornelius W. Wickersham, formerly on General Eisenhower's staff, entertained us and gave me the benefit of his advice. In Washington the Reverend Leslie Glenn assembled a host of Clayton's admirers, to several of whom I am immensely indebted – notably Mr and Mrs Glenn; Dr Paul Moore, Coadjutor Bishop of New York; Dr Thomas H Wright, Bishop of East Carolina; and Mr Coleman Jennings of Rigg's Bank. I am also much indebted to three of Philip Clayton's Canadian admirers: the late Major General G. P. Vanier (the former Governor General of Canada); his predecessor at Government House (the late Mr Vincent Massey, C.H.); and the former Lieutenant Governor of British

Columbia (Major General G. R. Pearkes, V.C.). All of them were generous with their hospitality and gave me their unstinted assistance.

Nearer home much help was forthcoming. Archbishop Lord Fisher of Lambeth wrote an inimitable account of his recollections of Philip Clayton at Oxford; whilst four ex-A.D.C.s supplied me with entertaining accounts of their days on Tower Hill: the Bishop of Coventry (Dr Cuthbert Bardsley), the late Bishop of Zululand and Swaziland (Dr Thomas Savage), the late Father Superior of the Community of the Resurrection, Mirfield (Father John Graham), and the Archdeacon of Derby (the Venerable J. F. Richardson). The Reverend John Durham, formerly Deputy Vicar of All Hallows; Miss Marguerite J. Coulson, the padre's ex-chief private Secretary; Mr Lancelot Prideaux-Brune and his son Mr Kenneth Prideaux-Brune read and criticized the whole book: their contributions were invaluable. That great Toc H supporter, Mr Barclay Baron, gave inestimable help in the opening chapters; it was a great misfortune that death deprived me of his further assistance. Father Graham, the last survivor of those most intimately concerned in the sad events recorded in Chapter XVII, read this chapter, made a number of suggestions which I adopted, and finally approved what I had written. At his own request, he was to have read the whole book; alas, that his premature death made that impossible. The Very Reverend Lord MacLeod of Fuinary helped me on some of Toc H's post-war difficulties, Mr Frank Gillard on the re-claiming of the Old House after the German occupation, and Mr Paul Paget and Mr Cecil Thomas on the re-building of All Hallows.

Others who have assisted me in various ways include the late Sir Otto Niemeyer, Sir Francis Chichester, Dr Trevor B. Heaton, Canon F. P. Halet, Canon E. G. Bucknill, the Reverend W. E. Drury, Canon H. E. Aldridge, the Venerable Archdeacon Alexander Cory, the Reverend Douglas Legg, the Reverend the Honourable Andrew Elphinstone, Mr Will Leonard, Mr Vic Blackman, the Reverend Henry Whiteman, Bishop F. R. Barry, the Reverend H. B. Brayford, the late Reverend Henry Moss, Mr Stanley Clapham, the Reverend Ray Beck, Mr Frank Gales, Mr Donald Cockrane, and Mr Peter Le Mesurier.

Finally, my thanks are due to the late Sir John Murray for many helpful suggestions, to Mrs K. West, literary adviser to John Murray, and to my secretary, Mrs C. S. Byers, for much useful work on the typescript.

T.L.

Lessudden
St Boswells
Roxburghshire

July, 1971

In the Family Circle

'I was born in a bush.'[1]

Philip Thomas Byard Clayton was born at Maryborough, Queensland, on 12th December, 1885. His parents, Reginald Byard Buchanan Clayton and Isobel Byard Sheppard, were first cousins, and Philip was their third son, and their sixth and youngest child. Isobel, it seems, was resolved that the new baby should be a boy, for on her eldest son's tenth birthday she made this record in her Family Book: 'Dec. 11th yesterday was Jack's birthday, his 10th. He has indeed been a pleasure to his mother, I had half hoped that the 10th might have given us another son, but he lingers on the way. Reginald overheard our two boys remarking upon why all their birthdays should be in December. "Oh, I know," says Hugh. "There are young birds in all the nests now; so this, I suppose, is the season for babies of all sorts."' But if the eagerly expected child lingered it was not for long, for Isobel's next entry records his birth. 'Dec. 20th. The day after writing my last gave us another son, Dec. 12th, Saturday. I went out driving (coaching myself) coming home about 5.30. Was taken ill at 6.30 and the boy born at 9.30. Thanks be to God all well, no Doctor needed – nurse good. Boy strong and Healthy and pleasant looking – my husband and sons full of tenderness – truly my cup overflows with gladness and blessing.' Then she records lovingly an early exploit of her eldest boy. She had, it appears, expressed a strong desire to have fish for dinner; whereupon Jack went off all alone determined to gratify his mother's craving. 'Dear God,' he prayed, 'put a great fish upon my hook': and when his prayer was answered with an outsized cod, he had all his work cut out first to bring his catch into the shallows, and then to land it. This done he laboured to carry it home, until at last a dishevelled but triumphant son presented himself at his mother's bedside with the heavy cod

---

[1] P.B.C., Autobiography: *The Children's Newspaper*, 17th January, 1931.

on a stick slung over his shoulder. This was his offering to his beloved parent and his baby brother.

'In origin the Clayton family is like Sam Weller's sausage, "wropt in mystery",' wrote the subject of this biography,[1] 'our antecedents are immune from interest. Beauty and fame alike have passed us by . . .' Yet this is scarcely accurate, for the name of Clayton is not without distinction. Perhaps the best known is Sir Robert Clayton, who in the seventeenth century amassed a fortune and became Lord Mayor of London ; but whether or not he is an ancestor is uncertain, and the founder of Toc H has never troubled to enquire. 'His record is not too exemplary,' he wrote, 'and his vast wealth has never lined my pocket.' It is, however, certain that from Stuart to quite recent times the estate of Old Park, Enfield, in Middlesex, was owned by Claytons, one of whom was Nicholas Clayton, the Presbyterian divine whose father occupied the property early in the eighteenth century. The Claytons of Old Park were undoubtedly ancestors, for they inhabited the place until the boyhood of Philip Clayton's grandfather, and it was he who sold the estate early in the present century.

The Sheppards hailed from Frome in Somerset, where since the days of Queen Elizabeth I, they had been engaged in the manu-facture of broadcloth. The mills were only sold by Philip Clayton's maternal grandfather rather more than a hundred years ago. Many of the Sheppards were Dissenters, and at least one, John Sheppard, was a well-known religious writer and lay preacher in Victorian times. Most Claytons bear the name of Byard; this commemorates Sir Thomas Byard, the famous Captain first of the *Victory* and later of the *Bedford* and the *Foudroyant*, who married a Sheppard to become Clayton's great grandfather. When not at sea Byard lived at his lovely west country home, Mount Tamar, overlooking the whole of Plymouth Sound and Plymouth Hoe.

Clayton's other grandfather, the Rev. Samuel Clayton, was both parson and squire of Farnborough Rectory, near Aldershot; and there Philip's father was born in 1844. Among young Reginald

---

[1] But Sam Weller's sausage was not 'wropt in mystery'. Can Dr Clayton have confused the passage from Dickens's *Pickwick Papers* with the well-known sentence (frequently misquoted) from Thackeray's *Yellowplush Papers*: '. . . my ma wrapped up my buth in a mistry'?

Clayton's earliest recollections were of riding as a small child to London on a six-horse dray and taking three days on the journey; of watching at the age of nine the troops paraded at Aldershot before marching away to the Crimean War, and the sad return of their remnant in the following year; and of witnessing in the spring of 1860, when he was sixteen, the great prize-fight between Tom Sayers and the American Heenan, which took place just beyond the bottom of his father's park at Farnborough. It was declared a draw at the close of the thirty-seventh round after the contest had lasted for over two hours. Reginald and his three brothers, all younger than he, were among the early pupils at Marlborough College some few years after it was founded; and several of them took leading parts in the revolt against the bad food when, for three days, the boys held the school and defied all the efforts of masters and police to dislodge them.

When Reginald was about sixteen his father decided that it would be good for his sons to emigrate to Australia in response to Queen Victoria's appeal for volunteers from English country homes to colonize the great new territory of Queensland. For Reginald there was but one regret; his enforced separation from his cousin, Isobel Sheppard, who was only twelve years old. In the rectory garden, these two young people plighted their troth by the splitting of a lucky coin; and ten years were to pass before he returned to claim her for his bride.

Northern Australia in the mid-nineteenth century was a harsh land: ten years in the backwoods would make or break a man. It made Reginald Clayton. His life was adventurous, and he has in part been immortalized by Rolf Boldrewood in the guise of Captain Starlight, the bushranger, in his classic *Robbery Under Arms*. He managed a sheep station near Maryborough on the east coast, which he leased from the young state of Queensland for an annual fee of sixpence an acre. The station included Mount Morgan of which a strange tale is told. If legend can be believed, one midday in the summer of 1882 two disconsolate prospector brothers, Thomas and Edwin Morgan, halted on the thirty-mile trail to Rockhampton, and cursed the ill-success of their journey, which had already occupied several weeks. Whilst Thomas began preparing the camp, his brother wandered off down the valley. As he trudged along, he idly swung his pick and smote a dark boulder. A chip severed from the mass glinted. One angry blow had revealed auriferous rock. Edwin promptly pocketed the chip and hastened back to his brother. They returned hurriedly to Rockhampton, but not before Reginald Clayton had seen them and detected their suppressed excitement. 'Sell your shirts and buy Mount Morgan,' they shouted, 'she's made of gold!' And so it was to prove. The manager of the Queensland National Bank sent a sample for assay, and this showed gold at the rate of 3,700 ounces to the ton. It was one of the greatest gold strikes in history.

The bank manager consulted a certain William Knox D'Arcy, son of a local solicitor, and he and the Morgan brothers formed the Mount Morgan Gold Mining Company with a nominal capital of a million pounds. In four years the £1 shares increased in value seventeen-fold, and before long D'Arcy returned to England with a great fortune.

Early in the new century and after protracted and difficult negotiations, D'Arcy succeeded in obtaining from the Shah of Persia an oil concession in the north border of the Persian Gulf, and the D'Arcy Exploration Company was formed. After several years of ill-success, and after D'Arcy had lost at least a quarter of a million of his own money, he and his fellow directors cabled their agent on the spot, G. B. Reynolds, instructing him to close down forthwith, before the rest of their funds were exhausted. But Reynolds knew that the tide of unsuccess was about to turn. He was confident that he and his men were on the point of striking oil. At all costs the cable must be ignored. He therefore declared that it would be unsafe, on account of possible errors of coding, to rely on a telegram; instructions of such grave importance could only be acted upon when confirmed in writing. This, he calculated, would give a month's reprieve. Meanwhile, drilling continued feverishly.

A month's respite was just enough, for on 26th May, 1908, he could write: 'I have the honour to report that this morning at about 4 a.m. oil was struck in the No. 1 hole at a depth of 1180 feet. Particulars re. gravity and quantity of oil flowing will follow but unless I get this away at once I shall miss the post . . .' A week later oil was struck in No. 2 hole at 1010 feet, with a pressure of gas, in Reynolds's words 'entirely beyond our control'. This was the real thing. Reynolds and his men penetrated what proved to be the biggest oilfield then known to man. 'Thus', wrote Dr Clayton, 'Abadan began from Broken Hill.'[1] Nearly a quarter of a century later, he was to visit Abadan as Chaplain to the Anglo-Iranian Company.

In 1870 Reginald Clayton, then aged twenty-six, having saved a sum sufficient to enable him to marry, determined to sail for home. He accordingly went to Brisbane, where he saw alongside the wharves a small barque flying the Blue Peter from her masthead; no luxury passenger ship this, but a new iron vessel of 300 tons just come out on her maiden voyage. Hearing that she was about to sail for England with a crew of eleven, counting the cook, cabin-boy and Captain, Clayton promptly booked his passage. Next day she set sail from Brisbane, and for seven long months was lost to view. Not until 8 p.m. on 24th June, 1871, did she tie up in the West India Docks. Young Reginald without delay took the train to Fenchurch Street Station. But he was in a quandary. His father had moved from Farnborough, and he could not remember the new address; all he could recall was that 'Milland' was part of it. He consulted a porter, who after much searching of time-tables, announced that there was a 'Milan' on the Continent. This not appearing helpful, Clayton resolved to make enquiries from his old home near Liphook. Here he bade the station fly drive him to Bramshott Rectory, where he was received by a strange maid and a Vicar who was not his father. 'Sir,' said Reginald, 'my name is Clayton and I am looking for my father, a clergyman. Can you help me?'

'Indeed I can, I know your father well. He lives in the next county. My name is Capes.'[2]

Reginald Clayton has himself described what happened next. 'My eyes just then caught sight of the cabby going back down a lane two fields away. The french window was open and I rushed into the garden and gave three of the loudest "Cooey Cooey Cooeys" I ever made. All the haymakers halted on their rakes and

[1] The reader who wishes to learn the whole of this astonishing story is referred to Henry Longhurst, *Adventure in Oil*, Chapter I, from which the above facts are taken.

[2] William Wolfe Capes (1834–1914), historical scholar; rector of Bramshott, 1869–1901; Canon of Winchester, 1894–1903. Fifteen years after this incident, Canon Capes, then a Governor of St Paul's School, offered Reginald Clayton a scholarship for one of his sons. 'I thanked him and said I might accept one if my sons could not win one for themselves,' recorded the proud father, 'but as they did succeed on their own merits, I had not occasion to again refer to him.'

pitchforks and passed it along, till by signals I saw the fly was
stopped and turning back.'

So at last Reginald reached Milland Vicarage, only about three
miles away, where he 'found the old Dad rather low because on
enquiry our barque, the *Harmodeus*, was reported overdue some
weeks previously'. Parson Clayton had told his parishioners –
some 130 in all, including infants – that if he had better news he
would ring the church bell to announce to them his son's safe
return; and this he now did. As the church and vicarage stood on
top of a steep hill above the village, they could only be approached
by steps or zig-zag paths. Hence at the sound of the bell, parson
and son were greeted by the apparition of old smock-coated
villagers toiling up the steps, unmindful of the parson's words,
and with no thought of the wanderer's return. They merely
thought it was a Saint's Day. On the following Sunday, a swelter-
ing July day, a thanksgiving service was held, and the whole
village crammed into the small ancient church, with its two low
galleries reached by ladders and steps from outside. As Parson
Clayton preached his sermon, the old gallery gave way at one end
and all the occupants began sliding into a heap. 'The Dad heard
the noise, looked up and rebuked them,' recorded his son.

> As it increased he again rebuked and even threatened them
> with the village constable next Sunday, when a ploughman
> contrived to get his head out of the squash of legs and arms to
> shout out 'Please, Sir, the Gallery's gied way.' Dad just went
> straight off into the Blessing, and came and helped to disinter
> the buried and struggling mass against the Church wall. No one
> was seriously hurt in the squash. One end had given way and
> the other end still held, but the difference in the two heights
> was a good eight feet and no man could help sliding down like
> a pack of cards.

Thus Reginald Clayton was united with his family; thus he was
united with the cousin who had waited for ten long years, growing
up and schooling herself to be the careful partner of a Queensland
sheep-farmer. On 25th June, 1872, at Frome in Somerset, Reginald
and his faithful Isobel became man and wife.

On 1st September bride and bridegroom sailed in the *Royal
Dane* bound for Brisbane. At first Reginald Clayton went into

partnership with his two brothers, Ernest and Sidney, who had bought a farm on the Mary river, opposite the town of Maryborough; and the three of them were notorious for the introduction in the district of the first modern farm implements – the mowing machine, the horse rake and the threshing machine. Here Isobel gave birth to three of her children. Her first, born in 1873, was christened Isobel after her mother, but was usually called Belle. Jack was born in 1875; his brother Hugh two years later. In 1877 Reginald Clayton sold his share in the farm to his brother Ernest who was getting married; and shortly afterwards he took charge of The Alpha Sugar Plantation, only a few miles away. At Alpha a fourth child was born but May died of dysentery before her seventh birthday. A few years later the manager of the adjoining plantation of Magnolia resigned, and Reginald Clayton secured the appointment. Here in 1883 Isobel had another daughter, christened Ivy; and two years later, on Saturday, 12th December, 1885, she gave birth to her sixth and youngest child, Philip Thomas Byard Clayton, the subject of this biography.

In the previous August, Reginald's father had died at Lynton in Devon. Consequently in 1886, when the family had been in Australia for some fifteen years and Philip was only a few months old, Reginald and Isobel decided to return to England. The change in environment, thought Reginald, would be good for the whole family, and both he and Isobel were anxious to have the children educated at home. So on one of the last few days of the year they set sail for England. Reginald had amassed in Australia a small fortune sufficient for their needs, from which he had set aside some few hundred pounds for their immediate necessities. But no sooner had they reached their destination than grave news reached them from Queensland. The Claytons' cedar-built house and stockyards had been completely destroyed by fire; the manager of their station had fraudulently sold off all the cattle and breed horses; and, worst of all, torrential rains and floods had ruined countless farmers, with the result that many banks, including the one where all the Claytons' savings were deposited, had failed. Everything in Australia had been lost; nothing was left but the few hundred pounds that they had brought with them to England. At the age of forty-two, with a wife and five children to support,

Reginald Clayton found himself in grave difficulties. Only two assets remained to him: a stout heart, and a noble wife whose spirit misfortune could not break. So Reginald and Isobel Clayton began their lives afresh. Australia was done with for ever, and the husband decided that he must, as the saying is, 'go into the city'. He started an agency in London for the export and import of goods to and from Australia. His city office was at No. 88 Bishopsgate Within; 'that lovely word "Within",' wrote his son Philip many years later, 'has been abandoned since those far days when I first knew the city as a supplementary office boy, daily receiving from my father's chief clerk 6d pay in lieu of wages for errands, or 4d only on Saturday, with the whole office closed at 3 p.m. My mother used to take me to the office in the summer from West Kensington Station to the Mansion House . . .' Although this business was not unsuccessful, it was up-hill work requiring patience and courage – virtues that Reginald and Isobel Clayton possessed in full measure.

But first a home had to be found: and after some searching they settled with their family at a house in Edith Road in the suburb of Fulham. The number was 104, a figure 'I can't forget,' wrote Philip in after years, 'since it was once the number of my home in Edith Road, to which the kind Police, or the Crumpet man of those far off days, or possibly the whistling butcher's boy, would bring me back from searching for a kitten or a hedgehog who was far from tame.'[1] Near by was Fulham Palace, residence of the Bishop of London. The occupant of the See at this time was the bewhiskered, imposing, but rather fearsome Frederick Temple, destined shortly to be translated to Canterbury. The Temples had two sons, the younger of whom, Billy, was only a few years older than the youngest Clayton. These two boys struck up a friendship in those early Fulham days which was destined to last as they went on their several roads – William Temple following in his father's footsteps to the Primacy, Philip Clayton to his remarkable life of 'walking with men while walking still with God'.[2]

At first, of course, life in Edith Road was hard. Money was short and the strictest economy had to be practised. Yet the children must be educated. That might have been a formidable problem had not the solution been near at hand. Their mother,

---

[1] Clayton to E. J. Putland, 14th December, 1960.
[2] Blair Bolles, *The Big Change in Europe*, pp. 344–5.

well-read and an accomplished linguist, would teach them herself. And this she did to such good effect that when the time came for the children to go to school they were not at any disadvantage. But then Isobel Clayton was a quite exceptional woman. Though small, she was a person of dominating character. She was a practised public speaker and possessed the remarkable art of reading aloud so as to bring any book to life; and no doubt this gift was of immense help to her when teaching the children their lessons. Moreover she was a woman of great moral courage, as was once shown to special advantage when a coal strike paralysed deliveries in and around Fulham. Isobel Clayton as 'District Visitor' was responsible for the well-being of her poorer neighbours, many of whom during the bitter cold winter days were suffering cruelly from lack of fuel. Strike or no strike this was not to be tolerated. So Mrs Clayton marched briskly down to the nearest coal-yard where loaded carts stood unattended, and before the very eyes of the astonished strikers harnessed two horses to a cart, mounted the driver's seat, and skilfully drove the wagon out of the gates and down the street. She went the rounds delivering where fuel was most needed, collecting and carefully noting the money as she went. The task completed, she returned to the yard, unharnessed, rubbed down and stabled the pair. She then placed the money on the office table. That done, without so much as a glance at the now somewhat shamefaced coal-heavers who had been silent witnesses of her audacity, Isobel Clayton calmly walked home. The subject was never referred to in the family circle; but their mother's temerity was not lost upon her children.

If life in Edith Road was somewhat rigorous, it could be fun too, for the Claytons were a fond and united family. The children were split into two age groups, the elder consisting of Belle, Jack and Hugh, the younger of Ivy and Philip; and the baby, inevitably perhaps, became the pampered darling of them all. He was known as the 'Sacred Nugget'; and later, when Isobel was teaching the elder children Greek, he was named 'Pelops' (or 'Ops' for short), presumably after the mythical King who was cut to pieces and served as food to the Gods.[1] Of the elder group, Belle, it seems, was always rather the cat that walked by itself. She was a strong-minded girl, and preferred to spend her holidays with one of her

[1] Or possibly after Philip of Macedon who in 338 B.C. conquered the Pelopponese?

aunts or uncles to joining her brothers and sisters wherever they might be. Yet her return home was always heralded with joy. 'Isobel has been away in Scotland for 2 months staying with an aunt,' wrote her mother to a friend. 'She is now home and we are so glad to have her. She is very short and square but has a sweet face and manner. Jack is tall and he's grown out of his fat. The two little ones are our amusement and delight. Ivy is the good looking one of the family. . . .'[1] The two 'little ones', Ivy and Philip, usually went away with their elder brothers, Jack and Hugh, and frequently the school holidays were passed at Goodwick in Pembrokeshire. There the elder boys would fish, shoot or play cricket, whilst the younger children, called by their brothers 'The Bobrii' (plural of Bobus), were provided with long switches, with which, at the call of 'Bobrii', they were entitled to chase their elders and, if they could get near enough, to switch them as hard as they were able until they cried 'Pax!' These Welsh holidays were very popular, but the children found the long train journey irksome: so they were wont to pass the time by inventing rhymes at the various stations, such as 'Caenarvon Junction, Important Function', whereupon they would promptly descend with avidity on the food baskets. An outstanding treat was a great tea of Welsh pancakes. Heaped plates were set before each person, and once, when offered more, little Philip said plaintively, 'If you would put me out of the window and let me run round the lawn several times, I might be able to manage it.' His brothers kindly obliged. It was at Goodwick, probably in the summer of 1893, that Philip wrote about the earliest letter that can still be seen in his childish hand.

> Dear Isobel Furlong did come here yesterday [and] is going to come again today to see me about taking us to Dinas at Newport at my expense.
> We caught 60 Fish one day in the boat and what boat do you think it is? Why the old ROCKET that used to lie on the beach near the lifeboat. We have not found any strawberries in the lane this time going to Manorowen on Sunday.
> Goodbye, your loveing [*sic*]
> Philip Clayton.

[1] Mrs Clayton to Monckton, 28th May [1890].

'And what, little man, are you going to be when you grow up?'
asked a well-intentioned lady of the youngest Clayton. 'I'm going
to be a clurgaman,' was Philip's prompt reply. Even at an early
age he knew his own mind. At an equally early age he learnt to be
something of the rebel that he was throughout his life. Among the
Claytons' friends who shared these holidays in Wales was a lad
named Otto Niemeyer, some two years Philip's senior, destined
to be a Director of the Bank of England and a financial genius.
Long afterwards he recalled those far off days when he and
Philip Clayton were together in Pembrokeshire, and when the
Great Western Railway extended their line as far as Goodwick.
'We resented their approach,' wrote Sir Otto many years later,
'and took some pride in removing their wooden surveying pegs.
We also possessed an air gun, which was frequently trained to
precipitate apples in the neighbouring orchard, access to which
was (otherwise) out of bounds. So even at an early age he was
temperamentally "agin" the authorities and interested in schemes
for their discomfort.' These two boys were at school and Oxford
together and their friendship endured.

2

St Paul's and Oxford

'Time is God's patience.'[1]

When the three Clayton boys grew to school age, they were sent first to Colet Court, then as scholars to St Paul's. This great public school had been founded in 1509 by John Colet. Dean of St Paul's with part of the fortune left him four years previously by his father, Sir Henry Colet, a wealthy mercer who had been twice Lord Mayor of London. Colet Court was established some three centuries later by James Bewsher as a preparatory school for St Paul's. When the Claytons were there, St Paul's was at the height of its fame under the High Mastership of F. W. Walker. The son of an Irish hat manufacturer claiming descent from George Walker, Londonderry's famous defender in 1689, he had been High Master of Manchester Grammar School until his election to St Paul's in 1876. Walker was a genius; but he was also something of an eccentric. Moreover, he was an intensely lonely man; his wife had died long ago after barely two years of marriage and had left him with a baby son and no other relative. His deep-toned voice was harsh, his language crude. He was not given to diplomacy and found it hard to tolerate minor social distinctions. Juniors feared him, and no assistant master claimed his friendship. But if Walker was formidable, at least one junior did not stand in awe of him. 'The thing which always filled me with wonder and admiration,' wrote an old Pauline to Philip Clayton some sixty years later, 'was to see you walking solemnly at the side of the Old Man before prayers, apparently discussing the most abstract subjects as pal with pal. In the whole of my seven years at St Paul's, I never saw the like: and when I heard later of "Tubby's" failure to be awed in the presence of a Field Marshal, it did not surprise me. I felt that one who could have strolled up

[1] P.B.C., *Portsdown Hill: Earthquake Love.*

and down unconciously with the High Master of St Paul's was a match for anyone.'[1]

Yet, despite his many imperfections, Walker was undoubtedly a great High Master. The numbers in the school rose under him from little more than two hundred pupils to six hundred and fifty, Paulines achieved an inordinate number of honours both at Oxford and Cambridge, and their first classical scholarship at Balliol was won in 1887 by Richard Johnson Walker, the High Master's only son. This brilliant young man – he won the Hertford, Ireland and Craven Scholarships at Oxford – had inherited a considerable fortune from his mother, daughter of a wealthy Manchester industrialist, and was always anxious to put his money to good use. Dickie Walker, as he was invariably called, was a great friend of Philip Clayton's at St Paul's, and when his constant companion was stricken with a serious illness – the expense of which was likely to cripple his hard-pressed father – young Walker paid doctors and surgeons out of his own pocket. Other of Clayton's associates at this time were G. K. Chesterton, already spotted as a budding genius by the prescient Walker; E. C. Bentley, whose masterpiece is generally regarded as one of the finest detective stories in the English tongue; Charles Brodribb, one day to be Assistant Editor of *The Times*, who introduced him to the world of journalism and literature;[2] E. V. Rieu, whose brilliant translations of Homer and the Gospels were to delight a wide public; W. H. Stewart, destined for the Church and to become Bishop in Jerusalem; and Geoffrey Whiskard, who became a Civil Servant of special distinction.[3]

The general testimony of his school friends seems to be that Philip was already what he has been ever since, the most socially-minded of human beings with a positive genius for universal friendliness. Such a character admits of no inhibitions or self-consciousness, and he assuredly had none. Whilst most of the young men sat in the School Debating Society in the trembling hope that they would not be called upon to speak, Clayton is remembered as a pungent debater ever ready to deliver an

---

[1] F. G. Finch to Clayton, 17th November, 1960.

[2] Clayton ran for a time a school magazine in opposition to the official *Pauline*.

[3] Another boy at St Paul's at this time was the future Field Marshal Montgomery, but he was by two years Philip's junior and they were not acquainted.

extempore oration on any subject, and eager to cross swords even with the redoubtable Chesterton, who already had a reputation as a formidable controversialist. At dinners he would jump up on to his chair and give the delighted company the song beginning 'Thairson swore a feud', which he always rendered with inimitable verve and gusto.

But of his friends at school, none was closer to him than a certain Cecil Rushton, whose promising career was to be cut short by early death in the First World War. The Claytons and the Rushtons were family friends, Mrs Clayton and Mrs Rushton having known each other before either of them married; then the Claytons had emigrated to Australia, and contact had been lost until the boys Phil and Cecil had met at Colet Court. In after life Philip wrote of this friendship:

> We were at school together, were day boys, to and fro. Picture us then, two small preparatory schoolboys, unkept to the verge of infamy, each with a satchel loaded with the lower rungs of knowledge. . . . The two small consorts held their course together to catch the confluence of the tide set school-wards, not dawdling until the corner of Auriol Road was reached, whence the great face of the school clock will be seen, and the period of permissible delay assessed. . . . In school-work, later on, Cecil and I were not much together. Our sea-fronts separated on either side of that Equator which girds the sultry climes of education. Mine led me to the more temperate zone of Mediterranean lore and literature, his lay across the thirsty sands of 'stinks': but out of hours we still were one; and learned our London side by side, one fat boy and one freckled . . .[1]

Encouraged by the boys' firm friendship, the two families had come together again and soon were constant visitors at each other's homes. Miss Dorothy Rushton, Cecil's sister, well remembers her first sight of her brother's friend at a children's party given by her mother in her London house in 1893. Phil Clayton, short but broadly and powerfully built and with a very deep voice for one so young, had come with his sister Ivy. This was the forerunner of other parties, many of them quite

[1] *A Man Greatly Beloved* from *Plain Tales from Flanders*.

uproarious. There was the occasion when they all sat down to play cards, and just as Philip had begun to deal his chair gave way beneath him, and he continued to deal from a sitting position on the floor, the Rushton family too much convulsed with laughter to come to his rescue; and later at a party at the Claytons' house, one of the less appropriate guests being Bewsher, the founder of Colet Court, when they played 'Musical Chairs' the game ended with Phil and Cecil rolling on the floor in playful disputation for the last chair.

It was about this time that the Claytons settled at Beaulieu in the New Forest. The house, Little Hatchett, was built on the lines of an Australian bungalow; and as befitted a family that had been for some years in Queensland there was always a dash of Anti-podean makeshift about the life they led there. Isobel Clayton, driving herself in a pony and trap, was invariably bustling about organizing her household and her village. Her husband, with his handsome face, his thick hair and luxuriant beard that were slowly turning white, loved to act the part of full-time gardener. He would don an ancient straw hat and venerable striped trousers with a green baize apron tied firmly round with string; then he would delight to be accosted by inquisitive strangers, to whom he would touch his hat respectfully and reply to their enquiries in broadest Hampshire. Sometimes he would accept with simulated humility the small tip they pressed into his hand. Then he would disappear with his wheelbarrow and garden implements, to re-appear later, resplendent in a black velvet jacket, to preside at the head of his table.

Into this gay family life came many of the Claytons' friends. One favourite pastime of the young people was what was called 'glog hunting', that is going out by night into the great forest to search for glow-worms. One of the company, in the manner of the 'Hunting of the Snark' would ring a large bell to assemble the searchers, each of whom was provided with a length of magnesium wire to wave around in competition with the soft glow of the quarry.

Among the young people Cecil Rushton of course was a fre-quent visitor. He had gone into his father's paint firm in Plaistow, whence he was wont to come to Beaulieu in 'the remains of what had once been a car on the re-construction of which he had been busy in his spare time'. This object, dubbed 'Collapsible Charlie', Cecil would in Philip's words 'coax with white magic' into covering the one hundred miles from Plaistow to Little Hatchett. The two friends were confirmed together. Alas, all that Philip could remember Cecil saying as they parted at the close was: 'Oh! I forgot, our cat had kittens yesterday!' 'But,' he ruminated, 'perhaps, as Talleyrand averred, words are chiefly given us to conceal our state of mind. I am writing of my friend, not a tract, but truly; and would not claim for him a meditative grasp of the unseen which was not in his nature. He had beliefs, and lived them more forcibly than most of us. But church once again meant stillness, and time consumed with nothing tangible to show . . . at this stage of our friendship I was in no condition to point him skywards, for at my second year at Oxford I was myself adrift, and could hardly complain that he was riding more and more loosely at his moorings.'[1]

Philip had done well both at Colet Court and St Paul's. 'His work and conduct have pleased me all the time he has been at the school,' wrote Bewsher when he left Colet Court, 'I hope he will have a good career at St Paul's.' That hope was certainly fulfilled, though his reports revealed that French was sorely neglected, and Greek Prose and Latin Verse 'his weakest compositions'.[2] Yet he left with a recommendation by the Examiners for election to a senior Foundation Scholarship and duly went up to Exeter College, Oxford, in the summer of 1905. 'My dear Phil,' wrote the delighted vicar of St Andrew's, West Kensington, who had coached him at St Paul's, 'With all my heart I congratulate you on your success at Exeter. May this new step forwards culminate, by God's blessing, in your faithful priesthood hereafter – and may you love Oxford as [do] all her true sons.'[3]

Clayton went up to Exeter in company with a party of Paulines among whom he was clearly immensely popular. A fellow freshman, W. E. Drury,[4] recalled in after years being introduced to him by another Pauline, Alan Judd; and how Philip Clayton began to be dubbed 'Tubby Junior' in deference to his uncle, the Vicar

---

[1] *A Man Greatly Beloved* from *Plain Tales from Flanders*.
[2] R. J. Walker to Mrs Clayton, 29th July [?1904].
[3] The Rev. E. S. Hilliard to Clayton, 24th January, 1905.
[4] Later Rector of Killeshandra, Co. Cavan.

of St Mary, Magdalen, who was generally known as 'Tubby Clayton'; and was – as he was a man of colossal proportions – much more deserving of the name. It was soon apparent that P.B.C. (as he was often called) was an ideal focal point round whom young men of diverse types and interests gathered, and undergraduates from inside and outside the College would drop in to see their friend at all hours of the day and night and invariably found a warm welcome. But his geniality was not by any means the only secret of his hold on his fellows. Whilst not in any way a prig he would fearlessly and, if need be, publicly uphold the strictest moral standards. Yet he did not belong to the 'pi set' and indeed thought them sometimes a little ridiculous.

This pious set were in the habit of holding prayer meetings in each other's rooms, and on one occasion they asked Drury if they might meet in his 'sitter'. He consented; but then, his courage failing, went out before the visitors arrived. They, finding their host from home, decided after some delay to make a start without him. In the midst of their prayers a protracted hollow groan was heard coming from the 'bedder'. The visitors, hurrying in, found the sufferer (whom they assumed to be their host stricken with sudden illness) curled up under the bedclothes, writhing and moaning in apparent agony. Whereupon the pious young men promptly knelt round the bed and began to pray earnestly. However, they had scarcely started before the patient threw off sheets and blankets; and behold, Philip Clayton, fully dressed and booted, sprang out of bed roaring with laughter at their foolish antics.

When the time came for those of their year to go out of college Clayton took rooms in the town with his friends William Drury and Alan Judd and a new friend, Charles Gordon Jelf, son of a Canon of Rochester.[1] These four young men formed a very happy company – except for two things. Jelf was a devotee of Bach, and drastic measures had to be taken to keep him from the piano; and Philip Clayton acquired a bitch. This bitch, the first of a long succession of distinguished pets, was named Hephzibah ('my delight is in her'). She was a young sheep-dog who had as yet not outgrown puppyhood. No one was much concerned when she ate Mill's *Political Economy*; but when she began to chew the land-

[1] It is sad to record that Jelf was killed in October, 1915, and Judd in March, 1918

lady's ornaments that was a much more serious matter. The outraged proprietress was furious; the offender's owner incensed by her lack of compassion. So Clayton and Hephzibah took lodgings with a more sympathetic landlady who, when Hephzibah found her carnations indigestible, sat up half the night to nurse her.

Now Drury was reading Modern History, and had accordingly joined the 'Stubbs', the undergraduates' Historical Society. To one of the meetings of this austere club, when papers were read and discussed, he took his friend Clayton – and lived to regret it. For Clayton arose during the debate, and delivered a heated harangue very little concerned with the papers under discussion. He denounced contemporary society in England in no measured terms, and forecast a revolution as bloody as the French. This was not the kind of contribution from a visitor to which the 'Stubbs' was accustomed, and the outraged Chairman required poor Drury to warn his friend not to talk in future of 'red fluid' at the meetings of the Society.

But these were not by any means the only friends that Clayton made at Oxford. Indeed, he probably had more friends there than almost any of his contemporaries. Only one more, however, can be mentioned here. He was 'a sober-minded and cautious young man', also destined for the Church; his name Geoffrey Fisher, and he was in later life to reach the highest pinnacle of his profession. When Primate of All England he recorded his memories of those undergraduate days.

It is difficult to describe with any precision what I recall of Tubby Clayton from the time when we were undergraduates at Exeter College, Oxford. He was two or more years my senior, and more than that older than I was; and he was almost more of an all-pervading and all-embracing radiance of originality than a distinct person such as I could know! Though indeed he was distinctive enough, and talked and laughed himself into our lives with the same exuberance that enlivened his later years.

There were other lively spirits of his own year or thereabouts; especially I remember Andrew Caldecott, later Governor of Ceylon, who had a most nimble wit and gift for versification even then. We juniors rather admired from an outer circle the extravagances and oddities of Tubby and his friends. The extravagances and oddities were all of the most innocent nature, but very intriguing with their mixure of drollery and adventurous imagination. And Tubby seemed to have such an immense store of knowledge, not only about things other people knew about, but about strange and outlandish things too. He was, of course, astonishingly widely read, and what he knew (or bits of it) kept popping out relevantly and more often irrelevantly, but always to our enlightenment and entertainment. Though a sober-minded and cautious young man, I enjoyed it all immensely, and though I did not understand it all, I regarded it as a continuous and gorgeous display of fireworks of an imaginative and copious mind. And Tubby made it clear in a most natural and ingratiating way that the Christian religion was always in the middle of it all; making it more many-hued and exciting than I had at that time imagined possible.

I can only remember one particular scene. One day Tubby gathered up an odd assortment of us: the assortment was always odd in his company, representatives of the hunting set and the drinking set and the working set and the pious set, all swept together into an unembarrassed group, talking about or doing what Tubby led us to do. So I found myself one of this assortment carried up after Hall into his rooms, conveniently placed, if I remember rightly, over the J.C.R. which made it easy for him to meet everyone frequently as they went to or from the J.C.R. After some time, Tubby suggested that we should try table-turning; and try we did. I seem to remember that the table was a very solid one and that we all did the right things and that the table never moved, or rather never moved of its own tabular volition. But the whole thing was a splendid mixture of the spooky and the hilarious, and I left earlier than most at about 2 a.m.

And throughout all his manifestation of a rollicking spirit, and along with his Pickwickian shape, he stood among us as a kind of wise owl – made a bit owlish by his glasses, but always wise. And indeed it was his wisdom that carried us along with him most. He seemed even at his most frivolous a sage among juveniles, a very understanding senior helping to jolly along his juniors in a most acceptable spirit and without a sign of

superiority. And if that was what he was with us, it is perhaps
what he had always been with everybody – a very wise and
devoted disciple of the Lord, who knew all the tricks which
delight adolescence, and played them all with a gusto, while
always seeing far beyond them and helping the ordinary
unimaginative kind of Englishman to see beyond them too to
Christ and the Christian religion.

But if much of Clayton's life at Oxford was gay and perhaps a
little frivolous – 'I was myself adrift,' he has admitted in *A Man
Greatly Beloved*, his tribute to Cecil Rushton – both he and
Rushton were soon to find consolation in the work of the Bermondsey Mission, started by that very remarkable man, John
Stansfeld, or The Doctor as he was always called.[1] Clayton has
described modestly his work in this field. 'By this time I had
attached myself to the tail of that most Christian comet which led
far wiser men to Bermondsey. Neither *Across the Bridges* nor *A
Student in Arms* had yet been written, but the Franciscan figure of
Dr Stansfeld had passed, like the Pied Piper, through the 'Varsity'
and bidden us to the boys' club at 'Dockhead', 'Gordon' and
'Decima'. Myself, I could contribute nothing to the spirit of that
spot, and was as much out of place as an American arriving at
Oberammergau by aeroplane. But one thing Bermondsey owes
me. I took Cecil there for his first few visits.'[2] That was certainly
something; but in point of fact Clayton for some time devoted
every Thursday evening to work in the club 'with which his own
missionary spirit, trailing a cloak of delicious whimsy, was
perfectly in tune'.[3] Indeed, his and Rushton's connection with the
mission was only broken by the outbreak of war.

In a less frequented street of Oxford there existed in those days
a small barber's shop, the proprietor of which delighted in discussing politics with an abandon unknown to the 'Stubbs'. There
Philip Clayton would repair, partly to be shaved, but more
especially to enjoy heated arguments on subjects of topical
interest with the politically-minded barber. Unhappily the
man's ideas were brighter than his blades. The result was

[1] For Dr Stansfeld, see Barclay Baron, *The Doctor: the Story of John Stansfeld of
Oxford and Bermondsey*.
[2] *A Man Greatly Beloved* in *Plain Tales from Flanders*.
[3] Barclay Baron, *The Doctor*.

bloodpoisoning. When the time came for Clayton's Final Honours Examination in theology, his face was covered with boils and swellings. He was seriously ill, and it was only with the help of drugs that he struggled through those grim days. In due course, when the results were published, his brother Hugh and several of his friends accompanied him to the Examination Hall, where the lists were posted. He hardly dared hope that he had passed at all, and the absence of his name from the bottom of the list seemed to confirm his worst fears. Gradually, and almost despairingly, he raised his eyes higher, but with no reward at all until he came to the topmost group of names, and there at last his was to be found. He had been awarded a First Class.

3

Westminster and Portsea

'Life is first an owing, then a giving.'[1]

When Clayton came down from Oxford in 1909, he received an invitation from Dr Armitage Robinson, the Dean of Westminster, to become one of his 'Y.G.s', or Young Gentlemen, as he was wont to call a succession of London students whom he took to live with him in Dean's Yard. In his youth Robinson had been domestic Chaplain to the learned Dr Lightfoot, Bishop of Durham, whose custom it had been always to have some six or eight divinity students lodging with him at Auckland Castle, where they read under the guidance of the Bishop's chaplains, and obtained some experience of parochial work in Auckland and the surrounding parishes. They were treated as members of the Bishop's family and he would never receive any payment for their board or tuition. Dean Robinson followed this custom in Westminster; and among his Y.G.s before Clayton's arrival had been such men as the lovable Dr Parsons, afterwards Bishop of Hereford; C. F. G. Masterman, who became a member of Asquith's first ministry in 1908; Malden, destined to succeed Robinson as Dean of Wells; and the saintly Gore, superior of the Community of the Resurrection, Mirfield, and Bishop successively of Worcester, Birmingham and Oxford.

The title of Y.G. was said to have been the invention of Father Richard Rackham, also of the Community of the Resurrection, who had lived at the Deanery of Westminster for some years as a combination of secretary, chaplain, A.D.C. and companion all rolled into one. Rackham was a brilliant New Testament scholar and a most delightful man; unfortunately, he was a victim to chronic asthma which often laid him prostrate, but it could never bow his noble spirit or cool his warm heart. Being what he was, he was universally beloved and he seemed to love all men. But if he

[1] P.B.C., *Toc H Journal*, January, 1928.

could be said to have had a favourite, it was probably the exuberant Philip Clayton who, though constantly getting into all manner of scrapes, was generally considered the most brilliant of the Y.G.s of his day. The other young men of the time were the late Dr Douglas Bryan-Brown, a strangely silent man who subsequently spent half a lifetime as a medical missionary in China; Dr Trevor Braby Heaton, the well-known anatomist of Oxford and a fourth who was not a pronounced success and whose name, fortunately perhaps, is lost in oblivion. His offence apparently was referring to Rackham as the Shepherd of Israel in allusion to the first verse of Psalm 80, Joseph being the Dean's first name.[1] The quip was not well received and the jester did not remain long in Dean's Yard. The three survivors were promptly nicknamed by Rackham, PB, BB and TB; and after fifty years Clayton still remained PB to Dr Heaton (TB), the only man in the world, perhaps, who did not habitually call him Tubby.

The Dean himself was undoubtedly a great man. He was an extremely versatile scholar, in the Cambridge tradition of Lightfoot and Westcott; a good classic, a great theologian, and a distinguished antiquarian and medieval historian. He had an impressive voice and was a magnificent preacher. His outward appearance was somewhat formidable, with his tall, ascetic figure, flowing grey locks, massive rock-hewn features – rather like an elderly Savonarola – and an expression of rapt impassivity. Perhaps he was a shade proud, possibly a trifle vain; but there was ample excuse for complacency, for he was only in middle age and at the height of his powers, with the reputation of being one of the very few outstanding men in the Church of England of his time.[2]

Life at the Deanery, according to Dr Heaton's recollection, was very pleasant. The Dean was invariably kindness itself to his young guests, who had few duties, apart from their studies, except occasionally to take some less important visitors round the Abbey and make themselves useful at the Dean's evening parties, which were usually agreeable. One day, shortly before the death of King Edward VII, the Princess of Wales (soon to be Queen Mary) came

[1] 'Give ear, O Shepherd of Israel, thou that leadest Joseph like a flock . . .'
[2] I am much indebted to Dr Trevor B. Heaton for these memories of Dr Armitage Robinson and of his days with Dr Clayton in Dean's Yard, Westminster.

to tea, bringing with her the two young Princes, Edward (afterwards King Edward VIII and later Duke of Windsor) and Albert (afterwards King George VI). The tea was not a hilarious affair; but afterwards Clayton and Heaton were told to take the two boys over the house, and this went off with considerably more *éclat*. It was probably the first time that Philip Clayton met the two Princes, whose destinies were to prove so diverse, and whom in after years he was to know so well.

A delightful room on the first floor was set aside as a Common Room for the Y.G.s: this had a french window leading out to the leads over the cloister and the cloister roof, which was exposed to what sun there was and was a great attraction to visitors. The students were also given a key to a private door leading through the Jerusalem Chamber to the Abbey, so they naturally spent much time there and came to know and love it well. Clayton, with his flair for archaeology, became something of an authority. Comper was installing his exquisite stained glass in the windows of the nave, and Dr Heaton recalled the heated arguments between PB, BB and TB as to their merits compared with those of medieval glass. 'PB, who alone knew what he was talking about,' wrote Heaton generously, 'had little difficulty in defeating either or both of us on this and many other points; but he was never puffed up with excessive spiritual pride, nor we with undue modesty.'

One unfortunate *cause célèbre* developed during Philip Clayton's residence in Dean's Yard. When George Meredith died in May 1909, the wish was widely expressed by the press and leading men, including the King, that he should be buried in Poet's Corner. But permission was refused by the Dean on the grounds that Meredith was a declared atheist. The papers were furious and took their revenge by referring to the offender contemptuously in a parody of Wordsworth's banal line 'A Mister *Robinson*, a clergyman'.[1] His Y.G.s naturally took the Dean's part, and Clayton was particularly exasperated by the reiterated use by the press of the *cliché* 'our national Valhalla'.

All this time Clayton was supposed to be reading for Holy Orders following his First Class in theology at Oxford. In fact, most of his time was taken up in writing a learned work on the encaustic medieval tiles in the pavements of the Abbey Sanctuary,

[1] It is only fair to add that a Memorial Service for Meredith was held in the Abbey.

which had not hitherto been adequately described. With the wise encouragement of the Dean, Philip Clayton set about this work with immense enthusiasm; and when in due course the thesis was completed, he read it before the Society of Antiquaries at Burlington House. It was adjudged an oustanding performance, and resulted in the author being elected a Fellow of the Society, a remarkable tribute to a man of twenty-five. Dr Heaton, who with Bryan-Brown 'was present on the great occasion and basked in reflected glory,' wrote thus of their return to Westminster. 'I well remember coming back to the Deanery after it was over . . . to invade Rackham's bedroom, and tell him all about it; and I can still see him there, sitting up in his horrible, thick, flannel pyjamas, coughing and spluttering, his poor little thin, eager face aglow with interest and excitement and pride; while Clayton of course played down his own achievement, and merely concentrated on making fun of all the bigwigs.'

About this time the Dean went to Jumièges in Normandy. He was anxious to trace such similarities as he could detect between the great Cathedral there and the meagre surviving relics of the old Norman Abbey of Edward the Confessor at Westminster; and he took Clayton with him as well as an ex-Y.G. who was an architect. The former, with his laurels from the Society of Antiquaries still fresh upon his brow, was of course in his element. Efficient and resourceful, he took charge of everything; and, thanks very largely to his considerable archaeological knowledge and less largely to his execrable French, managed to bring a rather difficult commission to a triumphant conclusion. 'Now that Tubby is so well-known as a friend to all the world,' wrote Heaton long afterwards, 'he may perhaps be thought rather miscast as an antiquary and archaeologist; but he would certainly have made a very good one and, of course, his proclivities in this direction have been given considerable scope on Tower Hill, to the great advantage of future generations'.

But the happy family in Dean's Yard was soon to break up. In May 1910 King Edward VII died. The Dean, always something of a valetudinarian, became convinced that his health would not be equal to the responsibilities of the coming Coronation, and incontinently resigned; whereupon he was translated to the more complete tranquillity of the Deanery of Wells, where he continued to live in perfect health for more than twenty years. Poor Rackham went with Robinson to Wells; but he soon had to be transferred to a sanatorium in the Mendips, where shortly afterwards he died. Clayton was among the last to visit him. Bryan-Brown qualified as a doctor and went off to China. P.B. was made deacon in the parish church of Guildford on St Thomas's Day 1910 by Bishop Ryle, and ordained in his Cathedral exactly a year later by Neville Talbot's father who had just succeeded Ryle in the bishopric of Winchester.

But the decision to take holy orders had come only after much doubt and hesitation. When he was at Oxford, Clayton was agnostic. 'I was myself adrift,' as he himself confessed.[1] When he came down in 1908 he was still uncertain about ordination. Whilst in this state of indecision, Philip had taken a teaching post at Colet Court, his old school, and at the same time, through the kindly intervention of a fellow Old Pauline, G. K. Chesterton, had secured work as a free-lance journalist in Fleet Street. It was at this point that he had received the invitation from Dr Armitage Robinson to become a research student at the Deanery, Westminster, and so came under Richard Rackham's beneficial influence. It was Rackham who finally cured his doubts; it was Rackham who, in Clayton's own words, 'convinced him of the Call to serve society as an interpreter of Christ and His Church, to stand amid their lives and circumstances with the open Gospel and the hand of friendship; to go about and do good where one can, keeping oneself from being conformed too readily with the world of welfare, which aims at altering circumstances rather than souls. This was the only vocation known to me by personal aspiration, I dared to read it as implying that I should be ordained.[2]

Early in 1909 Canon Bernard Wilson, the Vicar of Portsea, had written to Philip's father to say he would almost certainly have a vacancy on his staff in 1910, and urging that his son should go to a good theological college first for a year's training.[3] Six months later, he wrote to Philip himself that he would be 'extremely glad if you are able to come to us next year. I think you

---

[1] See footnote 1 on p. 16.
[2] Clayton, *Siddy: Major Guy Sydenham Hoare, Mark I and Mirfield*, p. 8.
[3] Wilson to Reginald Clayton, 5th February, 1909.

would like the work and do us good.'[1] Thus encouraged, Clayton went down to Portsea for an interview with the redoubtable Wilson. This interview he has amusingly but perhaps apocryphally described. The first person he met at Portsea was the former Captain of his College Boats, also out to obtain the one vacancy. The audience with the Canon was brief, and Clayton was told that he need not stay the night. Then the other candidate, full of hope after his rival's discomfiture, entered the Vicar's study. But the rejected applicant had barely reached the hall when uproar broke out aloft. The study door flew open and the Captain of Boats came precipitately down the stairs, whilst Wilson thundered from the top, 'You dare to come here engaged to be married! You dare to try to get on my staff, knowing you're not a free man.' Then he espied Clayton. 'Come up here, you,' he roared. 'You won't be any use to us, but I'll take you on to teach him. Perhaps you'll lecture on something. That wouldn't do us any harm. You're not engaged, are you? All right, come here.'

But tragedy was to intervene. Some two months later Canon Wilson had a stroke and on 17th October he died. The new vicar was Cyril Forster Garbett, one day to be Archbishop of York; and soon after his appointment he wrote to Clayton that he welcomed 'the opportunity of carrying out any arrangements made by Canon Wilson'. He added: 'I shall want you to concentrate at first on the Parish Church Group of the C.E.M.S,[2] it will be difficult as they had a bad start. . . .'[3] So Philip Clayton began his clerical career as one of the many curates of St Mary's Church, Portsea.

But before leaving the Deanery of Wesminster, let his old friend and companion of those days Dr Heaton, pay his tribute.

In all the years since then, I have found him to alter not in the least at heart, and in other ways less than almost anyone I have known: in his twenties he was already the same jolly, fat, genial, boisterous, noisy, sentimental, impetuous, enthusiastic, warm-hearted creature that he is still. All his geese are swans, and always have been; and most of us, being geese, like him all

[1] Wilson to Clayton, 5th August [1909].
[2] Church of England Men's Society.
[3] Garbett to Clayton, n.d. and 15th November, 1910.

the better for that. Without any enemy in the world and [with] friends all over the world, with malice towards none and a smile (or rather a roar, as from some infuriated elephant) for all, he remains humble and simple and devout, and absolutely sincere. At the same time, I do not doubt that even now, in spite of all his experiences, he would admit that he owes something to that year of 1909–10, to the quiet discipline of the Deanery of Westminster, to the inspiring daily proximity of the great Abbey Church, and to the friendship and example of two such men, so great and so different, as Joseph Armitage Robinson and Richard Rackham.

The town of Portsea is modern; but the parish of St Mary, Portsea, formerly called St Mary, Kingston, is ancient. In the Middle Ages it was appropriated, together with its daughter church of St Thomas of Canterbury in Portsmouth, to the Priory of Austin Canons at Southwick, founded by Henry I. In 1538 the Priory was dissolved, and in 1544 the revenue and patronage of each parish was transferred by the Crown to Winchester College. The history of Portsea Island is of course dominated by the growth of Portsmouth, which expanded rapidly with the docks towards the end of the seventeenth and in the early eighteenth century. The town of Portsea, which arose to house the dockyard workers, had a population of over 25,000 in 1801 and 120,000 in 1881; but the surroundings of St Mary's Church, including the extensive vicarage grounds, have remained comparatively rural and 'still constitute an oasis in the midst of row upon row of little houses'. This oasis, on which Clayton wrote a scholarly article, is all that remains of medieval Kingston, for the old church in which Isambard Kingdom Brunel was baptized in 1806 and Charles Dickens in 1812, was demolished in 1843 to be replaced by a mean brick edifice which in turn was replaced by the present imposing parish church, completed in 1889.[1]

The modern parish of Portsea was virtually the creation of an exceptionally able vicar, the patriarchal Edgar Jacob, who went there in 1878 and remained until his translation to the See of

[1] *The Work of a Great Parish* (Ed. Garbett), Article I 'The Ancient Parish' by the Rev. P. T. B. Clayton, F.S.A., pp. 1–27; Smyth, *Garbett*, p. 64.

Newcastle in 1895.[1] When Jacob came to Portsea, he found the spiritual life of the parish at a very low ebb. His predecessor, Vicar Stewart, had been there for nearly fifty years and had long been quite incapable of the arduous duties of his office. The new vicar found a population of some 20,000, a tumbledown, neglected and empty church, and one curate: when he left seventeen years later the population had almost doubled, there was a magnificent new Church of St Mary (largely built through the generosity of Jacob's wealthy friend, W. H. Smith), several mission churches and twelve curates. Jacob was succeeded in 1895 by the ambitious Cosmo Gordon Lang, later to be Archbishop of Canterbury, who was followed six years later by the boisterous Bernard Wilson. Wilson worked himself to a sudden and premature death in 1909, when Garbett was appointed to succeed him.[2] This was the golden age of Portsea parish, which can be said to have started with the arrival of Edgar Jacob in 1878, and ended with the departure of Cyril Garbett in 1919. Thus when young Clayton joined Garbett's staff as a Portsea curate in 1910 he counted himself lucky to be able to work his apprenticeship under a great vicar and in a great parish.

To appreciate why Portsea was indeed a great parish, it is essential to have some impression of what was Portsea parish in those days.[3] It was, as Canon F. P. Halet explained, 'a now vanished enclave in a now vanished world'. There were fifteen curates, not one of whom would have been accepted had he been ordained and 'defiled' by a first curacy elsewhere. 'We either went there at 23 straight from the egg,' as Halet has put it, 'or we didn't go at all.' It was understood that the curates should stay for not less than four years, and most of them stayed considerably longer; that they would remain single; and that in no circumstances would they dream of ever looking seriously at any girl in the parish. Though Garbett had socialistic leanings, to him class was class and he would not for one moment countenance his curates marrying beneath them. They were all alike in that they were all

---

[1] Jacob was Bishop of Newcastle (1895–1903) and of St Albans (1903–1919). He died in 1920.

[2] *The Work of a Great Parish* (ed. Garbett) Article II 'The Modern Parish' by the Rev. C. F. Garbett, pp. 33–60; Smyth, *Garbett*, pp. 64–80.

[3] For much of what follows I am indebted to Canon F. P. Halet, Vicar of Beeston, Nottinghamshire. See also Smyth, *Garbett*, Chap. IV.

gentlemen (as the word was then understood), that they had all been to a public school (except Garbett who could never forget that he had been a grammar school boy), to either Oxford or Cambridge, and to one of the major Theological Colleges. In this last respect Clayton was a unique exception. That sort of background was quite usual for the clergy of those days, the argument being that if fifteen young men were going to live happily together in a close-knit and arduous collegiate life, it was essential that they should all speak the same language and with the same accent. But if in many ways they were all of a pattern, in other ways the curates were dissimilar. Some like Clayton were scholars; some like Edge-Partington athletes; at least one, Oswald Hunt, was a saint. They were not chosen for their achievements – Garbett once turned down double First because 'he was not the sort that would fit in' – but each was selected for some individual potential that he possessed or was thought to possess, which would, it was hoped, develop beneath the external uniformity.

A very full account of a curate's life at Portsea under the stern discipline of Cyril Garbett has been given by his biographer and by Dr Chase (afterwards Bishop of Ripon) in his contribution entitled 'The Clergy House' in *The Work of a Great Parish*. This has been admirably condensed by Canon Halet. 'There was a Celebration (Voluntary) in the Parish Church at 7.30 every morning, followed by Matins (compulsory parade) at 8.10. Breakfast was at 8.30, after which until Sext at 1.0 we were supposed to be wholly immersed in reading and writing.' The mid-day meal was the only formal one of the day, after which there was a a free hour from 1.30 to 2.30 for recreation. The account continues:

At 2.30 we went out visiting: usually house to house visiting, and we all had to keep detailed notes of every house we visited, and 2.30 meant 2.30; woe betide the man whom C.F.G. found still in the Vicarage or in the grounds at, quite litterally 2.31. . . . We came back to high tea at 6.0 p.m. and were out again at or before 7.0 either to Clubs, etc., or else for more visiting, at the only time when the men would be at home. Evensong was sung (choir boys) every night at 7.0 but nobody went to it except the curate on duty, 'the man on course' who was responsible for taking it: the rest of us either said Evensong privately or joined together, some of us, to say it in the Vicarage chapel just before high tea. At 10.0 p.m. there was cocoa and biscuits, followed by Compline at 10.15. The rest of the day was our own. . . .[1]

Preaching was severely limited to about once a month and the sermon had to be written out in full and placed on the Vicar's desk not later than Thursday evening. This was collected on Friday, and Garbett's comments – often severe but never discouraging or sarcastic – were of lasting value.

Every Monday morning the junior curates – those, that is to say, who had been less than two years at Portsea – had to hand to the Vicar a printed form, known irreverently as 'the Washing List', completed to show how each had spent every hour of every day (except for the one off-day in every seven) in the previous week. 'For the morning he will have put down what books he had been reading and what time he gave to them,' explained Bishop Chase; 'for the afternoon the time spent in visiting (a) from house to house, and (b) special cases; for the evenings the time spent (a) visiting, and (b) at clubs. By these means the Vicar was able to see that each man is dividing up his time in the proper proportions, and that he is not neglecting any part of his work. To many such a time-table may at first sight seem uncongenial; his experience shows that it's extremely useful, so much so that many keep it up after they are officially absorbed, as a check themselves; without its self-criticism they find it so easy to waste and squander their time.'[2] Such was the rigid discipline enforced upon his curates by the redoubtable Garbett.

It will be remembered that when the Vicar was writing to his prospective new curate before his arrival he told him that he would be required first of all to concentrate on the parish church group of C.E.M.S., which will be a 'difficult job'. But it was soon found that Clayton's special aptitude at this time was with young men, and characteristically, his two contributions to the volume under Garbett's editorship entitled *The Work of a Great Parish* were 'The Ancient Parish' and 'Lads and Young Men'; and in consequence most of his best work in the Parish was done for and among these.

[1] Smyth, *Garbett*, pp. 107–9.
[2] *The Work of a Great Parish*, p. 70; Smyth, *Garbett*, pp. 110–11.

A fellow curate, later Canon E. G. Bucknill, wrote:

In the work of a priest Philip Clayton was supreme: his speciality was the Genus BOY. He loved boys for their own sakes, instinctively and sincerely. . . . They flocked round him, drawn as by a magnet. He had a way of calling everyone 'Old Man', which in others might have been an affectation. In fact, it was tempting to some admirers to copy Tubby's manners; result, a mannerism which could be repellant. He gave everyone the impression of remembering them perfectly; and no doubt, through his best years, this was true. But at a Portsea Reunion I noticed he had a young man in tow whose duty it was to take names down in writing, as the master passed from one veteran of St Mary's to another. Anyhow 'he calls his own sheep by name' (St John, 10:3) was his instinct and his ideal.

'A Parish that neglects its boys', wrote Clayton in article V in *The Work of a Great Parish*, 'is like a country that fails to develop its mineral resources,' and Portsea was peculiarly rich in that special kind of material. Moreover as he reminds his readers, 'The Founder of our religion, be it said with all reverence, was a young man: and deep down in the heart of youth there is always towards true religion an answering fire.'

Most of his boys were apprentices preparing to take employment under the Admiralty in the dockyard. The dockyard schools had two faults that were 'painfully apparent': first, the education they gave was far too 'narrowly utilitarian', even English History being made an optional subject; and secondly, in all but very exceptional circumstances 'influence' was a deciding factor in promotion to the highest places. Outside the dockyard, the boys came from a diversity of trades, in most of which 'the wages are as perilously low as the hours are long and uncertain. Some firms simply exist on the exploitation of boy labour. . . .' It was from such boys to whom life is 'prematurely serious' that Clayton's club and class members were drawn. Each district had its own club with Bible Classes included; that at St Boniface Mission was named *The White Company* after Conan Doyle's novel; St Mary's Mission was *The Red Company*; and St Barnabas' *The Blue Company*. These Portsea boys' clubs certainly attracted the lads and young men of the district; and, remarkable as it may seem, the Bible Classes were larger than the clubs of which they formed a part.

'After a boy had attended the *White Company* Bible Class for a year, he was compelled to attend the Confirmation Classes, although he was left entirely free in regard to Confirmation itself, and non-communicants were not debarred from holding office in a club of which they were members.'[1] It was largely due to the genius of Philip Clayton that these clubs were made to thrive. He taught the boys and lads of Portsea to be good Christians, good citizens, good friends, good husbands: he taught them the virtue of unselfishness, of service and of faith. 'Happiness,' he said with the Apostle Paul quoting his Master, 'lies more in giving than in receiving.'[2] 'Any opportunity of service', he wrote, will secure to a boy 'those opportunities of sacrifice and self-expression that fire and fan his loyalty and enthusiasm.'[3] He certainly fired and fanned their enthusiasm for their pastor, whom they soon came to count as their friend. And lastly faith – the faith that will remove mountains, the faith that is achieved only through constant prayer. 'The great bow of life lies to your hand,' he told his young listeners. 'You, not we, must draw it, and shoot the shaft that will stay the evil genius of the world. You can grasp the bow yourself, but you cannot bend it. See, over your young grip, eager and yet impotent alone, there steals, through prayer and sacrament, the scarred Hand of the Master Bowman. Now, indeed, the great bow bends; the great cord twangs; the great shaft is sped. You can do all things – in Christ that strengtheneth you.'[4]

In the summer of 1913 this remarkable curate, whose influence on the youth of the parish was so profound, organized a fortnight's camp in the New Forest. The success of this experiment was phenomenal. Those glorious, happy summer days of long ago were still vivid fifty years later in the memory of at least one active participant in the camp. He remembered how, on his first morning immediately after breakfast, he was summoned to the parson's tent, handed saw, hammer, nails, axe and crowbar, and

[1] *The Work of a Great Parish* (ed. Garbett) Article V *Lads and Young Men* by the Rev. P. T. B. Clayton, pp. 116, 114, 117. Smyth: *Garbett*, p. 105.

[2] *Acts* XX, 35.

[3] *The Work of a Great Parish* (ed. Garbett), Article V, *Lads and Young Men*, p. 124.

[4] An Address given by the Rev. P. B. Clayton, Curate of Portsea, at a Mass Meeting for Lads at Southampton on Sunday, 28th September, 1913.

then led forth to a glade in the forest. This was to be the site for the camp's Church, and two crosses, knocked together from the silver birches that abounded, were to be set up, one on the spot where they stood, and the other about fifty yards up the glade. The work was soon completed, and the simple forest House of God came into being. 'I can still see Tubby standing there,' recalled Vic Blackman, 'head bowed, eyes closed, hands clasped in prayer. What a revelation that was to me, standing a few paces behind him. Just Tubby and I and two simple wooden crosses. No stone colossus and timbrell trusses, but massive oaks with their intertwining branches overhead and the blue sky overall. It was at this moment that I fully realized how great was the influence that this remarkable man had over me and how near we were to one another, to nature, and to the Creator of all.' On the first Sunday Garbett travelled down especially to take the early Communion Service in the forest church. By this time he had come to appreciate to the full Clayton's true worth: it is much to be regretted that he had not appreciated this earlier.

Shortly after Clayton had been put in charge of the Boys' Club, the Vicar had announced that he was coming to see the club at 7 o'clock that night. Clayton went over to the club and soon returned to report that the boys had told him that more of them would be there by 7.30, so he had altered the time. The effect on the Vicar of this announcement was electrical. Garbett stared at his curate incredulously, and then exploded, 'Have I heard you correctly? *You* have *altered* the *time*! Do you presume to alter my time-table? I suppose it has not occurred to you that I have other things to do tonight?' 'Smarting under the lash of his sarcasm', writes Garbett's biographer, 'the junior deacon went miserably out into the garden, wondering whether he had not made a terrible mistake in entering this grim and humourless profession, and whether it would not be better for him to offer his resignation without delay. Then one of the other curates, a close friend from Oxford days – Maurice Pryke, the gentle Modernist of the Clergy House – came out and walked with him in the garden and comforted him. As a result, Tubby remained on Garbett's staff until 1919, although in fact he spent the last four years of his curacy as an Army Chaplain on the Western Front.'[1] Here, too, it seems,

[1] Smyth: *Garbett*, p. 123.

he could rile his Vicar. From France he wrote through the club magazine to say that he was glad to hear that his 'old Vicar had started smoking a pipe'. Cyril Garbett found this patronizing and slightly insolent; and, if rumour does not lie, the offender received a letter reminding him that he was only loaned to the army and that he was a Portsea curate still. But, if his curate's slightly disturbing personality sometimes disconcerted the Vicar, Garbett subsequently admitted to the Rev. H. E. Aldridge, later Canon Aldridge, the curate who was perhaps closest to him, that intellectually Philip Clayton was by far his (Garbett's) superior.

Indeed, the Vicar's respectful feelings towards his subordinate soon became reflected in the other curates. A newcomer to the Clergy House would have been struck by the outstanding personalities of two of its occupants. One of these was the Vicar himself, C. F. Garbett, 6 ft. 2 ins. tall, alert, energetic, a stern disciplinarian, and obviously a man to be reckoned with; the other, a much shorter man of heavily compacted physique, about whose body, face, mouth, voice and ways there was something round, rotund. 'There was something all-embracing about him,' Canon Halet has written, 'he was obviously a big man on a short vertical scale whom you simply could not "miss" and who was no less obviously "Tubby". And it soon became evident that to all this he added a very good mind, alert, cultivated and informed, which, as a (then) fourth year incumbent of the staff he could ventilate at will.' In a few weeks the stranger would have noticed that the formidable Garbett accorded his subordinate something of a status of his own. As has been said the Portsea curates, though chosen for some personality in their own right, were one and all subject to the same rigid discipline and drilled to conform to the same pattern. Thus Edge-Partington might be 'the one curate who could tease Garbett with impunity'.[1] But he was not permitted to live, as he wished to do, in the slum district of St Faith's: he had to continue living with and like his fellows. Henry Paget Thompson, one day to become the historian of the S.P.G., might have outstanding gifts as an organizer, and did in fact organize on special occasions, yet he was just an ordinary curate of Portsea with his district and his set routine. Ralph Seacombe might early show a

[1] Smyth, *Garbett*, p. 126.

pronounced interest in mission work, yet he for his Portsea days must accept the same training and the same disciplines as the others. To these rigid rules there was one exception, P.B.C. He lived, ate and prayed with the other curates; indeed, he was the Bursar of the Clergy House and an extraordinarily efficient one too. But for the rest he was given considerable licence to go very largely his own way. His fellows kept to their schedules; but Clayton kept no hours at all. He was continually up half the night, reading, writing or talking; and many a curate kept late in the parish was thankful for the convenient ground-floor window of his bed-sitting-room after the door was closed.

This placing of Philip Clayton by Garbett to some extent apart from the others undoubtedly had its effect on his colleagues; they liked, they admired him; but maybe they were just a little in awe of him. '. . . though I was in close touch with him as a fellow curate, and living in the same Clergy House, I was not specially in touch with him,' wrote Canon Aldridge, 'I am not sure whether any of us were; he was a bit of a law unto himself and went his own way. This was, at any rate, the impression of one of his fellow curates.' Again: 'I knew Tubby well enough at Portsea, and, on and off, thereafter. . . .' Canon F. P. Halet has recorded, '. . . I have in recent years met him but very rarely, on and off, yet it is true that if we did so tomorrow it would be as old-timers, not as strangers; and his autographed portrait is amongst my household treasures. Yet we were never *friends*, in the full sense of the word as I understood it; perhaps Tubby is one of those chaps who knew too many people to have many intimates, and at Portsea he had precisely one: Alfred Llewellyn Jones, and he is no longer with us.' 'Tubby was one of 16 curates when I came to the Parish,' the Rev. Gordon Hooper noted, 'and there were other giants on the staff – the saintly Oswald Hunt, Llewellyn Jones, large, strong and musical, Edge-Partington, sportsman and humourist who worked in the slum area, H. P. Thompson, supreme organizer, specially with children, G. A. Chase, late Bishop of Ripon, L. H. Lang, later Bishop of Woolwich, etc., but so far as I remember Tubby made no great friendship though he had a holiday in Austria with Llewellyn Jones.'

Yet they all liked and admired him tremendously for his kind heart and boisterous ways; and Alex. Cory, the only junior curate,

it seems, who could stand up to Dr Garbett,[1] long remembered
his first Christmas in the parish, when he found himself almost
alone in the vicarage with no friends or relatives to take him in
over the holidays. 'What are you doing with yourself?' asked
Clayton; and when Cory told him he had nowhere to go, 'Come
along with me,' he said, and took him to his home at Beaulieu.
'I well remember the kindness of the welcome that waited me
there,' related the unexpected visitor long afterwards when he was
Archdeacon of the Isle of Wight, 'and the adventurous journey by
which we got there, going by train to Netley and then getting a
boat to row across Southampton Water, while Tubby sang sea
shanties. This was a typical act of thoughtfulness and kindness
that we learnt was part of his make-up.'

'Those of us who shared the Clergy House with Tubby knew
we had a good friend in him,' recorded Canon Aldridge, 'and
when he let himself go he could be very good fun.' And as, like
Paul of Tarsus, P.B.C. was, in spite of shortness of stature, a man
of immense physical strength, the fun could at times be strenuous.
One day, for instance, as the curates were gathering in the
parquet-floored dining-room and were laughing and joking as
they awaited the appearance of the Vicar, there was suddenly a
pause in the general babel of conversation, broken by the remark,
à propos of nothing in particular: 'Rotund – yes, that's the word!'
The speaker was H.A., as Harold Aldridge was known: the person
described was P.B.C., who had just appeared. What happened next
nobody ever quite recalled. Chairs flew in all directions, there was
a clatter of crockery, the slither of footwear on the polished floor;
and, amid shouts of laughter from the assembled curates, the
offender found himself hoisted on to Clayton's shoulders and
through the window – $11\frac{1}{2}$ stone of him – onto the grass below.

Whilst the curates of Portsea were thus disporting themselves,
terrible events were passing in France and Belgium. From the date
of the declaration of war until 21st August, the British Expeditionary Force had been transported to the Continent without the
loss of a single man or ship. Three days later the whole British
Army was fighting the battle of Mons. By that time it was abun-
dantly clear that France's famous 'Plan XVII' had completely

[1] Smyth, *Garbett*, pp. 125–6.

D

failed. Their armies on the right were retiring in some disorder; their armies of the centre and the left were in full retreat towards Paris. The British Army, cut off and beset by overwhelming odds, was in dire peril of complete destruction. Sir Winston Churchill has recorded how at 7 o'clock on the morning of 24th August he was sitting up in bed in Admiralty House working at his boxes when Lord Kitchener appeared at his door. In a flash the First Lord knew that he brought evil tidings. 'Bad news,' said Kitchener heavily, and handed a telegram to his colleague. It was from Sir John French, and stated that his troops had been engaged all day on a line roughly east and west through Mons, but that they had held their ground tenaciously. A message had come from the French General Officer commanding the 5th Army that his troops had been driven back, that Namur had fallen, and that he was taking up a line Valenciennes – Longueville – Mauberge. 'It will prove a difficult operation, if the enemy remains in contact,' commented French, and 'I think that immediate attention should be directed to the defence of Havre.' 'I did not mind it much,' recorded Churchill, 'till I got to Namur. Namur fallen! Namur taken in a single day – although a French brigade had joined the Belgians in its defence . . . If strong fortresses were to melt like wisps of vapour in a morning sun, many judgments would have to be revised . . . Where would it stop? What of the naked Channel ports – Dunkirk, Calais, Boulogne? "Fortify Havre,' said Sir John French. One day's general battle and the sanguine advance and hoped-for counter strike had been converted into "Fortify Havre". "It will be difficult to withdraw the troops if the enemy remains in contact" – a disquieting observation.'[1]

With these tragic events upon the battlefields of Europe, the days of Portsea were soon to end. The curates went out as chaplains. The irrepressible Edge-Partington was among the first to go;[2] and Clayton was sent to be in charge of St Faith, a slum area of Portsmouth, in his place. The young here were very different from those he had been dealing with at the Parish Church. 'My word, this is a tough crowd,' he remarked to his assistant, the Rev. H. J. K. Burdett, as they walked home one evening: yet, as

[1] Churchill, The World Crisis, Vol. I, pp. 265–9.
[2] Smyth, *Garbett*, p. 133. Canon Smyth is, it seems, in error in saying that he was the first.

Burdett recalled, 'that tough crowd won more rewards for gallantry than all the rest of the parish put together.' He further pondered how Clayton would have tackled them, had he had the opportunity. But that was not to be, for Philip's days at Portsea were numbered. Early in 1915 he went to France as an Army Chaplain. 'I shall miss your son very much,' wrote Garbett to Mrs Clayton. 'I was sorry to spare him even for a time, but I felt very clearly that he was the right man to ask to go in response to the Chaplain General's appeal. His work has been wonderfully blessed these four years, and he has been a help also to all of us clergy, not least to his Vicar.'[1]

So Clayton, aged thirty, went to France an unknown curate, certainly with a reputation for having a winning way with youths and young men and possibly for being something of a scholar; but that was all. Then suddenly and without warning, like Paul on the Damascus road, he came face to face with God and was told what he must do. That work, as we shall see, he so nobly accomplished that he returned from France in a few years with a name revered in every land that speaks the English tongue.

[1] Garbett to Mrs Clayton, 8th January, 1915.

4

Poperinghe

'The Old House was a home for Jesus Christ in Flanders.'[1]

Philip Clayton's first visit to France was brief. In the spring of
1915 he went out as Chaplain Fourth Class, and was on the staff
of No. 16 General Hospital, which occupied a vast hotel on the
cliffs above Le Treport overlooking the Channel. At the end of the
summer he was relieved by John Macmillan, afterwards Bishop
first of Dover and then of Guildford, and spent his short leave at
his parents' house at Beaulieu. It must have been with a sense of
relief that he in due course received orders to rejoin the B.E.F.
and he embarked at Folkestone on 10th November. 'I've never
seen the main strength of the British Expeditionary Force before,'
he wrote to his mother from on board the leave boat, 'and a most
inspiring sight it is . . . One or two of the men are tipsy, but all the
rest are sober and a bit in the dumps, like boys going back to
school. One wonders how many of them will see Folkestone
again.'[2] Two days later he reported from Montreuil that he had had
'an excellent interview' with Bishop Gwynne, the Deputy
Chaplain General. 'He is sending me, not to Guards Division, as
before arranged, but, by special request, to work under Neville
Talbot somewhere in the Ypres Salient.'[3]

Neville Talbot, a son of the well-known Bishop of Winchester
of that name, had gone out from Balliol to be Senior Chaplain to
the 6th Division. At first Bishop Gwynne intended that Neville's
old friend should be padre to 'some Buffs and Bedfords', as Philip
told his mother a shade despondently, 'but I hope, please God, to
find better work to do than mere parades and funerals.'[4] However,

[1] P.B.C., *Toc H Journal*, March 1928.

[2] Clayton to Mrs Clayton, waiting on the boat at Folkestone, Wednesday, 10th
November, 1915, 4 p.m. *Letters from Flanders*, (ed. Barclay Baron), p. 10.

[3] Clayton to Mrs Clayton, G.H.Q., Friday, 12th November, 1915, 2 p.m. *Letters
from Flanders*, p. 11.

[4] Clayton to Mrs Clayton, Chaplains' Quarters, C.O. 1st Leicesters, 6th Division,
B.E.F., 14th November, 1915, Sunday afternoon. *Letters from Flanders*, p. 13.

he was soon able to report more cheerfully about his future work. 'Possibly . . . I shall be moved back a few miles to run a kind of Church hut in a town through which many troops are continually passing. . . .'[1] and again ten days' later: 'Talbot is trying to get an empty house for me in the nearest town, where I can both live myself and start some kind of homely club for a few of the multitudes of troops who pass to and fro. I'm strongly in favour of this. . . .'[2]

And so the two friends, Neville Talbot and Philip Clayton, in their search for a suitable house came to the little town of Poperinghe, a few miles west of Ypres. The amenities of this place were not impressive: a canteen run by a Wesleyan chaplain, many *estaminets* good and not so good, and a great divisional show called 'The Fancies'. This was renowned for its singing, and for the performances of two Belgian ladies, known respectively as 'Lanoline' and 'Vaseline' – to whom two more, 'Chlorine' and 'Glycerine', were later added – 'who could neither sing nor dance, but at least added a touch of femininity' and 'provided the sole real recreation for officers and men.'[3] In the centre of this little town was the *Grande Place*, very broad but not very *grande*, with five narrow streets leading off from it. 'You could scarcely shout across the Square: you might all but shake hands across the Streets.'[4] Here the two chaplains might be seen walking side by side over the cobbled way, and a comic sight they must have been for they were so unlike in size and shape that they might well recall the figures of Barnabas and Paul, whom the wild highlanders of Lycaonia mistook respectively for Jupiter, the Majestic father of the Gods, and Mercury, the small, swift young messenger of Olympus; for the one stood six foot five without his field boots, and the other, in the telling words of Barclay Baron – Clayton's life-long friend and supporter, 'Barkis' to all his friends – 'reversing Euclid, had "breadth and thickness but no length" to speak of'.

The two Army Chaplains made their way across the big square to one of the narrow roads leading off it, the Rue de l'Hôpital.

[1] Clayton to Mrs Clayton, Wednesday night, 17th November, 1915, *Letters from Flanders,* p. 15.
[2] Clayton to Mrs Clayton, Friday afternoon, 27th November [1915], *Letters from Flanders,* p. 21.
[3] Clayton, *Tales of Talbot House,* p. 13.
[4] ibid., p. 9.

In this unimposing thoroughfare stood a great empty mansion, the property of a certain M. Coevoet Camerlynck, a wealthy brewer of the town, who was anxious to retire to more peaceful quarters in the south of France. But his eagerness to depart did nothing to blunt his business acumen. He asked a rental of 150 francs a month, and stipulated that the tenants should make the house weather-proof, which was indeed imperative as the back had been ripped open by a shell from the Pilkem Ridge direction.[1] The premises were almost dangerously close to the firing line. 'True the Boches are less than ten miles away on three sides of us, and don't let us forget it from time to time,' Philip told his mother. 'But if they shell this place, one or other of their own billets gets a return of the compliment with interest from our "heavies". So that the game is, on the whole, unprofitable from their point of view.'[2] The owner further stipulated that the tenants should extricate from a small front room a gigantic safe which, on account of its immobility, had not been taken with the furniture. 'I am very busy living with one of my battalions in billets,' Philip reported to his mother, 'and taking over a jolly house which is to be the Pusey House of the place, when we have swept it out and bunged the hole where the shell hit it.'[3] A party of Bedfords, summoned to assist, managed with some difficulty to remove the safe; and then a party of 'male housemaids' from the same quarter descended on the house in order to put it to rights within, while the London R.E.s repaired the shattered wall and roof.

It was not long before gifts were pouring in to furnish and beautify this new club for the troops. A Scottish lady sent crates of furniture and provisions. Others in Bristol, and Teddington despatched books, pictures and all manner of necessities – cooking-utensils, curtains, tablecloths, waste-paper-baskets, clocks, vases – all designed to make the place an attractive and comfortable retreat from the filth and misery of war.

At first there were some doubts as to what the club should be

[1] Furthermore, as Mr Baron has told us, this item, in spite of the German origin of the damage, figures to the tune of 2,000 francs in the bill for dilapidations presented to Talbot House at the end of its tenancy.

[2] Clayton to Mrs Clayton, Talbot House, Monday, 6th December, 9.30 a.m. *Letters from Flanders*, pp. 24–5.

[3] Clayton to Mrs Clayton, Tuesday, 30th November, 1915. *Letters from Flanders*, p. 22.

called, and the name Church House was suggested. Fortunately wiser counsels prevailed, and, on the advice of Major-General May, that bleak designation was abandoned. Finally it was decided to commemorate a sad event that had taken place that summer. In July 1915 there had suddenly been launched upon the Allies around the Château of Hooge, due east of Ypres, a devilment intended to succeed where gas had only just failed a few months previously; this was liquid fire, and it had descended for the first time in the early dawn of 30th July on a battalion of the Rifle Brigade who suddenly found themselves standing in a bath of flame. The whole company had perished in a matter of minutes. In the afternoon a futile counter-attack had been made, and in this forlorn endeavour there had fallen a young man whose life might have meant much to the post-war world. His name was Gilbert Talbot, and he was the youngest and most brilliant of the sons of the Bishop of Winchester. It had been Gilbert's ardent wish to become a great Christian statesman, and he was thought to have all the attributes needed to fulfil his ambition. 'I loved Gilbert,' Lord Balfour wrote to his parents, Bishop and Mrs Talbot, sixteen years later, 'he was always delightful to me, and I cherished the most confident hopes that if he tried he could do great things for his country. He *has* done great things – the greatest and most enviable – but not in the way I expected.'[1] A few days later his body had been recovered by his brother Neville, who with others had crawled out between the lines to retrieve it. Later they had given him burial in Sanctuary Wood, 'the most pitiful parody of a wood or a sanctuary in Europe.' Soon afterwards the grave had vanished and 'the ground resembled nothing so much as the surface of the moon under a strong telescope'. Who better to commemorate, asked General May, than this brilliant youth and good Christian? And so it was decided that the new club for the troops should be known as Talbot House after the gallant young officer who had fallen at Hooge a few months previously.

On the 15th December the House was opened without ceremony and without acclaim (as the Chaplain proudly announced to his mother).[2] In a few days the Corps Commander, Lord Cavan,

---

[1] Balfour to Mrs Talbot, October, 1931.
[2] Clayton to Mrs Clayton, Talbot House, Wednesday morning, 3.30 a.m., 15th December, 1915. *Letters from Flanders*, p. 27.

came to inspect the premises. Cavan was Clayton's cousin; his mother, daughter of a rector of Ayot St Laurence in Hertfordshire, was Philip's godmother; so general and priest were very close to one another. Soon officers and men came flocking to see the club and to experience the joys of peace and comfort which it offered amid the horrors of its surroundings. 'From each Officer we demanded five francs for board and lodgings on the Robin Hood principle of taking from the rich to give to the poor. For this sum the officers secured on arrival from the leave train at one a.m. cocoa and Oliver biscuits, or before departure at five a.m. a cold meat breakfast. The bedrooms were communal, save for the dressing-room, which we turned ambitiously into the "General's bedroom", on account of a bed with real sheets. In the rest, stretcher beds and blankets provided more facilities for sleep than a leave-goer required, or than a returning officer expected.'[1]

As far as possible the club was run on civilian principles, 'a home from home where friendships could be consecrated, and sad hearts renewed and cheered, a place of light and joy and brotherhood and peace'.[2] Thus discipline was not maintained by martial orders, but by light-hearted notices that arrested the attention and won the readers' hearts.

IF YOU ARE IN THE HABIT OF
SPITTING ON THE CARPET AT
HOME, PLEASE SPIT HERE.
THE WASTE-PAPER BASKETS ARE PURELY ORNAMENTAL.
BY ORDER.

and when a Sapper had been lending a hand at the Old House and had inadvertently taken away the Chaplain's penknife instead of his own:

IF THE SAPPER WHO HELPED ME YESTERDAY, AND LEFT HIS
PENKNIFE IN MY ROOM WILL APPLY TO ME HE WILL RECEIVE TWO
APOLOGIES –

1. AN APOLOGY FOR THE TROUBLE I AM GIVING HIM

2. THE APOLOGY FOR A KNIFE WHICH HE LEFT BEHIND.

At the top of the stairs, the following notice was displayed:

[1] Clayton, *Tales of Talbot House*, p. 28.
[2] ibid., p. 36.

NO AMY ROBSART STUNTS DOWN THESE STAIRS

and at the foot

COME UPSTAIRS AND RISK MEETING THE CHAPLAIN.

He who was sufficiently courageous was greeted by a legend over the door of the Chaplain's room which read: ALL RANK ABANDON YE WHO ENTER HERE.

In this room hilarious parties were held, officers and men mingling in unselfconscious friendliness. Naturally this free-and-easy style often produced amusing incidents. One afternoon there was a knock at the padre's door, which was then opened timidly by a middle-aged R.F.A. driver, looking for all the world as if he were in search of a five-franc note. The chaplain asked what he could do for him. 'I could only find a small Cambridge manual on palaeolithic man in the library,' came the reply. 'Have you anything less elementary?' Clayton turned to the young Oxford undergraduate from St John's College – for duration a wireless operator with the artillery – who was sitting beside him, and noticed that his own surprise was nothing to the boy's astonishment. 'Excuse me, Sir,' he blurted out, addressing the driver, 'surely I used to attend your lectures at . . . College?' 'Quite possibly,' replied the newcomer, 'mules are *still* my speciality.'

When the House opened, the staff consisted of an N.C.O. and four men of the 17th Field Ambulance; but after a few months these were replaced by guardsmen under Sergeant Godley of the Coldstreams. These too were soon changed and the staff question was a constant headache to the chaplain of Talbot House. But, in addition to the padre, there was throughout its life one member of the staff who was destined to be permanent; and it is now time that the reader should be introduced to a real old soldier who had been known to the Army off and on for more than thirty years under the official designation, No. 239, Pte. Pettifer A., 1st, the Buffs.

Private Arthur Pettifer of the Buffs when we first meet him is quite an elderly man, having enlisted as a band-boy in 1885, the year of Clayton's birth. Before the war he had been long settled with 'the missus' and 'the nibs' in South Hackney where he drove a capacious cart. 'Trust an old infantryman,' commented his employer, 'to find something in peace-time which keeps his feet off the ground!' Then at the outbreak of war he got down from his cart and rejoined the Buffs. In November they were in France and spent that winter in 'the bracing locality of "Armonteers"', reaching Ypres early in the following summer. In November 1915 Pettifer was instructed to report as batman to a new chaplain, to whom at their first interview he frankly declared his total inability to meet any domestic needs. This notwithstanding, he soon developed unique capacities in that direction. But the most remarkable capability of this remarkable man was his genius for making friends among old and young alike. To the children of Poperinghe, who greeted him joyously as he walked down every narrow street, he was a devoted companion. They it was who affectionately dubbed him 'le Général'; and as 'general' or more shortly 'Gen' he became universally known. To the poor, the needy, the distressed of the little town, he was always the good neighbour who brought succour, often at considerable risk to himself, in their times of trouble.

One dark night in March, 1918, shortly after midnight the whole of 'Pop' was awakened by a series of terrific explosions. Several heavy shells had obviously landed on the town. In a few moments Pettifer, lighted candle in hand, was standing by Clayton's bed. He was visibly shaken. 'There's a woman scream-ing somewhere, and I can't-a-bear it,' he declared. Without a moment's delay they both, with overcoats over pyjamas, rushed out into the street to find it twenty yards away blocked by debris. Cyril's Restaurant had been blown bodily into the road; and as the wreckage was showing signs of subsiding still further, they and other helpers made all haste to extricate the victims. A man, a woman and a child, the sole survivors of the eleven inmates of the house, they brought to safety. By the first grey light of early dawn the completeness of the catastrophe was revealed. Madame Cyril was rescued alive, but she died within a few hours. The decapi-tated body of her husband was recovered; his head could no-where be found until the following day, when it was discovered in the house opposite – 'blown by a grim jest of death across the narrow street and through a broken window'. It was such gruesome toil as he underwent that dreadful night that made 'le Général' so beloved of all the inhabitants of the little town that suffered so grievously from man's inhumanity to man.

It has been said that Pettifer was on the permanent staff of Talbot House. And so he was until the autumn of 1917. Then suddenly the blow fell. Drafts of men at home were being kept back, and the halt and the lame in France were being summoned to base. Among the thousands so summoned was Private Pettifer, late of the Buffs. His master made frantic efforts to recover him; but the padre, powerful in Flanders, had small influence at the base, 'where friendship was a fable', and they went unavailing. And then early one morning some months later Clayton awoke to find his faithful batman 'standing like a spirit, grave and outworn, at the bed's foot'. The 'Gen' told him that he had merely called in to see him, that he was up the line digging as best he could with a lot calling themselves Camerons, but who were really a Labour Company. He had wanted to be sent back to the Buffs, but his medical report was not sufficiently good and so he had descended to this. His master was furious when he heard his old batman's story and he took prompt and vigorous action. What happened is best described in Pettifer's own words:

I was taken away, that was September 17, 1917, from Tubby and sent to the Base to be re-classified, with a letter from 'im to 'and in, to have me sent back to 'im again. I 'anded the letter in to one of the sergeant-majors there, but whether the letter got 'anded in or not, I wasn't sent back to Tubby. So I was marked P.B. [permanent base] and put to a labour company in the Camerons, and got sent up to Dickebusch, an' I knew that if I could get down to Tubby I should be orl right.

So after some bit of trouble I managed to get a pass to go into Pop; and o' course made my way straight to Tubby. So 'e ses to me, 'Noa I've got you I'm goin' to keep you.' So I said to 'im, 'You can't do that, I'm only on a few hours' leave and I've got to go up the line working' (we were makin' a road called Warrington Road just off Hell Fire corner).

Tubby ses to me, 'You come with me and we'll go and see a doctor.' 'E took me to see a doctor in the 'oo dee Furnes', an' 'e went in first and saw this doctor, and 'e ses I'm unfit to travel. An' next day they sent a despatch rider to Tubby to say 'send Pte. Pettifer back' – Tubby sent a messenger back to say 'the doctor's orders are, he's unfit to travel' – and then my transfer from the 2nd Army to the 5th came through an' I was sent to the company; and the nex' message was 'send Private Pettifer to bring his kit away!' An' I went up and got my kit, and the Captain 'ad gone on leave that mornin', or I dessay I'd 'ave got a tickin' orf. I guess 'e knew it was a wangle.

Thus Clayton and 'the Gen' were reunited. They were never again separated for any length of time until the faithful batman's death thirty-seven years later.

OUR MATCHLESS ARMY.

5

The Upper Room

'The throne of a most Divine Master
served by most human servants.'[1]

'Welcome met me at the door, Happiness lived within, and the Peace that passeth all understanding could be found by those who sought it in the Upper Chamber.' Thus wrote Lord Cavan, the Commander of the XIV Corps, of the Old House at Poperinghe. And it is of this Upper Room that some account must now be given.

Obviously, to fulfil the requirements of the young and enthusiastic padre, Talbot House must needs have a Chapel. At the outset this was on the first floor; but after a couple of weeks or so, it was, at the suggestion of Padre Crisford of the London Rifle Brigade, transferred to the big hoploft, which was approached by a ladder from the floor below. Before the move could be completed many difficulties were raised, for practically every one who was consulted pronounced the attic wholly unsafe for the congregation of large numbers of people. 'After this', declared Clayton characteristically, 'we asked no more questions, but opened the Chapel therein without more ado!'[2]

Then the Chapel had to be equipped. In the garden they found a disused carpenter's bench, which Clayton with great intuition at once set aside as the altar for the worship of the Carpenter. 'This was our altar always, whence tens of thousands have received the Sacrament, many making their first Communion and not a few their last.'[3] The Bishop of Winchester, Neville Talbot's father, sent out some splendid old hangings, dark red and dark green, which long before had beautified the private Chapel at Southwark, of which he had previously been Bishop. These were hung so as

[1] P.B.C., *Toc H Journal*, January, 1928.
[2] Clayton, *Tales of Talbot House*, p. 68.
[3] ibid., p. 20.

to form a baldachin, beneath which on a rough dais was set the carpenter's bench, rescued from the garden. A reproduction of Perugino's 'The Crucifixion' formed the altar-piece; other gifts for the altar and sanctuary were a silver-gilt chalice with a veil of Flemish lace, two great wood candlesticks carved from old bedposts, and a frontal of green and gold worked by some nuns of Haywards Heath. These and other relics, the gifts of friends known and unknown, lent beauty and dignity to the little Chapel. No communion rail – 'that painful obsession of the modern church furnisher'[1] – was allowed to separate ministrant from recipients: and on the same principle many offers to construct a pulpit were firmly declined. A great gilt candelabrum was suspended from the loft's central beam: this, with sconces on the side walls, illumined the whole Chapel in a warm glow of light. Music for the services was at first supplied by a portable harmonium; and in Holy Week, 1916, Godfrey Gardner, organist of the Royal Philharmonic Society, then a lieutenant in the Suffolk Regiment and destined to die gallantly on the Somme in July of that year, came for a week's duty to Talbot House, and managed to extract every note possible out of the tiny instrument. 'Thus it was,' recorded the Chaplain, 'that the homely beauty of the Chapel, with its inward gift of hope and fellowship, drew many who learnt their hunger in the grimmest school which the spirit of man has yet experienced; and yet, hardened by indomitable will to withstand the brutalizing obscenities of war, softened to appraise our simple seeking after sweetness and light.'[2]

The Church in the hoploft was opened early in 1916, and soon the services were attended by large and enthusiastic congregations. '. . . They nearly brought the Chapel floor down on Sunday with their numbers,' the Chaplain proudly reported to his mother in March. 'The House is indescribably full, mostly now of six foot men, as Jonah and his lot have moved up.'[3] On Easter Day of that year, Sunday, 23rd April, there were ten Celebrations of Holy Communion from 5.30 a.m. onwards. In view of the lively state of the line, no estimate could be made of the numbers who would be

[1] Clayton, *Tales of Talbot House,* p. 70.
[2] ibid., p. 73.
[3] Clayton to Mrs Clayton, Talbot House, 10th March [1916]. *Letters from Flanders,* p. 39. The 'six-foot' men were the Guards Division and 'Jonah' was the Rev. Llewellyn Jones who had taken the place with them originally intended for Clayton.

able to attend. In the event all hopes were surpassed. 'Not only was every Celebration furnished with joyful guests, but so great was the throng, and so divergent their estimates of time, that the whole of the floor below the Chapel was full of congregations waiting to replace that already above,' he recorded. 'Single-handed as I was, I could do no more than Lift and Break and Give without pause from 5.30 until after noonday, those that were fed being about four hundred men.'[1] To at least one present on that historic occasion it meant the end of his doubts as to what his vocation should be. 'We crowded into the Upper Room to greet the Risen Christ,' wrote a young soldier called Douglas Legg. 'Many more were waiting below to kneel at the altar before the Lord Himself. Reverently, almost lovingly, the little bent figure of Tubby administered the Bread of Life and the Cup of Salvation. "This is My Body – this is My Blood." When I think back to that Easter Day I have often wondered at the supernatural strength that must have been given to Tubby on that occasion; for he showed no sign of fatigue. I like to believe that many men felt a call to Holy Orders on that wonderful Easter Morning. We were glad when we saw the Lord. Even so send I you. My decision had been made.' The young soldier of 1916 became in due course vicar of a Surrey parish; but the events of that Easter Day were still vivid in his memory half a century later. The Chaplain undergoing his herculean task conjures up the vision of the weary Moses having his arms stayed by Aaron and Hur so that Joshua might discomfit Amalek and his people with the edge of the sword.[2]

But the Chapel was used by all sorts and conditions of men, and it was not always crowded.

One summer day in 1917 a young Sapper, a carpenter by trade – Clayton could never forget that Jesus was a Carpenter – returning to his unit after suffering a slight dose of gas, entered the Old House shortly after 5 o'clock in the morning. The padre was up and surprised to see him. 'My dear Leonard, where have you come from?' 'Short hospital spell; I'm just rejoining my Company,' came the reply. 'Have you been able to receive Communion lately'? 'No.' 'Would you like to?' 'Yes.' 'Reserved Communion or would you like the full service?' 'If possible, the full service, please.'

[1] Clayton, *Tales of Talbot House*, pp. 77–8.
[2] Exodus, XVII, 10–13.

'We climbed to the Chapel', records Sapper Will Leonard, 'and he did his priestly job, from the first prayer to the Blessing, for one lone soldier. It sticks in my memory over the forty-three years since.'

Another 'lone soldier', a signaller in the Royal Artillery, came full of hate and loathing for everything that life had in store for him. But let him tell his own story:

> I knew fire, gas and water, at Ypres, Somme, Messines, Cambrai and St Quentin; once wounded and twice gassed. I had memories of battles, bombardments, blood and hate when our regiment was ordered to muddy Flanders opposite Passchendaele to face more. After months of bombardment and little progress, I had my second dose of gas from shells accurately lobbed around our observation post, and I was sent away to the rear of the line to rest awhile. During this short stay at Regimental H.Q. I visited Toc H Poperinghe, and sat glum and filled with hate for the Germans and the whole set up. I was alone and just bottled up all this something within which was nothing short of murderous! Up came a Padre, who turned out to be the Rev. P. B. Clayton. 'Come soldier', he said, 'nothing is too sour but it can be sweetened.' He sat with me awhile, and then invited me to the Upper Room and there he said a simple prayer. . . . The gassing had left my eyes blood-shot, and Tubby suggested that when 'I got safely out of this hell', I might at the Government expense go to Australia. All that he said changed a hateful heart to a grateful one and I returned to my unit that evening thinking deeply on those things revealed to me by this cheerful, spiritual, understanding Priest of Christ's Church. The outcome of all this was that in 1920 I went to Australia, entered Bendigo Theological Hostel, and thence for my finals in Ridley College, Melbourne. During my last year in the latter college Tubby Clayton visited us and I sat opposite to him at dinner; so I told him how we had previously met at Talbot House, and how filled with gratitude I was for his guidance. He humbly replied: 'Let us always remember Toc H, its anagram is To Conquer Hate.'

The one-time signaller in the Royal Artillery is the Rev. Henry Whiteman, later Rector of Marston Trussell in Leicestershire.

The chapel, Talbot House, Poperinge, during the First World War
In the garden of Talbot House, *c.* 1915

Little Talbot House, Ypres, 1917

The back of Talbot House, March 1916

Yet a third 'lone soldier' recalled many years after the marvellous influence of the Upper Room:

Thirty years ago, I was lonely and afraid, and felt that I had not a friend, until I opened the door of the Upper Room, one Sunday, because I heard singing, and I nearly closed the door again because the room was full, but someone saw me, and said 'Don't go away, come right to the front' which I did, and then I found a friend. Which has lasted till now. And I trust will go on to the end. By his persuasion I was confirmed in the Upper Room. And spent two happy days at the Old House, and in that Garden, where all was Peace in the midst of war. And when I joined my unit in B Camp at Vlamertinge, I was telling the boys of my experiences. We were among the trees then, it was a small wood. There were not many birds about in those days because of so much shell-fire. And while I was talking to these men, in the quietness of the trees, they were all amazed, and so was I, to see a bird suddenly appear, and fly straight on to my shoulder and stay there. And their eyes seemed to say, 'Surely this man is blessed' and I surely felt, I was, ever after. Because then I had no fear. No, not any more. Because I knew that it was a message from God, to say, 'Fear not, for I am with you always.' This is the truth as it happened in April 1916.[1]

Another records his visit to Talbot House and what it meant to him in the summer of 1917. This man had trekked up with his fellows from the Somme; and, knowing where the wagon lines were to be pitched, as they passed down the Rue de L'Hôpital in Poperinghe he asked the Sergeant's leave to quit the column for a visit to the Old House. The padre was out visiting the several batteries stationed near by – his parish, as he called them – but Neville Talbot showed him round and knelt with him in the Upper Room. The young soldier, Frank Gales by name, was able to attend several times more before his B/241 Battery was moved up in readiness for the assault on 31st July; and this entry in his diary tells what Clayton and his club meant to him, as it meant to countless others in those terrible days: 'It was cruel until the 4th August when in the evening we were told we were being relieved for six hours, so I made my way to the wagon-line. I was

---

[1] Written by Sergeant J. Bennett on 20th January, 1946.

determined I should spend Sunday morning at Talbot House, so I hurriedly washed and shaved and set off for Pop; reaching P.B.C. by 10.30, lorry all the way. I was made so awfully welcome – a hot bath, a complete change of clothes which I had brought with me, a lovely bed with white sheets, and up for 7.30 H.C. in the delightful chapel. Matins at 10.30 when the ever resourceful P.B.C. crammed in a Baptism Service (3 R.E.s).'

'I shall never forget a certain Service in Talbot House,' wrote Colonel Frank Worthington of the Royal Army Medical Corps to Padre Clayton shortly after the war. 'The sequel to it was the successful carrying out of a job picking up and carrying wounded which lasted some days, and appeared next door to impossible. Incidentally, I never expected to see the finish of it personally. Everything went right in the most remarkable way, and arrangements that I made when hardly able to think fitted into each other with a perfection that my brain could never have achieved. What I regarded as doomed to failure, involving many besides myself, turned out a success which amazed me. I saw many strange things during the war, but that has left a mark which I can rely on remaining. I shall never believe again that a duty is impossible. I got a bar to a D.S.O. over it, but few people would understand if I told them how I got it in Talbot House.'[1]

'How well I remember when our Division (58th London) came to Poperinghe in September 1917 to be in readiness for the Passchendaele offensive,' wrote a certain Philip Hancock to Clayton many years after the war:

> On the Sunday evening about six of us (all pals) were looking for a service somewhere and happened on Talbot House: what a wonderful home-like atmosphere the place had. We were told by some other Tommies on entering that the little room upstairs was crowded out and we should not be able to attend service. We were just on the point of turning away disappointed when we saw you making your way down the staircase packed with fellows. I can see you now and hear you singing the hymn which was being sung at the time in the Upper Room, 'Praise my Soul the King of Heaven' – and you did. 'Don't go away,

[1] Worthington to Clayton, Forward Districts, St Pol, France, 27th November, 1919. I have to thank Colonel Worthington's widow for having sent me a copy of the letter for publication.

boys, we are having a second house, there will be a second service.' So we waited and thank God we did. The memory of that quiet Sunday evening service helped us over many dreadful and difficult days which followed in that awful month of St Julien and Langemarck. Some of the boys went under, but their last days were cheered and their hearts made glad by the message of Toc H, and we talked of these things in our dug-out afterwards.

One young subaltern wrote to Clayton years later:

I don't think you ever realized what it meant to me when I ran across Toc H and how, probably unknown to yourself, you helped me to find my way back to the Carpenter's shop, where I won good shelter from the stormy blast of the many temptations which beset us youngsters over in France. From the day I met you I began to realize that I could not afford to play ducks and drakes with my soul, and it was you, dear Tubby, who pointed out in your quiet and wonderful way, not only the folly of my actions, but also showed me the Lord and Master with His Crown of Thorns regarding me with sorrow and pity. You did not even speak to me; but it was just your good example. And since then I have, thank God, played straight; and have been rewarded by the love of the best of wives, a comfortable home, and a good billet. As I go on now, my one wish, in order to try and repay God (if such a thing is possible) for His loving kindness, is for service in and through Toc H.

And here in very truth is a manifestation of Christ in Flanders. On Sunday afternoon, 19th June, 1917, a young rifleman, Basil Lawrence, sat down to write to his *fiancée*. Like many men at that terrible time he had suffered much from fear and from the almost greater fear of seeming to be afraid.

This week I have again been privileged with a view of the reality of the help of Christ at all times; on Whit Monday [May 28th] I was at Talbot House (a place I have often mentioned) and was telling the Padre there I had been unable to communicate the previous day, so after a talk he asked whether I would like a service in the Chapel. I was able to go up and have a good long quiet time for prep. and self-examination, and then made use of the privilege of Confession. I mean in the presence of a Priest. I shall never forget it in all my life. It was the most wonderful experience I had ever had because *it was the most humiliating*. The Service that followed was naturally made the more real. I have had to mention this because it affects what followed – you see we were going into serious action about which you have read this week. Before the action I spent a couple of days [on] trench garrison duty and still had that same nervous feeling which of course was noticed *as usually*. However a couple of days out of the line and then again for action. We were in the assembly trenches, and then zero moment arrived announced by two deafening explosions followed by all the guns opening. Fritz was dropping his heavies near by and we dreaded the walk across the open to get to the other trenches, but during the intervening time I got one of those wonderful visions of Christ – of His Passion and Crucifixion – of His great Love, and by just fixing my eyes on that vision of the Cross I was calmer than ever before, so much so that as I happened to be the leading man in the team I went calmly across the open and into our old front-line trench. Then – from my old critic – 'Basil, you are getting better.' What a difference it made! Of course we proceeded on 'over the bags' and on to our objective and the business went on. The night was fair considering the position we were in; but early during the following evening we were subjected to the worst bombardment I had ever been in, during which I was able to pass humorous remarks with the others. Why? Because I had had a vision of Christ with extended arms in front of us all and instead of bearing all our sins, He was bearing all the harm from the shells, and I knew they would be diverted from us – I even said to the others, 'Lads, if any drop near us they will be duds.' Sure enough, and to me it was only because of faith, two dropped on the parapet and *were duds*, otherwise we should have been 'goners'. When it got quiet one of the team said, 'Basil, did you say the usual?' I said, 'Yes of course' – while the critic came up and shook hands and I knew God had given me the victory over fear and nervousness. . . . I shall never forget it in all my life.

Poor young man. On 4th November of that year, 1917, Basil

Lawrence was killed in Flanders. Six years later the woman who was to have been his wife sent to Dr Clayton this extract from one of Basil's letters – 'a very much treasured one,' as she told him. 'He gave me permission to pass on anything he had written of his experiences when I thought it might be helpful and I can safely do so to you. This one will show you what tremendous help was given to him. . . .' May it tell others what Talbot House and its Chaplain meant to this young rifleman in France more than fifty years ago.

Then there was the strange experience of the man in the 2nd Durhams, a frequent visitor to the Old House, who later became Chief of Police in Kuala Lumpur, and was an active member of the Malayan Group of Toc H when Clayton visited the district during his world tour in 1925. He then recorded his 'little experience of Pop' in 1918. The Durhams had been given the task of retaking Elsenvoir Chateau in Scottish Wood, a necessary preliminary to an altogether bigger operation to regain Kemmel. The task was successfully completed, but only after the battalion engaged had had a bad time. Whilst they were resting however, the enemy broke through. Casualties were heavy and reinforcements urgently required. The future Police Chief knew the ground; he was the man to take the reinforcements up the line. They must arrive before daylight, or the Germans on a certain ridge would observe their positions and quickly put them out of action.

. . . After certain difficulties we reached the vital spot exactly on daybreak. It was beautifully quiet, so I carefully went forward to have a quiet look-see, when it appeared that every gun in the Salient opened out. A literal wall of shells impeded our progress. The other unfortunates in the line had to be reinforced. We could not afford to lose even a foot of ground. I just stood still for a moment and quietly asked the Elder Brother to take us through. Do you know, Tubby, I don't think I ever felt so happy or calm – that's all, just at peace. I fell in the troops, and gave the order to move off. The ――, who was a soldier before I was, said it was madness; at any other time I should have taken his advice, but on this occasion I ordered him to go behind and at all costs to keep the troops all together, and on no account to have stragglers. I knew that this was really contrary to all legitimate formation under the circumstances, but I felt impelled to give the order. We started off, I a few yards ahead, with about four hundred troops behind. The barrage seemed to increase in fury, and some good way ahead this appeared to be a wall of falling shells. I was never so calm and happy. The troops did not seem to have the wind up. We reached this hellish wall when part of it suddenly disappeared, perhaps a gap of twenty or thirty yards only; we all got through, without a scratch, and with a loss of one bicycle. When I arrived with my draft the C.O. of the little crowd of survivors appeared amazed and said something like, 'How did you bring them through that, Sonny?' I replied, 'I didn't.'[1]

That was his experience of war, following the teaching of the Old House. The recollection of those days was vivid with this man seven years later; it was, we may be sure, firmly implanted in his memory for the rest of his life.

On one occasion General Plumer was found by the padre sitting alone and thoughtfully in the Upper Room. 'A good place for rest and quiet after a particularly heavy day,' came the reply to the Chaplain's anxious query. On another, shortly before 3 o'clock one afternoon, a young soldier, a total stranger to them all, came to the Old House and asked rather diffidently if he might spend a short time in the Upper Chamber and be quiet. The padre showed him the way and asked if it would be any help if he accompanied him. Yes, the young man told him, it would. His father had died a few days before and, owing to his regiment being moved, the son had only just received the news. The funeral was taking place at 3 o'clock that very afternoon. So Clayton conducted the Burial Service with a congregation of one, at the very time that the same rites were being administered in a country churchyard in faraway England. At the conclusion of the short service, the mourning son went away with his sorrow a little assuaged.[2]

It was perhaps some such lonely soldier that Clayton had in mind when he wrote his humble lines, *In the Upper Room*:

[1] ———to Clayton, Chief Police Office, Kuala Lumpur, 10th November, 1925.
[2] Clayton to Mrs Clayton, Monday, 10th April [1916]. *Letters from Flanders*, pp. 49–50.

He might have been a gardener or a groom,
He came in shyly and he proved sincere:
Then we climbed up the ladder to the Room,
I started to interpret what was there.
'Nay, 'tis no place for talking,' the man said.
He stoopt and knelt: ashamed, I bent the knee.
The Room, eternally inhabited,
Received two men. There surely now were three.

Such humility, such sense of inadequacy, such sense of frustration, remind us of the apostle Paul and the constant feeling of failure that haunted him throughout his life. 'The good which I want to do, I fail to do'; he told the Romans, 'but what I do is the wrong which is against my will; and if what I do is against my will, clearly it is no longer I who am the agent, but sin that has its lodging in me. I discover this principle then; that when I want to do the right, only the wrong is within my reach. In my inmost self I delight in the law of God, but I perceive that there is in my bodily members a different law, fighting against the law that my reason approves and makes me a prisoner under the law that is in my members, the law of sin. Miserable creature that I am, who is there to rescue me out of this body doomed to death? God alone, through Jesus Christ, our Lord!'[1]

In May 1916, the Archbishop of Canterbury (Randall Davidson) visited France and held a series of conferences with the army chaplains; one of these was in the garden of Talbot House. Afterwards, in 'an exceedingly upper room, a long garret transformed into a chapel,' recorded the Archbishop's chaplain, he confirmed a number of men presented to him by the padre. 'That place is a place of many memories, and among them both here on earth, and beyond there must surely remain that of the old Archbishop sitting in his chair, with the lighted candles behind him as the darkness came on, and the candidates kneeling before him, whilst outside in the street there was the ceaseless rumble of troops moving up to the Salient and the intermittent sound of firing.'[2] About one hundred and fifty chaplains were at the gathering in the garden, and thirty-seven candidates were

[1] *Romans*, VII, 19–25.
[2] Bell, *Davidson*, II, p. 780.

confirmed by the Primate. 'Cantuar was perfectly delightful,' Philip told his mother, 'and as simple as a Mission preacher with them.'[1]

In March 1917 a pencilled message was found in the Upper Room. It had been left by a soldier before going up to the Salient. There is no evidence as to his identity. No one can tell whether or not he perished in those hideous days. Out of the past, therefore, speaks this unknown voice: 'Will you pray very earnestly for me that I may have strength given me to do that which is right and to make an effort to help others; not so much by what I say, but by my whole life. I have wandered away very far, but I want to put things right; and the prayers of Talbot House will mean much to me.'

Some eighteen years after the war a great public meeting was held in the Town Hall at Woolwich. It was presided over by the Mayor, and practically all the senior officials of the British Army were present. They had met to do honour to Lord Cavan, the former Corps Commander of the Salient, and now Field Marshal and Chief of the Imperial General Staff. When Cavan had been in command of the XIV Corps, he had come frequently to Talbot House for rest and peace; and now, when called upon to speak, he recalled with extreme reluctance in his voice the misery and horror of that ghastly year of 1916, *The Blood Test*, as Sir Winston Churchill has called it.[2]

Lord Cavan told his audience how in the early spring of 1916, he came away from the trenches after having spent the whole of a grim day witnessing destruction descending upon his men. As he left the line, the torrential rain, the bitter cold, and the evening Hate began to break his spirit. He had long been a stranger to despair; but as he made his way down the shell-torn road, he felt that the Salient was doomed, its fate certain. As he came to this terrible conclusion, he recalled the fate of the luckless General Sir Horace Smith-Dorrien who, demoralized by the agonies suffered by his troops from the German's first gas attack in the spring of 1915, had written to General Sir William Robertson, Chief of the Imperial General Staff, advocating a withdrawal to a point near Ypres so as to avoid further massacres. The reward for his

---

[1] Clayton to Mrs Clayton, nd. [*c.* May 20th, 1916]. *Letters from Flanders*, p. 59.
[2] Churchill, *The World Crisis*, Vol. III, Part I, Chapter II.

humanity had been immediate; the same day brought a telegram directing him to hand over his command to General Plumer. 'No reason or explanation was vouchsafed,' as the *Official History of the War* succinctly put it![1] And the ironic outcome was that, following Smith-Dorrien's retirement, Plumer was forced to carry out the very withdrawal that his predecessor had advocated.

As Lord Cavan pondered those tragic happenings of the previous year, his car came to the outskirts of Poperinghe. There a switch road, avoiding the shelled town, would take him straight back to his Corps Headquarters in Château De Lovie. Instead, he left the car, instructing the driver to take it back to Lovie and explaining that he himself would follow in due course. Buttoning his trench coat round him, he walked directly to the doors of Talbot House and entered. He was greeted by Clayton's batman, Private Pettifer, who asked Lord Cavan whether he wished to see his master. 'No,' came the General's reply, 'I have come just to try to say my prayers'; and without more ado he climbed first the stairs and then the ladder that led to the Upper Room. Here he saw one officer and three men kneeling at benches. He knelt down himself and prayed, as he had never prayed before, that Almighty God would give him comfort, self-reliance, courage, and would take away despair. He never knew how long it was before the answer came; but come it did, and he found himself, as he described it, being then upheld. At first came quiet, a sense of peace, confidence revived. He felt as if an overwhelming burden had been lifted from him and that he was free and strong once more. He rose from prayer, refreshed, renewed; knelt again to render parting thanks, descended the stairs, went out into the darkness and walked alone back to his Corps Headquarters. From that day until this meeting in Woolwich, he had made no mention of that visit to Talbot House. But now, as Chief of the Imperial General Staff, he felt that it was right and fitting that he should publicly declare that he owed the whole of his subsequent career to that one visit to the Upper Room. But for the strength then vouchsafed to him from God, his fate might have been similar to Smith-Dorrien's; he might have thrown up his command rather than lead troops committed to the hopeless task of holding the Salient; and he indignantly told his hearers that it was the politicians of Lloyd

[1] *Military Operations: France and Belgium*, 1915, p. 507.

George's Cabinet who caused the Salient to be held at all, and that it was an indefensible position.

Thus we see something of what the little chapel in the hoploft of the Old House and its Chaplain meant to the men who came to Poperinghe in the awful years of the First Great War.

6

'Slumming'

'It is historically true that the
greatest opportunities spring from
the greatest tragedies.'[1]

It must not be thought that Clayton's war-time activities were
confined within the walls of the Old House. As with St Paul the
world was ever his parish, and so it was in Flanders during the
war years. He would go, what he called 'slumming'; that is to say
visiting the troops in the surrounding areas, enquiring after their
well-being, ministering to their needs, and often under fire giving
them Communion. Thus in the late summer of 1916 he became
attached, quite unofficially and by chance, to the 141st (East Ham)
Heavy Battery, R.G.A., the headquarters of which were at Cat
Farm, near Vlamertinghe, midway between Poperinghe and
Ypres. He happened to run into Battery Quarter-Master-Sergeant
Thorpe of the 141st, a man of resource and initiative, who subsequently reported to his Commanding Officer, Colonel L. H.
Higgon, that a chaplain he had met had asked whether a service
was ever held in the Battery. The B.Q.M.S. had been obliged to
say no; whereupon the chaplain had announced that, if the C.O.
would give his permission, he would hold a service in rear of the
guns at 3 p.m. the following Sunday. Colonel Higgon readily
agreed; and as there was not much firing that day, a fairly large
congregation was assembled to greet the unknown chaplain. At
first no chaplain appeared; then, at last, after a long and tedious
wait on a very hot August afternoon, they saw coming through
the long grass a sweating and rotund figure, laden with gas-mask,
bags of hymn-books, and other impedimenta; followed at some
distance by Private Pettifer, also laden with books and with the
portable harmonium – the 'groan-box' as Clayton called it – that
gave an apology for music to the proceedings. The service began

---

[1] P.B.C., *Toc H as Earthquake Love : Earthquake Love.*

at once, and all went well until the sermon; then, just as the preacher was about to start, a small dog trotted up and sat himself down immediately opposite and facing the preacher. Every time the preacher opened his mouth to speak, the dog began to bark. When this absurd situation had gone on for some time, Clayton relapsed into silence. Then, fixing his eyes on the stranger, he addressed him solemnly in his well-known booming voice: 'If you will be good enough to let me finish what I have to say, your turn shall follow.' He then looked back to the congregation and continued with his sermon. The dog never uttered another sound. 'Ludicrous as it may seem after this lapse of time,' wrote Colonel Higgon, the C.O., 'I am quite convinced that that little human and humorous touch helped to sow the seeds of a friendship between Tubby and the members of 141 Battery that has existed for forty-five years and has, I hope, served us all in good stead.'

After this Clayton became a regular visitor to the Battery, coming, circumstances permitting, every Thursday. He would arrive at the farm in the evening, hold a service in the barn, go round to the men on the guns, have supper with any disengaged, and hold an early celebration the next morning. On one occasion when Colonel Higgon noticed that their visitor had been issued with a goodly ration of sausages and bacon, he asked him, half-jokingly, whether he was doing all right. 'I assure you,' came the reply, 'I am not doing at all badly for a high-church curate on the first Friday in Lent!' But he did not come solely to bring religion to the men; he brought recreation also. Frequently he and the 'Gen' would stagger in heavily-laden with a portable cinema, a screen and a number of films which would be entrusted to Tommy Glanfield, the popular sergeant-major, for safe keeping. The entertainment was never censored by the padre, and often proved to be saucy French farces which delighted men who had scarcely set eyes on a woman since they left home. Many times performances were interrupted by 'straffing'; on at least one occasion the screen was torn to pieces by shrapnel – but a new one was soon forthcoming.

Clayton's affection and regard for these men of the Heavy Batteries was profound. In the summer of 1916, Neville Talbot and others having gone south in training for the Somme, the chaplains of 4th class rank, among whom Clayton was still numbered, found themselves under a new superior, the Rev. C. E. Ensell. The new D.A.C.G. called a meeting of chaplains at Talbot House to meet their superior officer and to arrange their spheres of work. After the opening prayers, Ensell, the soul of consideration towards his chaplains, said unconcernedly: 'Oh! Clayton, you are doing two Heavy Batteries, I see. I want you to take on some extra units. Please hand over your Heavies to . . .' Clayton heard no more. He fainted. 'I woke up on the floor,' he recorded, 'with solicitous faces of fellow chaplains gazing down at me. I revived rapidly. . . .' The embarrassed Ensell, no doubt anxious to conclude the meeting, promptly gave way. 'Clayton, if you are feeling strong enough, I gather you wish to keep the Heavies? Of course you can. I didn't know you wanted them!' So he retained his Heavies and took on extra work as well.

Clayton's roving commission took him to all sorts of places, where he made a wide variety of contacts. Almost always his visits were welcomed with enthusiasm; but there were exceptions. Amongst his special friends were the Railway Operating Department, or the R.O.D. as they were usually called. One of the least pleasant of their duties was the running of what was known as the Ypres Express, a nightly train laden with stores and ammunition, which was hauled up into the Salient as far as circumstances permitted. Behind it was a second engine, heavily armoured. This was a very necessary precaution, because, if things became too hot, it beat a hasty retreat – if possible with, but sometimes without, the train. One evening the padre came across the train halted in the gloaming; and, under the mistaken impression that the driver was a special pal of his, whom we will call Bert Atkins, knocked on the door of the engine and enquired if Bert Atkins was there. No answer. So he knocked again, and then a third time he even more loudly summoned Bert to show himself. But still silence reigned. Then he incautiously took a large stone and flung it at the door. This had an electrifying result; the door was flung open and a furious non-Bert appeared armed with a coal shovel with which he struck the intruder on the top of his steel helmet. 'What the hell are you knocking my engine about for?' he shouted, 'I'll Bert Atkins you, you. . . . !' The padre sank down on the side of the track whilst the train clanked off slowly into the gathering darkness.

But Clayton's peregrinations were often attended with danger far graver than a shovel on his tin helmet. He totally ignored shell-fire. If he was minded to go to a place and if it was humanly possible, he went, regardless of the consequences. His survival is a miracle. That is perhaps a cant phrase; but undoubtedly Clayton would have endorsed it, for he was fully persuaded that he was sent into the world to do God's bidding. It was all the more miraculous because Clayton never acquired shell sense, that intuition born of experience which told you when and where the next shell would fall. The Germans were people of fixed habits. If they shelled the road between two points at 10 a.m. on Monday and Tuesday, one could be reasonably sure they would shell it at 10 a.m. on Wednesday; the wise man, therefore, passed that way either before 9.45 or after 10.15. Not so Clayton. He had no idea of time, was never known to look at a watch, and would be sure to be along that stretch of road at 10 o'clock in the morning. The result was that he spent many very uncomfortable moments in all sorts of handy refuges; and on at least one memorable occasion he perforce held a service in a huge shell-hole with portable harmonium and prospective organist.

On another occasion, having celebrated in the morning at the headquarters of the 154th, then situated at St Eloi, and being determined to minister to men in the more forward sector, Clayton with the ever-faithful Pettifer in attendance proceeded down the long, muddy slope that led northwards to Ypres. Having reached about half-way, they surveyed their chances of crossing an exposed field that divided them from an embankment, into which a number of caves and tunnels had been cut and propped with planks to give shelter to the men of that sector. Over this field there had been an intense bombardment. This had momentarily stopped, but at any time it might begin again. Should they make a dash for it? They decided to do so; and, just as the shelling re-started, they slithered, rolled or tumbled, breathless and drenched with wet mud, into the largest tunnel. Immediately, the gas curtain was dropped behind them. The scene that greeted them was strange and awesome. 'No eyes which have looked upon these things in actuality can ever hope to find their like in any church on earth,' Clayton wrote, 'the intense reality, the humble eagerness, the unity of aim, the thought of one another, the constancy of friendship thus for ever knit, were like great shafts of light streaming upon a dark and narrow way, whereupon a Figure all-commanding stood plainly to be seen. The crouching men, outlined in candlelight, against the background of the oozing boards upon the yielding carpet of moist clay, made this the Food of Immortality indeed, delivered within the Sepulchre itself. Death stood without and knocked, but Christ within forbade his instant entry; for, even as we knelt, such sound came very near.'

Death stood without and knocked. When some eighteen men had received Communion, Clayton and the subaltern in charge went to move the curtain. Something resisted their efforts. They pushed harder and together. Suddenly the curtain fell aside to reveal the dead body of a young soldier that had half fallen against it. He had been manning the farthest gun and had followed his comrades, trusting to be in time to communicate. But before he could be admitted, death had touched him – so gently that he seemed to be asleep. He was about eighteen years of age and known to them all.

With a sad heart the padre enquired if there were any others who had not been able to receive. He was told that, about fifty yards away over an exposed part of the embankment that was being heavily shelled, there were four signallers unable to leave their post. Without a moment's hesitation he made his perilous way thither and proceeded to minister to them in the open. All five, their tin hats removed and entirely unprotected, knelt in the Presence. Whilst they did so a colossal shell burst with a deafening roar only a few feet away, tearing the earth asunder and filling the air with steel and slime. Yet those men knelt oblivious to what was passing around them, whilst the priest ministered the Chalice, recited the Lord's Prayer, and rose to give the Blessing. His task done, he stumbled down the embankment where Pettifer awaited him, and together they went on their way.

Once Clayton was enabled to visit the Fleet at Scapa Flow, and at a grim moment in its history. This is how it came about. In January 1916 the Ypres Salient was a mass of stagnant waters in the winter rains, the drainage having been damaged and the pumping station put out of action by mines and shelling. At this unpropitious moment, Corps Headquarters announced that a party from the Royal Navy was on its way to pay a visit to the Salient. Soon afterwards the contingent arrived, and were billeted in Talbot House. They declared that they came as visitors, that they were to return to their respective stations in the Home Fleet after a week or more of fun in Flanders, and that they would be expected to talk about all they had seen of trench warfare.

It was up to their hosts, the 6th Division, to entertain their guests, and accordingly a raid was duly staged. As often happens on such occasions, awkward moments occurred; thus a machine gun crew got knocked out, though their gun was not seriously damaged. Unfortunately a Petty Officer, whose point of vantage was near this distressing incident, forgot in his excitement that he and his party were to be mere spectators. The guests determined to lend a hand. The Petty Officer and some junior ratings rallied round the gun, persuaded it to function, and before long were causing widespread irritation in the enemy lines. The Petty Officer, much to his surprise, received the D.C.M., thus surely becoming the first R.N. rating to win in Flanders this soldierly award.

When the naval party were leaving, they asked whether their visit could be returned by some of the friends who had entertained them in the Salient, and three or four months later an official invitation from the Admiralty was duly received. The first party reached the Grand Fleet at Scapa Flow just in time for the Battle of Jutland, and three gunners went down in the *Queen Mary*. The second party of six, including Clayton, left France just when news of the battle was most gloomy, and two days after Kitchener was lost. 'At one of the worst moments in our history', wrote Philip Clayton long afterwards, 'when Kitchener had gone down off Marwick Head in H.M.S. *Hampshire*, and Russia was abandoning her allies, I saw the Fleet licking its wounds at Scapa. Never did any body of true men more doggedly "disown discouragement".'[1]

In the spring and summer of 1918 there was a series of appalling set-backs to the allied cause. In March the Germans imposed the Peace of Brest-Litovsk on a shattered and bolshevik Russia. A

[1] Clayton's letters to his mother describing this trip are published in *Letters from Flanders*, pp. 60–77.

he Prince of Wales lights the first Toc H lamp in the Albert Hall, 1923

Tubby Clayton with the Prince's lamp, 1922

Tubby Clayton at Talbot House, Trinity Square, at the outbreak of the Seco
World War

few weeks later Ludendorff launched his long-expected attack which shattered Gough's 5th Army and hurled it back behind the Somme. By 5th April the enemy had driven a great wedge between our 4th and 5th Armies. Petain, pusillanimous as always, was anxious to abandon his allies to their fate and to save his own troops by falling back on Paris. It was this emergency that drove the hitherto reluctant Haig to urge the appointment of Foch as supreme commander of all the allied forces. In mid-April the second German thrust, under the command of Prince Ruprecht of Bavaria, was delivered with the utmost vigour in the area of Ypres; the outcome was rapid and momentous. In the south, the Messines ridge and Mount Kemmel were quickly taken, and northwards the vital junction of Hazebrouck was seriously threatened. It was at this terrible moment that Haig issued to his troops the famous 'Backs to the Wall' message. 'In these two great battles, 120 German divisions had fallen on 58 British, who suffered 300,000 casualties.'[1] In May the third stroke fell, this time on the French along the Aisne, and by early June the Germans once more stood on the Marne.

Just before midnight on 'the Saturday before Low Sunday'[2] whilst these events were running their bloody course, an urgent signal was received ordering the padre to close Talbot House forthwith and to return home immediately. Clayton, faced with this ominous situation, consulted, so he tells us, the morrow's Gospel which 'seemed to make it plain that no good shepherd, if worth his salt, would turn upon his heel and leave his sheep when wolves were in the offing'. He rapidly came to the conclusion that 'this Gospel contrasted oddly with the signalled order and that in consequence the order must be ignored'. He therefore sent a brief reply to the Provost Marshal Second Army, asking him to explain to the Chaplain General – in terms courteous but firm – that his subordinate had no intention of obeying his orders, and that he was prepared to take the consequences. This of course might have had serious repercussions for Clayton. Fortunately, however, he found in the Provost Marshal an unexpected ally, who knew the value of the Old House and of its founder. He cabled promptly

---

[1] Feiling, *History of England*, pp. 1071–2, where these events are brilliantly summarized.

[2] Saturday, 6th April, 1918.

and tersely: 'Essential to the morale of the Ypres Salient that Talbot House remain open.' Thus it was decided; and 'Everyman's Club' was at the last moment saved from extinction just when it seemed to be most needed.

But in fact the Germans had reached high-water mark. By mid-August the tide had turned, and the enemy realized that the struggle against the ebb was beyond their dwindling strength. 'Few scenes could be more like the mouth of hell,' wrote Clayton nearly forty years later, 'than were the craters lined with blood-stained bodies which met our eyes when we re-took the hill ten days before September ran its course.'[1] In October the Germans were suing for peace. In November the holocaust came to a sudden end after more than four years of death and destruction.

One day early in November 1918, the officer in charge of Railway Construction in the district around Poperinghe descended upon the little town to enquire if the chaplain of Talbot House would give his men some Sunday services on the other side of no-man's-land, an area popularly known as Macedonia. Accordingly, on Saturday afternoon, 9th November, two days before the Armistice was signed, the padre sallied forth from Poperinghe on a thirty-mile trek, hoping to catch the French return leave train as it passed through. As it happened, however, he was picked up by a lorry on its way to Ypres, and then by a French flying tender that took him on the rest of the journey. The tender, so Clayton affirmed, was carrying stores, a goat, a grandmother, her daughter and two babies; and he was nearly suffocated. 'Charitably, we will put it down to the goat,' he said, 'though I doubt it.' So this strange assortment of human cargo was bumped and jolted over the devastated area of no-man's-land, where the most terrible desolation met them as far as the eye could see. The trees at first were scarred, then blasted, later just stumps, and finally there was nothing. At first houses were roofless, then scarcely recognizable, later mere pieces of wall with dug-outs against them, later no more than heaps of rubble, and finally nothing. People dug among the ruins to uncover here and there the remains of floors and cellars; but as other more noisome remains were also thus uncovered,

[1] Clayton to Sir Campbell Stuart, 15th March, 1954. 'The Hill' of course refers to Mount Kemmel.

prudent men refrained from such activities. Amid all this scene of desolation, perhaps the most evil-looking things were the tanks. 'They seemed like monsters of the iron age, frozen in the act of springing,' recorded Clayton a few days later. 'A child could read in their shattered contour what each had purposed, and how each failed. You can almost see their brown driving bands wrenching in vain to lift free of the fatal pool, or their noses peering desperately over the insuperable bank.'[1] For the rest, there were wire tangled and rusted, rotting sandbags, shattered wheels, trucks broken down and abandoned in the mud, live shells piled in great heaps, crates of ammunition, duck-board tracks, decaying horse and mule carcasses half buried in surface graves, emitting an indescribable stench; and here and there were to be seen plain rough-hewn crosses that had somehow survived the holocaust.

But gradually as the tender bumped its way onwards the scene of extreme desolation began to give way to something less bleak. The wagon at length reached the broad highway leading from Menin to Roulers. Along this the padre dropped off and thankfully bade farewell to his former travelling companions. Here, complete with flask, biscuits, and 'Church essentials', he made his way on foot to the old, battle-scarred German van which served as mess for the men engaged on railway construction. 'They are all in their element,' he recorded, 'heaps of real big engineering at last, miles of destroyed track, broken bridges, etc., and *carte blanche* to get it done quickly. Shop, as they talk it, is full of fascination.' It was a Sunday morning; but with tasks on hand so heavy and so urgent there was no prospect of Communion that day. A late evening service was the most that could be hoped for. So Philip Clayton determined to join one of the reconnaissance parties that was to set out at dawn on the following morning; that historic day, 11th November, 1918. This was not without danger, for the fighting still continued. The previous day the Germans had been said to hold the Scheldt, and to occupy an unassailable position along its banks; now they were believed to be in full retreat. But who could tell? The position was obviously perilous. As the party of engineers approached the river, ominous signs of recent fighting and desperate shelling were painfully apparent, and Avelgem by the riverside looked, so Clayton recorded, as

[1] Clayton, *Letters from Flanders*, p. 169.

though a tornado had struck it. The bridges across the river were down, so they could go no farther by road. Moreover, the line was mined every few yards with traps so cunningly contrived that it was death to meddle with them. Some detonated from time to time, to the peril of the engineers repairing the track. Along the steep embankment, also extensively snared, the intrepid party picked its way, only to find after some time of cautious advance that the track ended suddenly in nothingness. Yet another bridge had gone. But by a rare piece of luck they saw a hundred yards upstream a gang-plank bridge resting on floats made out of petrol tins. This had miraculously escaped the enemy's onslaught, and by it the party crossed into the front line from which the Germans had only just retreated.

Here too, of course, a scene of desolation greeted the new-comers. Almost the first thing they encountered was the remains of a sugar-beet factory with half its machinery looted. What remained looked highly suspect, so Clayton and his fellows left ill severely alone. At first no sign of life was to be seen anywhere, until at last a small boy of about twelve emerged from a Roman Catholic Church. He greeted the strangers excitedly in queer, scarcely comprehensible French. He had just been to Mass. Yesterday the hated Boches had passed that way for the last time. The windows of his home had been shattered by a mine on the railway, but mercifully the shell nearest the house had not exploded, so the house was safe. Only the cowhouse had been blown up; but as he had a week's holiday from school, he would help his father to rebuild it. Farther on, they came to a railway-man's cottage. The man welcomed the engineers with rejoicing. His wife was making a savoury dish of horsemeat, which would be, they said, their first meat meal for two long years. And so at last the little party reached the more populous and less devastated areas where with tears of joy mingled with their cheers village after village sallied forth to greet the engineers and the relieving troops. The men, weary though they were, stepped out boldly, some helped by the cheerful music of their bands; those who had no bands whistled or sang snatches of war-time songs. 'They do not look proud,' Clayton recorded at the time, 'but infinitely patient, and kindly, and domestic, and withal there's a little twinkle in their eyes. I see some old friends among them, but they

are mostly younger brothers,' he added sadly, 'most of my generation lie quietly asleep with the tanks keeping guard over their
slumbers.'[1]

About 10 o'clock the party reached Oudenarde to find it in
strange confusion. Shells had been falling in the street from both
sides whilst it changed hands, and the Germans still held one end
where the roadway ran over a low bridge across a narrow stream.
By the water's edge lay the bodies of some twenty American
soldiers who had fallen victims to the German traps. The firing of
the early morning had ceased; and now an ominous silence ensued.

Clayton, with time heavy on his hands, hammered on the
shuttered door of an Oudenarde shop, through the window of
which he had seen a vast horde of German mouth-organs. After
a few moments two terrified women emerged from the cellar;
whereupon he handed them all his spare cash and filled his pockets
and haversack with mouth-organs. These he distributed to every
man he met, pledging them all to learn to play before peace was
signed. And as he did so, the hitherto unheard call 'Cease Fire'
sounded down by the broken bridge at the bottom of the street.
It was as if God's voice had cried: 'See, I make all things new.'
Surely the people thus redeemed would live with an ever-growing
strength of purpose, the old internal feuds and hatreds forgotten
in the new family life. Surely from that moment onwards all
would be well with the nation and the race. No shadow of doubt
or hesitancy lay across that dawn.

Thus thought Philip Clayton on that historic November
morning in 1918. How strange sounds that optimism in the grim
world of the present. Yet it never crossed his mind – it perhaps
never crossed the mind of anyone on that first Armistice Day –
that there were in store for humanity torments and tribulations far
graver than any they had yet endured in all the exigencies of war.

[1] Clayton, *Letters from Flanders*, pp. 174–5.

7

Knutsford

'I was with many of my friends
residing in a jail.'[1]

One afternoon a few days after the signing of the Armistice, two
young men were engaged in animated conversation in the main
street of Poperinghe. One of them was Douglas Legg, a soldier
already encountered in the Upper Room, and destined to be
ordained a few years later; the other, the irrepressible P.B.C.
Clayton announced that he proposed to go to Dunkerque and
would like his friend to accompany him. 'How on earth are we to
get to Dunkerque?' asked Legg. 'Every available form of transport has left Pop – the Army has taken everything on wheels on
their victorious march into Belgium.' This seemed for a moment
to nonplus his companion; but for a moment only. 'Ah, I know,'
Clayton suddenly exclaimed, 'we will ring up for a Light Engine
from the R.E.s to take us to Proven.'[2] 'To hear Tubby on a field
telephone,' recorded Mr Legg, 'is something one can never
forget. Charm, bluff and diplomacy were brought into full play.
He got his Light Engine!'

And so there soon came puffing down the main street to what
was left of the station of Pop a British Light Engine driven by
two grinning R.E.s. The Chaplain's greeting was effusive, and
his friend was bade to climb up and seat himself on the coal
tender. Mr Legg has confessed his childhood ambition to ride on a
real railway engine, but he never imagined that his wish would be
fulfilled on a W.D. Engine in Belgium. Whilst Legg was settling
himself on the coal, Clayton took his place beside the driver and
fireman on the footplate. The engine started slowly, but gained
speed rapidly. Legg set his teeth and clung on as best he could as
the engine bumped and lurched along the crazy track. Fervently
he prayed for a speedy deliverance. Meanwhile, Clayton, su-

---

[1] P.B.C., *Here and There*, No. 45.
[2] At Proven they would catch the train to Dunkerque.

premely happy as it seemed in the comparative comfort of the footplate, drew out from a capacious folder a pile of papers, which he handed up to the harassed Legg. They were some of the drafts of Clayton's forthcoming book, *Tales of Talbot House*. 'I grasped these very precious papers feeling slightly sick,' Legg has recorded, 'I have never been quite sure why I was privileged to have a first glimpse of what was to become a famous book. I only know that I was very thankful to reach journey's end, and to hand that precious document back to its owner.' Later, when the book was published, the author presented Mr Legg with a copy, on the flyleaf of which he had written several well-intentioned compliments, among which the word 'gallant' figured prominently. 'I often wonder', Mr Legg commented, 'if he used the word "gallant" in recollection of that mad journey from Poperinghe to Dunkerque. Certainly for me, personally, the clinging on to that tender was the most gallant thing I ever did for the Old House at Pop.'

One morning early in 1919, the Rev. W. H. Stewart, one day to become a bishop, but then a London parish priest and Secretary of a Government Committee concerned with the employment of conscientious objectors, was rung up in his room at the Home Office by Sir Geoffrey Whiskard, the Secretary of State's private secretary, bidding him come to his office immediately. In Sir Geoffrey's room, Mr Stewart found Philip Clayton who had just crossed from France with the mud still on his boots. Thus there assembled three old Paulines who had been together in the School fifteen years before.

The story Clayton had to tell his friends was this. During the war years some hundreds of officers and men serving in the Salient had given in their names at the Old House as being anxious, if spared, to offer their lives to the ministry of Christ and His Church. Thus encouraged, he, Clayton, had drafted a scheme for a Test School which had been amended by the Archbishop's former Chaplain, John Macmillan, acting liaison officer between the Archbishop of Canterbury at home and Bishop Gwynne, the Deputy Chaplain General, in France. In 1917 this scheme had been submitted to the church authorities in England and the bishops had for the most part approved it. It entailed, of course, a grave financial responsibility, because, whereas a few men would no doubt be able to provide some or all of the cost of their training, many obviously would be totally unable to do so. The roll of candidates begun at Talbot House, which had subsequently swollen to considerable proportions, had recently been transferred to Bishop Gwynne's General Headquarters in London.

Shortly after the Armistice, a young Oxford don, Frank Russell Barry, later Bishop of Southwell, was seconded from his corps to the D.C.G.'s office to arrange for the collection of candidates from their respective units as soon as possible after demobilization. So efficiently did he effect this that by December it was possible to establish in France two temporary schools for these officers and men, the officers' school under the command of the Rev. E. K. Talbot at Radingham, the men's under the Rev. F. R. Barry himself in the old Lewis Gun Camp at Le Touquet. The men's school, staffed by a group of chaplains especially detailed for the purpose, opened its doors shortly before Christmas 1918; but it started work under severe difficulties, for no educational books were available. Nevertheless, all being eager to learn and to prove their worthiness, many perplexities were overcome, manifold short-comings excused. During the last week of the year Philip Clayton, who had been detailed to the men's school under Frank Barry, drove up from Poperinghe with a lorry-load of furniture and other gifts. He was given the formidable task of transforming two lecture-rooms hung with diagrams of Lewis guns attacking Gothas, into a chapel and a common-room for the students, many of whom were friends from the Old House days. Lectures were various, '. . . some by instructors so learned that men rubbed their eyes,' as Clayton has told us, 'and others by educational adventurers who skated precariously across the thin crust which covered their consummate ignorance. I was myself notorious for a series of three lectures embracing the history of the world. The first ranged from the Creation to the death of Julius Caesar; the second to the Reformation, and the third to the Armistice. My colleagues, however, were far better equipped and included some far-sighted men of real capacity.'[1]

Soon after Christmas, when pressure upon the Government to send the army home was becoming irresistible, it was felt that the time had come for the Church to redeem its pledge. That it

[1] Clayton, *Plain Tales from Flanders*, p. 43.

redeemed it effectively was thanks largely to the splendid work of Canon Partridge, Secretary of the Central Church Fund, whose task it was to find the necessary funds. Philip Clayton's mission in England was to find suitable quarters at home to which both sections of the Test School could be transferred. He had already been to Lambeth Palace to harangue the Archbishop of Canterbury; indeed, when his Grace showed signs of cutting short the interview because of a summons to see the King about the funeral arrangements for little Prince John, Clayton joined the Archbishop in his car and continued to hold forth all the way to Buckingham Palace. He had already reported to Canon Patridge. He had also already sought out his old friend, Dr Leonard Browne, who had acted as first Honorary Treasurer to Talbot House and had been invalided home a year before; and the two of them had set out to find, as soon as possible, a building in which about five hundred men might be suitably housed and taught. This odd quest had been unsuccessful. Hence Clayton's presence this day in Sir Geoffrey Whiskard's room in the Home Office.

The three old friends pondered the problem light-heartedly. Whiskard murmured a shade tentatively that there were quite a lot of empty prisons to offer, whereupon Clayton assured him that they would soon be filled now that the army was being demobilized. Stewart, equally tentatively, reflected that there was quite a good line in asylums available. 'Oh, don't bother about that,' came the reply, 'they are demobilizing the Staff too.' But as the choice seemed to rest between prison and asylum, P.B.C. preferred the former; and by the time he left the Home Office, arrangements had been made for Knutsford Gaol to be placed at his disposal.

No sooner had he gone than he received an urgent summons to appear forthwith before Bishop Taylor Smith, the Chaplain General, at his office in Whitehall. He had overstayed his leave. The Bishop opened his speech of rebuke by reminding Clayton severely, and perhaps a trifle sententiously, that he was a soldier, and that his offence was grave. This delighted the unrepentant defaulter, who promptly asked for an extension of leave – and of course got it!

Thus dismissed by higher authority, Clayton and his friend Browne made their way northwards to inspect their acquisition. They reached Knutsford, the 'Cranford' of Mrs Gaskell's novel, shortly before midnight and in a snowstorm. Clayton, quite undaunted by such small inconveniences, felt, he tells us, like Scrooge awaking from his prodigious course of nocturnal instruction: 'I am as light as a feather, I am as happy as an angel, I am as merry as a schoolboy, I am as giddy as a drunken man.' The massive ugliness of Knutsford Gaol fascinated him; and he and Browne promptly reported that it offered 'complete accommodation for anything up to 700 men ready at the shortest notice', and that they found it 'clean, light, warm and easily made cheerful . . . a disciplined atmosphere for real work, the place itself something of a test of sincerity and a valuable deterrent against snobbery. . . . A good neighbourhood, homely, quiet and bracing.'

Towards the end of February, F. R. Barry was demobilized, and early in March he crossed from France to become Chief of the new venture. His first impression of Knutsford prison was in sharp contrast to Clayton's and Browne's. 'Conceive this building empty of all but dirt,' he recorded, '. . . damp, filthy and forbidding – desolate galleries of dismal cells, desperately unlighted and unfurnished. Everything was beastly and repulsive, the "whitewash" front, the atmosphere poisonous, the dank vacancy sepulchral. There was nothing about it which did not make you shudder. We shall never forget the horror and disgust struck into us by the sight of our new home. The faith of Tubby had leaped to its possibilities; to some of us they were not so apparent. There was a moment when it seemed so impossible that anything could ever be done with the place that we were tempted to throw down our cards.' But men accustomed to four years in France were not to be daunted by such trifles, and all lent a hand. New plumbing was needed, and the plumbers had celebrated the advent of peace by going on strike; the lighting was totally inadequate and had to be renewed. Willing hands soon set these things to rights. Plank beds, even when covered with blankets, were still hard, but were gradually replaced by something less comfortless; and the commissariate, at first crude and uninviting, was soon improved by the importation of a splendid body of W.A.A.C.s.

The prison-yard, the inmates' only playground, was grim enough until – with the coming of spring – the kindly neighbours beautified it with their flowers. The execution-shed was locked;

beside it was the burial-place of men who had suffered death for their crimes. The ground was destitute of any sign of faith. Nothing but a series of initials and dates on the wall marked where each man lay; broken bottles and jars, odd lengths of drain-pipes, and other discarded litter lay across the graves in degrading disarray. A grievously-wounded Scottish soldier, F. M. D. Watt, so smashed up that every movement caused him pain, who was destined to live only two years more, charged himself with the task far beyond his strength, of clearing the heaviest rubbish and converting it into a small garden. 'So, during the first spring of Knutsford School,' wrote Dr. Clayton many years later, 'this obscure corner, which had been ill-omened, became a place of quiet dignity, infinite pains and almost loveliness. . . . All memories of early Knutsford fade into insignificance beside the precious tribute paid by the priestly soul of that much wounded Scotsman to the graves of criminals unworthy of reprieve.'

'We were full of the sense of real pioneering,' recorded the 'Chief' long afterwards, 'there was an *élan* and exhilaration which set us along in a sheer rush of joy. We knew we were doing something worthwhile. It is well in these days of ordered civilization and comfort, which was then unimagined, to recall those weeks of our adventurous youth. Our brotherhood was forged in a readiness to take big risks and attempt impossibilities. It was a fellowship of vision, because it had seen a vision of Fellowship. We have not been limited here by a fixed tradition. But those who brought Knutsford from across the Channel have bequeathed to us an "active service" spirit which – however changed be the conditions – we are pledged never to let die.'

Knutsford School was divided into houses, each known unromantically by the lettering on the part of the prison which it occupied. Clayton's house, he tells us, was B.IV. It comprised among its twenty members a Colonel, a Naval Commander, several junior officers, a Q.M.S., some N.C.O.s and others. This seemingly ill-assorted group was typical of the occupants of the other houses, all of whom had voluntarily come together in their anxiety to learn how they could best serve the Church of Jesus Christ on earth. And an arduous service it certainly was. The day started with Reveille at 6.45 a.m. followed by morning prayers in the parish church at 7.30 and Holy Communion a quarter of an hour later. Breakfast was at 8.15, and half an hour's Bible reading followed at 9.30. From 10 o'clock till noon was devoted to lectures. The midday meal was served at a quarter to one, to be followed by two hours of games and tea at 4.15. Lectures were given from 5 till 7 o'clock when supper was served: 8 o'clock to 9.30 was given over to private study, followed by evening prayers in church at half past nine. Lights were out at 10.45 p.m.

The students who had submitted themselves to this rigorous life were fortunate in the staff of the School assembled to instruct them. At their head was the Principal, F. R. Barry, later Bishop of Southwell; others included J. H. Nicholson, later to become Principal and subsequently Vice-Chancellor of Hull University; Mervyn Haigh, who in due course occupied the Sees, first of Coventry and then of Winchester; E. S. G. Wickham, Gladstone's grandson, who followed Barry as Principal of the School; and of course P.B.C. from whose inspiration the whole scheme derived.

It was not long before all those in the School, both staff and students, were feeling the impact of his forceful personality. The vast building was divided into four blocks converging on a central hall, which inevitably became a common meeting-place. And at least one former inmate retained many years afterwards vivid memories of Philip Clayton and his pupils in 'Piccadilly' as this central area was called. The Rev. H. B. Brayford, afterwards a Dorset parish priest, remembered P.B.C. mounting a chair one night and leading the whole assembly in the singing of 'There was a rich man . . .', the opening words of the song *Rogerum* which served Toc H as its anthem in its early years, the singer's deep voice echoing down the long corridors and the company taking up the chorus with uninhibited abandon. He also recollected him as a lone figure in the middle of the open space wearing a 'tin hat' and rubber cape, whilst men gathered on the landings above rained down on him jugs of water. On May Day he was to be seen – a conspicuous figure in the procession – impersonating Britannia under the disguise of umbrella, trident, shield and gas-mask. And he wrote and produced a full-blooded operetta entitled *The Bell Rock*, the scene of which was laid on board 's.s. *Champaignia* in mid-ocean between Lampeter and Limehouse'; in this he played Captain Clap-in-Irons, the hero of the piece. Because of these pieces of horse-play, some austere critics have condemned

Knutsford. But others did not take so narrow a view. 'I hold', stated Mr Brayford more than forty years later, 'that Tubby well understood that these men needed such nonsense now and then as a relief from the strain they were under.'

And let there be no mistake; they were working under very great strain. First, it must be remembered that those gathered at Knutsford were a mixed body of men – postmen, clerks, shop-assistants, weavers, boiler-makers, journalists, teachers and so forth – all of whom had passed through the moil of war; and now they had to live together as a family amid the discomforts of an abandoned gaol. 'That we did mix, and so very successfully,' stated Brayford, 'is one of the things I marvel at to this day. I hold it one of God's Mercies that Tubby was there during those months.' Next, this mixed assembly had to turn their brains, rusted with the skills of war, to the art of learning; each must try to pass his test examination in twelve to fourteen weeks. For Knutsford was not a Theological College, but a 'Test School', that is, as Barclay Baron wrote:

> A place where men who had been attracted, while on active service, by the possibility of holy orders, could test their abilities and their vocation for it. Some found that their 'sense of voca-tion' was confirmed at the School and proceeded steadily towards ordination. Others came to the conclusion that they were called to serve God and men in some other way than the Ministry; meanwhile they eagerly embraced the chance of training their minds at the School to whatever work might afterwards be theirs. Others, again, discovered – or were told – that they were not cut out to be pupils in the School at all; these did not finish the course but returned to some work for which they were better fitted in the world outside.

'Tubby took his part in the necessary teaching', Brayford has told us, 'and I was lucky enough to sit at his feet for lectures in English. I cannot recall a thing he taught, but I do remember that I learnt from him to love the English language.' But that was not what most impressed him about his teacher. 'Either praying or preaching,' he wrote, 'Tubby dwelt in the heavenly places, and since he did we were transplanted part of the way. It seems to me now as though he were looking through a door in heaven, and trying to beckon us to come and see what he saw. He prayed and preached so as to convey an utter certainty of our Heavenly Home.'

The Bishop of Southwell wrote down some forty years later his memories of those days: 'The whole idea of enrolling "Service Candidates" among men who had found their vocation in the first war was born into the same cradle as Toc H. This movement, which saved the parochial ministry of the Church from collapse when the war was over, was the child of Tubby's faith and vision and was mainly organized and sustained from Poperinghe.' After the Armistice, when the Archbishop of Canterbury (Randall Davidson) had pledged the Church that no one should be prevented by lack of money from training for Holy Orders, 'the way was clear for the Church at home to act, and for Tubby's idea to come true'. He continues:

Everything had to be done in a frantic hurry and everything had to be improvised from bottom. There was nothing ready-made to be taken over. And there Tubby's genius had its full scope. . . . It was Tubby who found the empty gaol at Knutsford – which became for hundreds their spiritual home – and inspired us to venture this wild experiment. Within a very few months the School was opened. A nucleus staff had already been assembled, and the furniture came the same day as the students who, long accustomed to fatigues, humped their beds from the goods-yard to their cells. So when Tubby came to join us he was regarded not as simply a member of that staff but as the Apostle and Founding Father of that great and exciting spiritual enterprise. He was, needless to say, the life and soul of the place; and behind all his exuberant mirth and laughter and the idiosyncrasies now known the world over, everyone recognized those silent depths which were the true sources of his strength. Without him the whole thing could never have happened at all. Without him it could have been something entirely different. His prayers had created it, and from first to last Knutsford owes more to him than can ever be told.

It was at about this time that Clayton had his first post-war contact with the reigning House, a contact that was to become more and more intimate as the years went by. Whilst at Knutsford he was summoned to Buckingham Palace to preach before King

George V and Queen Mary. Before the service, his kinsman, Canon Edgar Sheppard, Sub-Dean of the Chapels Royal and Canon of St George's Chapel, Windsor, warned him against preaching too long a sermon: 'I will indicate when you should stop,' he promised. To the visiting preacher it seemed as if he had scarcely started when Canon Sheppard coughed. He went boldly on until some minutes later the Canon coughed a second time. This surely must be his signal, so Clayton stopped 'as it were at a semi-colon', as he described it, and descended from the pulpit. 'That was rather an abrupt end to your sermon,' commented the King after the Service. 'I know, Sir, but I heard Canon Sheppard cough.' 'Yes, yes,' replied the King, 'it is a nuisance, he has a terrible cough and cold.'

But the ebullient Clayton had far more on his mind than the fortunes of the Ordination Test School lodged in Knutsford Prison. As early as 1917 he and other former inmates of Talbot House had resolved on establishing in London a club that would carry on the traditions of the Old House. At Christmas 1918 they had despatched cards to several thousand men whose names stood on the roll of 'Pop' informing them of their intentions. These were written in a humorous vein.

These cards, known as 'Tubby's Whizz Bangs', were enthusiastically received, as was Clayton's modest and light-hearted account of his experiences on the Western Front, published in 1919 under the title *Tales of Talbot House* – 'the very precious papers' clutched so anxiously by Mr Legg on the coal-tender between Poperinghe and Dunkerque. Thus encouraged, Clayton and his friends – when at work from Knutsford, when on leave from his sister Belle's flat in Red Lion Square – sought out all those they could trace who might be interested. And to the April 1919 number of the *St. Martin's Messenger*, the parish magazine of *St. Martin-in-the-Fields*, where his cousin Dick Sheppard was vicar, he contributed an article in his inimitable style, giving details of his plans for a re-born Talbot House, where Boniface the innkeeper of Poperinghe, could renew his activities in the heart of London.

Depose Nelson, remove the column, ungum the lions, deduct the fountains, wash out the National Gallery, and cease to

NOTHING is to be written on this side except the date and signature of the sender. Sentences not required may be erased. If anything else is added the post card will be destroyed.

I am quite well.

~~I have been admitted into hospital~~
  { ~~sick~~ } ~~and am going on well~~
  { ~~wounded~~ } ~~and hope to be discharged soon~~

~~I am being sent down to the base.~~

~~I have received your~~ { letter dated
     telegram "
     parcel " }

Letter follows at first opportunity.

I have received no letter from you
  { ~~lately~~
     ~~for a long time~~ }

Signature only } *Alfred J. Baines*

Date *29th may 1915*

[Postage must be prepaid on any letter or post card addressed to the sender of this card.]

ANYTHING may be written on this side, the other, the obverse, by the law of Ancient Lights, is the private playground of the long-suffering A.P.S.

I vote the forthcoming booklet on Talbot House a { sound } *scheme*
  { ~~rotten~~ }

I will { ~~try~~
   burrow } 2/6 to { get
     ~~rid of~~ } it.

By all means } T.H. should be set up in Town.
~~On no account~~ }

I won't { ~~stir a finger~~
   leave a stone unturned } to help.

You've got my RANK { ~~exactly right~~
   unutterably wrong }

I am now a { ~~Lance Corporal~~ } and hope to be
  { Field Marshal } discharged soon.

This address will find me { ~~till~~ } the { ~~girls~~ }
   come home.   { boys }

Road *Cray Street*(?)
Town *London*   Yours { ever
                   ~~never~~ }
County "   Sig. *Baines*

visualize Whitehall; then roll the surface flat (except for execrable *pavé*) and, with these trifling alterations, Trafalgar Square becomes the Grande Place of Poperinghe.

You must also, by the way, rebuild St Martin's, and put a shellhole through its tower, and a clock that declares for years on end that it is half-past five, thus reminding us of human fallibility in high quarters.

The real similarity between the two places is, however, more readily realizable, for Poperinghe Square was for four years to the B.E.F. what Trafalgar Square is to London – a big place through which well-nigh every man must pass on his pilgrimage; an open place wherein he takes his first or last or intermediate breather before getting to or from business; near enough to the scene of work to warrant and provoke a pause; remote enough to make the pause a pleasure reasonably immune from accident.

What is to happen, he asked his readers, to the place that had meant so much to so many? The fellowship of Talbot House was far too great to lose. His design was to find quarters in London where this fellowship could be revived and made to flourish. He had a very clear idea of the sort of place that was needed. His article continued:

The only great fault I find, as a parson, with London, is that there aren't nearly enough public houses in the place. There are places so-called, no doubt, but they are tied to one tradition as well as to one brewery. The innkeepers are all too humble to approach you or too proud to be approached. Where is the bustling Boniface of literature? He is bedimmed by a guinea-pig directorate; he is dehumanized by the shadow of shares-cum-dividends.

Our fancy leads us to a cosy house with a good A.B.C. downstairs; and upstairs, lecture room, library, games rooms, and 'grousing' rooms, together with a London Territorial Lethe chamber, where warlike reminiscences may merge wholly into imaginative art; in short, a junior Cavendish Club, though not quite so serious; Its membership (at 10s. shall we say?) would be the 4,000 already on the Communicants' Roll of the Old House (of whom some 500 are in London), reinforced

G

from the Civil Service and Territorial world – a class who, among the faithless, were surprisingly faithful to Mother Church, in inverse ratio, perhaps, to the care she has bestowed on them.

An inn without beds is like a song without a chorus, therefore we must have a hostel in our hostelry; for in London men are even more homeless than they were in Flanders. The only financial detail yet decided upon is that, when the water-rate question becomes acute, we are going to draw water in a dixie from the fountains of the Square. You see, we are practical prophets, and the smallest detail is thus completely envisaged.

All this is not yet. . . . Meanwhile, will St Martin cover the beggar with its ample cloak, and seek God's will concerning Talbot House in town?

Meanwhile, the Service Candidates' School at Knutsford must for the moment take first place and 'six months' hard labour', as Clayton put it, must be worked out in Cheshire before the work in London could proceed. In fact the hard labour was for far longer, for the School continued at Knutsford until financial stringency forced the Church to withdraw its grants; by then 675 candidates had been trained, 435 of whom were eventually ordained.[1] Thereafter it thankfully accepted an invitation from Mr Henry Gladstone to set up a smaller Knutsford at Hawarden, where it prospered for fifteen years and sent men forth to preach and to teach the Word of God in the far corners of the earth.

So at last Clayton was released to forward the work he was convinced he was called by his Master to fulfil, the re-establishment of Talbot House in the heart of London. As the Rev. E. S. G. Wickham wrote:

The two great outcomes of the First World War, which derived from Talbot House in the Ypres salient – Knutsford ordination Test School and Toc H, both attributed their existence to the Hand of God, both beginning their Foundation Prayer with the words: 'O, God, who hast so wonderfully made . . .' We suggest that those who were at the start of either movement, if challenged, would have said: 'That is exactly what we all feel. Of course there are human instruments, but

[1] Bell, *Randall Davidson*, II, p. 944.

our experience was of something behind and beyond mere human planning and achievement.' Further, if pressed as to the nature of their unique experience, they would have replied in terms of 'fellowship', some quite possibly using the phrase 'the Common Life'. Either term recalls Pentecost – Pentecost which created the 'beloved community' and gave to the word 'common', without superseding its old significance, the contrary meaning of something gladly and thrillingly shared.

8

The Re-birth of Talbot House

'Britain is littered with
Societies; but only God can
make a family.'[1]

'My eldest sister, Belle, was five feet square if squareness is a
measure for a lady,' wrote a teasing but fond brother. 'She had a
great heart and she loved the poor, among whom, with a cross-
grained obstinacy, she much preferred to live and have her being.'
She had a tiny flat of three rooms, 'none of them large enough to
swing a cat', in Red Lion Square. 'Belle's flat was just a doll's
house with three doors, and only men who had learnt to squeeze
themselves into the holes and corners of a trench found it a place
where they could take their rest.' To this 'microscopic habitat'
Belle's brother would go when on leave from France; to it, also,
would repair many of his friends from the Old House, whose
experiences of trenches made them appreciate its amenities, and
all of whom could be sure of a warm welcome.

To this retreat one night in early March 1919 came Philip
Clayton, and wearily flung down upon the floor a sandbag filled
with several thousand signed slips of paper, the names and
addresses written by the communicants at the Old House as they
reached the bottom of the precipitous stairway from the Upper
Room. Every man who had used Talbot House in war-time was
to be eligible to become a 'Foundation Member' of the revived
movement, and the Communicants' roll alone was evidence of
eligibility. The fact that a similar list of names had been lost in the
crisis of May 1918 made the surviving one more precious. But on
this particular evening Philip Clayton was tired and dispirited.
'What on earth shall I do with all this?' he exclaimed despondently, for, as he wrote later, it was 'just a crushed chaos of odd

[1] P.B.C. at *Birthday Festival, 1930.*

pencilled scraps which represented men I had known and loved, most of whom had not lived to be demobilized. I did not know who was alive, who dead. I stood confused and pondered whether after all the words meant much. I ponder still. Paul gave it up, this puzzling about men whom he had known, where they might be by now "whether in the body or out of the body, I know not. God knows".'

At this stage of perplexity, a loving sister came to Philip's aid with the comfort and strength he needed for the task that, as he firmly believed, his Master had set him. 'So it is really true', wrote her brother thankfully, 'that one old sister, who never learnt to spell, and never wearied and was always hopeful, and never thought of herself at all, was used within the mystery of God to exercise a tireless sponsorship towards innumerable muddy strangers who came to find a man who wasn't there, and then got caught up by a cup of tea into the purring song of a perpetual kettle on a gas-ring; and all the arts and wiles of Piccadilly, and all the light and pleasures of the town were dust and ashes by comparison with one old spinster, who just brewed their tea knowing that God intended in the future much to rely upon the men He brought.' And so, to the soft song of the purring kettle on the ring, Toc H was re-born in London, a weak, sickly infant indeed, but destined to grow to lusty manhood and to have a great career.

In September 1920, when *Tales of Talbot House* was published, Lieutenant E. J. White, the first London Secretary of Talbot House, could proudly announce that a great concourse of old friends had expressed their interest in the venture and their anxiety to help and support it; and that these, in addition to the students of Knutsford, included nearly two hundred officers (of whom seven were generals) and close on five hundred and fifty other ranks. Fortified by this encouraging news, Philip Clayton and J. H. Nicholson, his colleague on the staff of the Test School, travelled to London by the night train from Knutsford on Friday, 14th November, 1919, to attend 'a meeting of intimate confederates' called to consider future plans on the next afternoon.

Clayton had already issued an agenda for the meeting, drawn up in suitable military style. It was, indeed, headed *Operation Order*

No. 1. After giving the *Assembly Point, Zero Day and Hour,* it continued:

> *I. Information* The attack on the problem of re-opening Talbot House will be carried out by a Round Table Conference thirty in number, troops being drawn from Talbotousians past, present, and to come. The attack will be covered by a creeping barrage of business advisers, supported by expert Londoners. A Section of Clerical Tanks will co-operate. The operations will be under the direction of Gen. R. S. May, C.M.G., D.S.O., etc.

The notice then proceeded with *II. Intentions* and *III. Methods of Advance,* and ended thus:

> *IV. Nature of Country* The vital need of maintaining the old fellowship and extending it to the younger clerks, civil servants and students of London offers special opportunity for the initiative of all arms, and risks must be boldly taken.

It was signed 'Tubby, Chaplain; Issued on 8th November at the School, Knutsford. Copies to all concerned.'

During the course of the journey, as Mr Nicholson recalled in after years, his companion read to him a screed which he proposed to put to the meeting. There was, of course, only one copy in Clayton's not very legible hand. On arrival the friends went to the Royal Automobile Club in Pall Mall for breakfast. The most pressing problem facing them was how to get the paper duplicated in time for the meeting that afternoon. After some hesitation, Clayton luckily noticed quite close to the club the offices of an insurance company which had recently, so he tells us, paid 'without a murmur' the cost of a recent smash on his Clyno motor-cycle, which amounted to more than the premium for the past ten years. As this seemed the very place for which they were looking, they immediately passed through its august portals to the vast office beyond. The counter clerk glanced at them enquiringly. 'Please,' said Clayton, with his characteristic short laugh that somehow wavered between a chuckle and guffaw, 'Please, can I see the manager?' The Departmental Manager was forthcoming, and on his status being explained, 'I'm sorry,' said Clayton, 'but it's the General Manager I want.' Though no names had been given, and though the padre was not wearing a clerical collar, and gave no sign that he was in Orders, they were promptly taken by lift to the top floor and ushered into the General Manager's room. 'What can I do for you gentlemen?' asked the General Manager genially. 'I wonder', replied Clayton a shade dubiously, holding out his screed, 'if you can have this duplicated for us?' Mr Nicholson was at this stage expecting a curt dismissal; but by some miracle no such thing happened. Indeed, he was astonished to hear the Manager reply simply. 'Of course, how many copies do you want?', and to see him send for his personal secretary to have the manuscript deciphered to her. Whilst the stenographer was at her work, the Manager talked affably to his guests, first about the virtues of golf and fishing as hobbies for busy executives, and then about their future plans; and when the stencils were ready and approved, he kindly arranged to have several dozen copies sent round to the club.

Only at this stage did the visitor reveal his identity. Taking out of the waistcoat pocket of his 'best suit' (which, says Nicholson, was a 'shocker') a somewhat crumpled piece of pasteboard, he said 'perhaps you would like to know my name, and by the way I am insured with you, you know.' They tried to thank the Manager, Mr William Hurst, but he would have none of it. 'Come again', he said as they withdrew, 'whenever we can do anything for you.' And come again they did. Until late in 1926 when Toc H headquarters moved to Queen Anne's Gate, the Central Executive of Toc H met every month in the board-room adjoining the Manager's sanctum and William Hurst himself became the first Honorary Treasurer and one of the most indefatigable workers for the new cause.

It was fitting that the historic meeting held that afternoon should be presided over by General May, for he it was who, as a Staff Officer in Flanders, had decreed that the soldiers' club just opening should commemorate the name of the Bishop of Winchester's youngest son killed in the Salient, and be known as Talbot House rather than Church House – the bleak name with which it had been threatened. Now, to avoid confusion with the Talbot House Settlement in Camberwell founded before the war by Bishop Talbot, it was decided to adopt officially as the name of the new movement the signallers' affectionate diminutive, Toc H. Many thought it unwise to embrace so odd a name; but, contrary to the forebodings of the pessimists, the new style caught on, and has long been firmly established wherever the movement has its being throughout the world.

Among those at the meeting were Alec Paterson, of the Oxford and Bermondsey Club, a Foundation Member of Toc H; Canon Patridge, of the Central Board of Finance of the Church of England; John Macmillan, at that time Vicar of Kew and later to become a bishop; Dick Sheppard, Clayton's well-known cousin, Vicar of St Martin-in-the-Fields; Major Shiner, later to become first Warden of the first Mark, and later still Colonel Sir Herbert; and Lord Saye and Sele, who had been a frequent visitor to the Old House and to the Upper Room.

To the vast majority of those present that afternoon it was apparent that, whilst war-time fellowship and the spirit of Auld Lang Syne were very well in their way, they did not form a sufficiently enduring foundation on which to build a new and virile movement, the object of which, it was decided, must be first to enlist a youthful membership and then to inflame it with the ideals of comradeship and service. 'Youth made the Greatest Sacrifice', it was said, 'and it is to Youth that the world owes most in return.' This challenge was unanimously accepted, and a resolution to reconstitute Talbot House at the earliest possible moment was voted with enthusiasm. An Executive Committee was promptly formed; and thus, in the words of Barclay Baron: 'Toc H, a domesticated phoenix, is re-born from the ashes of Talbot House.'

Encouraged by these portents, the founder of the movement finally resigned his position at Knutsford and promptly took two premises that were, for a time, the twin homes of Toc H in London. At Effingham House in Arundel Street off the Strand were the offices of *The Challenge*, which described itself as a weekly Church of England newspaper 'with a difference'. From its inception on 1st May, 1914, and for some years afterwards it had been edited by Mr Barclay Baron: thereafter it had had a succession of editors, including Maude Royden, William Temple and Philip Clayton. But in spite of the efforts of all these gifted people, the paper had not flourished, and it came to an untimely end in 1922. Before that happened, however, the youthful Toc H eased

its declining years by taking over one of its three rooms for an
office, from which Clayton dealt with his rapidly rising tide of
correspondence. As the infant movement's popularity increased,
so mounted the enthusiasm of the man who has ever been its life
and soul; and from his tiny office off the Strand came a daily flow
of articles and pamphlets, whose whimsical humour caught the
attention and impelled the interest of those into whose hands they
fell. But not only by the written word did Philip Clayton seek
out would-be supporters: he was the movement's chief and highly
successful recruiting officer. 'Each casual bystander, each passing
acquaintance, must be told of this unique society, with no
prospects but that of its own certainty,' as Barclay Baron has well
told us, 'and his infectious eagerness and amazing personality and
fun constantly drew those he met in bus and tube and train and
shop into his exuberant following. The boundless optimism, outward irresponsibility and deep inward purpose of Armisticetide
remained with him, and made an appeal to the romantic and good-
hearted Londoner, which no cold arguments could have done.'

About this time, Miss Belle Clayton reported that a flat had just
become vacant three doors from her own on the top floor of No.
36, Red Lion Square. It was very small; it had five rooms; and the
rental was £175 p.a. Her brother gasped at the rent. But as usual
his zeal rapidly overcame his discretion, and he and three friends –
Herbert Shiner, Frank Wilkins and Arthur Pettifer – promptly
moved in to these new quarters. It soon became clear to the four
that, if ruin was not to overwhelm them, an additional hosteller
must be found to share the exorbitant rent. An advertisement in
the Agony Column brought a welcome addition to their number
in the person of George Spragg, a Shakespearian actor of vast
proportions, whose rendering of a war-time recitation, *The Hell-
gate of Soissons*, could count upon a rapturous reception from his
fellow-hostellers and their guests. And the guests were numerous.
The tenants were five; and five men in five rooms doubtless
sounded quite reasonable to the health authorities. But if those
officials had visited the premises any evening, they would probably
have encountered, not five, but more like fifty young men all
eagerly arguing, shouting, talking, laughing and drinking
innumerable cups of tea – the whole scene partly obscured by a
haze of tobacco smoke. They would have heard from time to time

the ringing of a bell in the sitting-room; and had they examined this, they would have found a length of cord attached to it which hung out of the window. To the other end of the cord was tied a label bearing the legend:

Toc H, the Rev. P. B. CLAYTON, formerly of Poperinghe and Ypres

All the would-be visitor needed to do was to pull the cord which rang the bell aloft and soon brought Pettifer (or perhaps the 'Innkeeper' himself) hurrying to the front door, anxious to give the new arrival a welcome that was strangely reminiscent of the padre's room in the Old House.

It was at about this time that a new power appeared on the scene; and it was as well he did, for he was destined to bring order out of the increasing chaos. The correspondence and the necessary organization were getting rapidly beyond the control of Lieutenant White, and the one or two who had been enlisted to help him. The typing requirements were also getting far too much for the Poperinghe typewriter, now 'shell-shocked and quite incapable'. Clayton looked at the machine quizzically, then at his bank pass book which showed a credit of some £19. He telephoned the firm that had made the machine in the dark ages, and their representative was sent to inspect it. The salesman, a wounded ex-serviceman, was asked to take the thing away and bring it back restored, or else another as cheap as possible. He vanished, soon to return with a No. 10, an old machine reconstituted. The price was £10. A few days later, a Mrs Payne, secretary to a hospital, called to say that she had a few free hours each day and was prepared to employ them typing for Toc H. But, alas, Mrs Payne gave one look at the typewriter and forthwith pronounced herself unwilling to touch a No. 10 reconstituted. An anxious summons was sent to the limping salesman, who took away the No. 10, and returned quickly with a newer model at £15. Clayton protested; whereupon the representative astonished him by forcefully agreeing: 'Yes, they are dirty swine,' he said with conviction. He was asked to enlarge upon this: 'They are,' he said. 'And I'm soon hoping to join another firm. What's all this you're up to, anyway?' P.B.C. told him what he could, and handed over a cheque which almost broke him. The salesman pocketed the cheque reluctantly and departed, promising to return after office hours. He was as good as his word, and that night he supped at Red Lion Square. They learnt his name at last – W. J. Musters; but he was soon 'Mus' to all his friends in the movement.

Three weeks later, Musters returned once more, this time to announce that he had left the firm and had an excellent new job ahead of him at £9 a week and commission. Meanwhile, he was on holiday. His girl was still nursing in the hospital in Scotland where she had nursed him and his shattered foot on his return from near Ypres. He was consequently at a loose end. Could he give his leisure to Toc H? He worked like a Trojan; and when, his holidays over, he left to take up his new appointment, P.B.C. and Mrs Payne looked wryly at each other. He had been so quick, so efficient. They could not face his loss. Yet it seemed they had no choice.

Another three weeks passed, and then out of the blue 'Mus' turned up once more. At first he was hesitant. Then he blurted out! 'I can't leave you like this. You'll never get ahead; so I'll resign my job and come and work for you. What can you pay me?' He was shown the bank pass book made up to that very day: the credit stood at precisely £36. '£3 a week for twelve weeks,' he was told, 'then I don't know . . .' What Philip Clayton was to live on meanwhile was not clear; but the newcomer, taking his courage in both hands, accepted the offer. 'I have written to the girl and told her that I think I ought to join you,' he said. 'She says she thinks so too; so we'll just wait. Talbot House was not born when I was in the Salient, but it seems a good thing. I'll take the job. Come on.' So Toc H acquired its first Registrar. It did not need to seek another for over twenty years. William Musters died suddenly on 16th January, 1941.

Meanwhile, the Central Executive was getting down to its task of projecting the movement to the post-war public. At first their aim was for a single House or headquarters, from which a body of men would go out 'carrying with them', in Barclay Baron's telling words, 'the Christian traditions of a single house, which was regarded as the material method of achieving a new spirit between man and man'. In the early spring of 1920 two posters appeared on London hoardings. The first defined the aims of Toc H thus:

1. The perpetuation of the Active Service of Fellowship.
2. The extension of this tradition to the younger generation.
3. The continuance of the House tradition in service, thought and conduct.

The second outlined the privileges, the second and third of which existed only in the minds of the Committee:

1. The incalculable asset of live friendship.
2. First-rate club premises and hostel accommodation at cost prices.
3. A Corner House for all estates of men.

It was to the attainment of these advantages that the Executive Committee now addressed itself.

The balance in the bank of Toc H at this time is said to have stood at slightly under £30. Yet the Committee cheerfully considered the problem of obtaining a large house to form its central club in Trafalgar Square. Many alternatives were suggested, and at an Executive meeting in December a discussion took place on the possibility of raising between £30,000 and £40,000 which was considered the approximate amount that would be needed to acquire the Guards' Club building in Pall Mall! The Committee resolved at once to open an appeal for £30,000 for the acquisition of suitable premises, and a campaign 'sustained more by personal enthusiasm than efficient organization' was promptly launched with that object in view. The Committee at the same time came to a second resolution of grave import. It was clear to them that much of the personal appeal for the required funds must be made by the man who had started it all in the Old House at Poperinghe. It would be the padre's task to interview important and wealthy people, his mission to present Toc H to men of power and influence as well as of goodwill. He was therefore sternly bidden by the Committee to provide himself with a new suit.

This, as P.B.C. has himself confessed, was not so easy for a man of his configuration. On demobilization he had been provided with a 'standard' suit from Gamages' 'as a final tribute from a grateful country'; but as it had apparently, so Clayton swore,

been made for a Guardsman, it was not a perfect fit. The difficulties of obtaining garments that would becomingly clothe his
rotund person were obvious. But the Committee was adamant;
the Appeal demanded a new suiting for their 'Chaplain-plus-
General-Secretary', and they were not to be denied. So Clayton,
bowing to the inevitable, regretfully set out for Southampton
Row, where he was told that tailors were to be found. After gazing
into a window for a time, he hesitantly entered the premises. 'I
want a suit,' he said, 'two trousers and a waistcoat and a coat. My
friends are sending me to see a lot of men with money. I want to
look impressive for ten years. The first Lesson last night,
Nehemiah nine, says that the Jews in the wilderness did not wear
out their clothes in forty years. I want a suit like that!' Tailors, of
course, do not make suits to last for forty years; they would be
ruined if they did. But a spherical clergyman in a 'standard' from
Gamages' could not be expected to be familiar with such mundane
matters. He must be humoured. At length the pattern of cloth
was selected, the fitting endured; and the victim was permitted to leave the premises for the last time to await the arrival
of the suit. In due course the faithful Pettifer was despatched to
bring it home. And there at last it was – two trousers, vest and
coat, in all their glory. 'I saw myself accoutred as never before,'
recorded Clayton, 'ranging with rich results in high Society,
a mode of compelling dignity. I heard the Clubs and Drawing
Rooms whisper, "How perfectly he dresses! Let us support
Toc H!"' Then Pettifer handed him the bill. It was sixteen
pounds! He fulminated against those who had insisted on such
extravagances.

But the members of the Committee were shrewd people who
knew what they were about. The appeal caught the popular
imagination and was astonishingly successful. Membership increased by leaps and bounds, and many prominent people gave the
movement their enthusiastic support. The Archbishop of Canterbury and Field Marshal Plumer, both old friends of Talbot
House, became its Presidents, and two more – Clayton's kinsman
Lord Cavan and Lady Grosvenor – its Vice-Presidents. Money,
too, flowed in; not perhaps quite hitting the target set by the
ambitious organizers, but enough for the movement to transfer its
tradition of open-house to the one-room office in Arundel Street,

somewhat more spacious quarters than the flat in Red Lion Square. It was clear that Toc H re-born was a sturdy infant rapidly growing towards maturity. Already his prescient sponsors were foretelling for the thriving child a prosperous life and a great career.

9

Toc H Expands

'Toc H is a man-hunt.'[1]

Early in 1920, Harry Moss, a trusted friend of the Old House in the Salient, returned home to receive one of the innkeeper's invitations to visit him at his sister's flat in Holborn. Moss accepted promptly, to receive the usual warm welcome reserved by Clayton and the 'General' for old Talbotousians from Poperinghe. But, like other visitors, the newcomer had to make himself useful, and he soon received his instructions. It appeared that No. 8, Queen's Gate Gardens, 'a mansion set in a land of stucco and museums far removed from the crazy perch of Red Lion Square' which had lately been used as a convalescent home for wounded volunteers from the South American States, had just become vacant. First thing on the morrow Moss was to call on the lady in charge of the premises and say: 'Mr Clayton sent me . . . and as your house is being cleared of wounded ex-servicemen, would you let us have the place rent-free for six months?'

Moss has described how, early the following day, he presented himself at the house in Kensington, to be greeted at the door by a nurse in uniform. Might he see the lady in charge? Alas, no, she was about to leave for the South of France and was busy packing. The visitor pressed his point. His mission was urgent. Eventually he was ushered into a large room before a lady in the uniform of a Red Cross Matron. He spluttered his request. But, horror of horrors, the lady replied that she had never heard of Mr Clayton. 'Blasphemy, never heard of Tubby Clayton,' recorded Moss: 'I quickly informed her in my best Sergeant-Major voice who Mr Clayton was – everybody in Flanders must have heard of him . . .' But it was no use. The lady had been in Flanders, so she said; but she still protested that she did not know of him. Moss, desperate, now craved permission to telephone and ask his principal to

[1] *Tubby on Toc H*, No. 16.

come over in person, and leave was granted. 'Meanwhile I sweated and fretted. At length there was a hell of a bang outside in the street and, looking out of the window, I saw a strange little creature climb or unfold out of a mechanical thing named, I fancy, a G.N. – Tubby himself clad in trench boots and a huge scarf more like a blanket enveloping him.' He was soon closeted with the lady of the house, to emerge triumphantly saying: 'Well done, Harry old lad! My dear fellow, we have the house for a year rent free.'

So the mansion became a centre for the movement and at the same time a hostel where those dedicated to its faithful service could live and work together. Thus was founded Toc H Mark I, the first full-sized embodiment of Talbot House in London. But so great was the flow of men through the house that a second migration was soon necessary; and within a few months Mark I was transferred to much larger premises at No. 23, Queen's Gate Gardens, a corner house of noble proportions, close to the Natural History Museum. Here was a true peace-time equivalent to Talbot House in the Salient, inspired, as it was, by its own Chapel, where the Carpenter's bench from Poperinghe, recently at Knutsford, now found new rest and service.

It was soon apparent, however, that a second Mark was needed; for in less than twelve months some 1,600 men had visited and about 400 had somehow managed to pass the night in Mark I, and the congestion must have been alarming. So later that same year, 1920, Toc H Mark II was opened in St George's Square, Pimlico. It was due to the generosity of the Duke of Westminster, (son of Lady Grosvenor, one of the two recently appointed Vice Presidents), that this was possible. Later the Duke most generously added the gift of the house next door.

But Toc H was spreading far and wide. By the end of 1920 its Chaplain had conducted inaugural campaigns for the establishment of Marks in Edinburgh, Newcastle, Durham, Goole, Manchester, Stockport, Liverpool, Birkenhead, Birmingham, Leeds, Sheffield, Portsmouth, Gosport, Maidstone, Brighton, Northampton, Swindon, Bristol, Cheltenham, Worcester, Oxford, Cambridge, Saffron Walden and High Wycombe. Toc H was catching on in factory, in mill, in workshop, in store; and early in the new year the founder could proudly boast to Lord Salisbury, shortly to become a trustee, that '. . . the whole movement is growing at a pace, and with an intensity, far beyond our expectations. . . . Several of our seventy Branches in England are now on their way to Houses of their own, and in London we have two further Houses in immediate prospect.'[1] It was becoming a national movement.

It was also showing signs of getting beyond the control of its leaders. Clearly, if Marks were to be opened all over the country, local secretaries must be appointed to give local leadership. Accordingly in June 1920 a letter over the signature of 'P. B. Clayton, *Padre and Hon. Sec.*' was sent out to leading provincial supporters asking whether they could act in their district as Local Secretary of the Movement. 'The step we are now taking in the formation of Local Branches all over the Kingdom', it stated, 'is one that is vital to the welfare and development of the new work, and it is of the utmost importance that Toc H should be represented by a Foundation Member whose sense of service and fellowship can be relied on.

'The geographical analysis of our old Communicants' Roll (with the addition of a few old friends of the House) is now at length complete. It has been a big undertaking for an amateur staff, but the foundations are well and truly laid. The districts which we have formed are – (a) London and the big provincial centres; (b) country districts which have been more sub-divided, in order that the Local Secretary may not find his small flock utterly beyond his reach.'

The response to this appeal was immediate and enthusiastic; and soon really first-class leadership outside London began to emerge. For example, Pat Leonard, who had returned from a brave and brilliant war service to be Chaplain of Cheltenham College, and was later to be for many years Suffragan Bishop of Thetford, was so impressed that he resigned his chaplaincy for the 'uncertain adventure of Toc H'. He was shortly afterwards transferred to Manchester where he was appointed Staff Padre. 'Our House at Manchester opens on Saturday next,' Clayton told Lord Salisbury, 'and I said God-speed to the wonderful Pat Leonard, D.S.O., its Chaplain, yesterday.'[2] Thus began a spell of fourteen

---

[1] Clayton to Salisbury, 3rd January, 1921.
[2] Clayton to Salisbury, 25th April, 1922.

H

years' service to the Movement that had had its beginnings in
those grim war years in the Ypres Salient.

But as the movement grew and progressed, difficulties inevitably
presented themselves. It was soon apparent that, if post-war Toc
H was to be a lasting force, it must at all costs avoid becoming
merely a body of ex-servicemen. It was essential that it should
capture the hearts and minds of a new generation, and in many
cases a very young generation thrust forward to assume responsibility unduly early in the place of elder brothers for whom there
had been no return. Yet many were slow to grasp this need, for
the bond of fellowship forged in war remained strong between the
older members, and was jealously preserved. Thus the London
Committee once passed a rule that none but an ex-serviceman
could be eligible for the wardenship of a London Mark. At about
the same time the 'Elections Committee', whose duty it was to
scrutinize all candidates' lists, disputed hotly for some hours the
application to Join Toc H of a Quaker who had been a conscientious objector, even though he was proposed and seconded by the
Founder Padre himself and Mr Barclay Baron. At length he was
admitted and later became Chairman of a district committee; but
the jaundiced judgement of his fellows was slow to give way to the
more tolerant and balanced perceptions of youth. It was clear that
the views of the younger generation had to be respected if the new
movement was to survive and prosper.

Yet in this, too, risks were inherent. 'Fellowship' as seen by
the older generation had been every man's contribution towards
the task of winning the war. No such bond united the young.
Yet, if Toc H was to be a living force, it must inculcate the
doctrines of 'Fellowship' and 'Service': 'service to society as a
whole and to less fortunate fellow-beings in particular', as Barclay
Baron has well put it, 'must take the place of the service of war.'
But the awful disillusionment that followed the Armistice had
antagonized the older and younger generations, led to the cult and
pursuit of ease and pleasure, and rendered the lesson of service
exceedingly hard to learn. Of organized 'social service' there was
in the movement in 1920, scarcely a trace. Later, as we shall see,
the leaders of Toc H solved this problem in their own way; but that
time was not yet. Meanwhile, a guide was needed to show them
the road they must take. Fortunately that guide was close at hand.

Early one Sunday morning about mid-summer, Philip Clayton and Alec Paterson met for Holy Communion with Dick Sheppard at St Martin-in-the-Fields, and stayed for breakfast. After the meal the three friends went into committee in an effort to enumerate the objects that should inspire the Toc H family. Sheppard had been too fully involved with his own great work to contribute concretely, but Paterson produced what he called *Four Rules of Life*:

'Each day:-
1. I will think for two minutes.
2. I will read for twenty minutes.
3. I will treat every fellow servant as a brother, not asking from what school he came or how his father earned his daily bread.
4. I will build a new and glorious future for my country, believing that the best is yet to be.'

No sooner had Paterson read his four *Rules* than Clayton produced from his pocket a crumpled slip of pink paper, covered with copious notes and amendments, and read out the following aims:

'1. To promote an active and intelligent sense of brotherhood among men of all classes.
2. To stand for the fullest development of the individual for every man [such] as may assure him security and opportunity within the growing framework of Society. Everyman both to think and act with judgment and unselfishness, not only as a neighbour but as a citizen.
3. To recognize the dominating claims of the spiritual factor in human life and to found on them a principle of reconciliation between man and man in the joy and service for the Common Good.'

On the scrap of paper were also listed methods by which it was hoped these aims might be achieved.

'1. The opening of a series of self-supporting Club–Hostels, where both residents and visiting members stand four-square in the unity of common life.
2. The establishment of Central Club premises, which in addition to the ordinary recreative facilities shall serve as a depot for the recruitment and training of social workers.

3. To bring the expert to the Group, thus educating both ourselves and what public opinion [we] can influence.
4. To spread the Gospel without preaching it.'

There followed a full discussion between the friends, from which emerged – largely from Clayton's crumpled pink manuscript – what became known as the Four Points of the Toc H Compass: FELLOWSHIP – to Love Widely, SERVICE – to Build Bravely, FAIRMINDEDNESS – To Think Fairly, THE KINGDOM OF GOD – to Witness Humbly.

The value of this has been well explained by the Rev. John Durham, who was many years later to become Clayton's Deputy Vicar at All Hallows: 'The points of the compass are not separate, each being isolated from the other, they are in fact inextricably linked. If I love a man I shall think fairly of him and serve him. To think fairly of him is part of loving him and one way of serving him. Through Fellowship, Service and Fairmindedness we come to know the truth about men, about Life and about God, Himself.' On another sheet, happily more substantial than his scrap of pink paper, Clayton set down the philosophy and the deep spiritual significance of Toc H as he saw them in those days:

Toc H is based on the idea that Christianity is concerned with a dual reconciliation, each involving the other. First, there is the reconciliation of man with God, and then the reconciliation of man with man. You cannot love men till you work alongside, and know how much you need them. The harder the common task, the deeper the common sympathy. The work of Toc H is, therefore, to bind in a single tether those who would else be poorer for their ignorance of one another. Civilian life sinks us all in one rut after another, according to the bedrooms we were born in, or the trades we follow; and class-war is a biological necessity under the circumstances, if we do not repent. Toc H thus aims not at the stampeding of the whole social system, but at the creation of a place and atmosphere in which the younger men at least may meet their otherwise unknown contemporaries and learn, on taking over, how much needs doing from the tired survivors whom they have come to relieve.

On the morning of 18th June, 1921, a passer-by might have

noticed two men in shirt sleeves at No. 8a New Cavendish Street, a large and somewhat shabby house near Oxford Circus, where they were busy packing pictures and books into crates for removal. One of them would have been instantly recognized by any member of Toc H: it was the indefatigable Barclay Baron. Furniture stood about the rooms in great disorder; it was clear that the premises were being vacated. In due course a heavy lorry drew up and the driver, ex-M.T., lent an expert hand in loading his van with the contents of the house. On one of his journeys across the pavement, he slipped his load and fell, laughing, against the tail-board. Whereupon a passer-by called out cheerfully: 'Take more water with it, chum!' This was good professional advice, for on his peak-cap was the badge M.W.B. – he was an employee of the Metropolitan Water Board. But at last all the gear was stowed and the lorry set off down Regent Street. At length it drew up at 123 St George's Square, then the Toc H headquarters, and the removers began at once to unload the contents. When they ended their task, Toc H had the right to add to its name on its letter-heading the somewhat clumsy words – 'With which is incorporated the Cavendish Association'. The two institutions had amalgamated. How this had come about must now be told.

In June 1911, in the week of King George V's Coronation, a meeting had been held in the Queen's Hall in London, presided over by Lord Loreburn, the Lord Chancellor, at which Dr Lang, Archbishop of York (later of Canterbury) and Dr Winnington-Ingram, Bishop of London, spoke. 'At that meeting', wrote *The Spectator,* 'there were 1,700 men who acknowledged by their presence that they were anxious to commemorate the solemn re-dedication of the throne to the nation and the nation to the throne in Christian unity by devoting their leisure more closely to useful societies under the inspiration of Christianity.' The outcome of the gathering was the formation of the Cavendish Club.

The Club took its name from the Duke of Devonshire, a loyal and enthusiastic member who supported it liberally, and was housed in pleasant premises in Piccadilly, overlooking the Green Park. Its members were of the type one would expect to find in a good West-End club, except perhaps that they were somewhat younger than average. One qualification for membership, rigidly enforced, was that the candidate must have been to a public school; another was that he was doing or was prepared to do some kind of 'social service'. Thus things stood till 1914. Then came the war. The vast majority of the Cavendish members joined up, and many never returned. The social-service work for which the Club had stood was not forgotten; but it was completely submerged by the call to service elsewhere. And when the Armistice came, the Club found itself in a new world. Its members no longer had either money or leisure. Furthermore, they had fought and suffered alongside men who would never be eligible for membership of a Piccadilly club. 'Social Service' in the old sense now seemed patronizing and meaningless. The younger members were no longer interested in such things, the older ones tried to revive the spirit of the place and dismally failed. In the post-war world, as they soon realized, the Cavendish Club had no real place. In due course it was wound up.

In 1913 a group of friends who had been responsible for the start of the Club, many of them distinguished figures, had decided to spread its ideas far beyond the premises in London. There was to be no longer merely a Cavendish Club, but a Cavendish Association – with precisely the same objects and the same call to service. On Wednesday, 5th November, no less than eleven public meetings were held to disseminate their views and doctrines in London, Liverpool, Manchester, Bristol, Sheffield, Nottingham, Stoke-on-Trent, Norwich, York, Carlisle and Exeter. The London meeting was held, as in the case of the Club, at the Queen's Hall, with the Duke of Devonshire, President of the Association and of the Club, in the Chair. The speakers were Dr Randall Davidson the Archbishop of Canterbury, Mr Asquith the Prime Minister, and the Rev. H. R. L. Sheppard Vicar of St Martin-in-the-Fields and Chaplain of the Cavendish Club. Of these four men, three were or became intimately associated with Toc H, as were Lord Salisbury who spoke at Liverpool, William Temple (then Headmaster of Repton, and later Archbishop first of York and then of Canterbury); and Lord Methuen (the old Field Marshal, then Constable of the Tower of London) who spoke at Sheffield; and Dr Lang (then Archbishop of York, who in 1928 succeeded Davidson at Canterbury); and General Plumer who spoke at York.

The prospects seemed good and 'Centres' were formed in all the cities and towns where meetings had been held. But the fate of the

Association ran parallel with that of the Club. Nine months after its birth, war broke out. For four years it struggled to swim against the tide. The end of the war found it poor and exhausted, many of its most promising supporters dead or dispirited. Mr Barclay Baron and the Rev. Hugh Johnston, later one of Dick Sheppard's curates, strove valiantly to save something from the wreck. But their efforts were vain. And then, just as they were considering winding up the Association, two members of its Committee, Alec Paterson and Dick Sheppard, made a startling proposal: why should they not open negotiations with a new movement that seemed to have the vigour and appeal that their's so conspicuously lacked?

And so it came about that the Cavendish Committee approached Toc H to see if an amalgamation would be possible. It was clear that there was much in common in the aspirations of the two organizations, though the Cavendish was far more exclusive, more aristocratic, more 'pre-war'. On the other hand, Toc H could do with a dose of the public school spirit, which was such a prominent feature of the older and weaker partner. Though amalgamation seemed the obvious solution to the Cavendish's difficulties, as Paterson and Sheppard clearly saw, they encountered fierce opposition. Nor was this entirely one-sided. On 21st May, three days before the meeting that was to reach a final decision, Philip Clayton wrote anxiously to the two enthusiasts for amalgamation, that it . . . 'would merely wreck our little Jerusalem, which, however tiny, is built upon a hill and is at unity with itself'. Yet, despite this pessimistic and short-sighted view, the joint meetings of the two Executives secured a favourable vote. The resolution, proposed by Lord Methuen and seconded by Dick Sheppard, was passed unanimously. And so the two organizations became one. There were, of course, still many problems to be worked out, many difficulties to be resolved; but with goodwill on both sides these were duly overcome, and the benefits that accrued to Toc H from its association with the sturdy Cavendish pioneers can hardly be exaggerated. They richly deserve the tribute paid to them by Mr Barclay Baron in 1922: 'Let us not forget the debt we owe to these pioneers; they initiated a system which still works, they gained the respect of many great schools, they sacrificed their leisure to give of their best to a cause which they believed to be immensely important. It is no fault of theirs that their horizon was limited, and no merit of ours that our horizon is a little less so. Our successors will wonder how we ourselves could be so short-sighted; let us only hope that they will give us credit for doing our best.'

Towards the end of that year, 1921, the leaders of Toc H, emboldened by the remarkable success of the venture, determined to hold a 'birthday party' in London. The year before, on 15th December, the date for the first opening of Talbot House in Poperinghe,[1] a few enthusiasts had gathered for a cheerful evening's celebrations. But now, twelve months later, something more ambitious was planned. Before the party a short service of thanksgiving was held in St Martin-in-the-Fields, attended by some seven hundred members from all over the country. The birthday party that evening was held in Grosvenor House, the great London home of the Duke of Westminster, so soon to be demolished to make room for a vast building of modern flats. Unfortunately the recently-appointed Patron of Toc H, the Prince of Wales, was India-bound on board the *Renown*, so could not be present. But he sent a message by the hand of his brother, Prince Henry, later Duke of Gloucester, who represented him. The Prince was welcomed by Lord Salisbury, a trustee of Toc H, and thanked by Private Pettifer, 'the Gen'.

The enthusiasm of this great rally of young and not so young, all bound together in love for their movement and by their determination to spread it far and wide, is well shown in the great Round Robin, measuring some two feet six inches square, which was signed that evening by every person present from Prince to the most junior clerk:

Address to be read at the Centenary family party of Toc H on the fifteenth day of December, A.D. 2015: Whereas it is as unlikely that we shall be able to join your festivities as that you will join us tonight, we indite this Round Robin to you. Not knowing you, we have the Utmost Confidence in you, and trust

---

[1] Some authorities state that 11th December was the actual date of the opening of the Old House, but Clayton's letter to his mother dated 15th December seems conclusive evidence that that was the correct date. See p. 43 and *Letters from Flanders*, p. 27.

that our Sentiments are reciprocated on the same terms towards all those whose signatures are attached – with the inevitable exception of those whose names have plagued you in your History Books. But like all great causes, Toc H is similar to the 'wood' in *Alice*, where names of persons are lost. To be serious in a document of this character would be unconvincing to the last degree. We therefore content ourselves with wishing all Many Happy Returns of the Day, and remaining your obedient ancestors of Toc H.

The original of this interesting document is carefully preserved at Toc H headquarters, in anticipation of the day when it will be read aloud to our descendants on the movement's centenary, 15th December, 2015.

10

Vicar of All Hallows

'The temple of Toc H is this All Hallows.'[1]

Towards the end of 1921 Clayton was showing, as he put it, 'signs of wear'. Hearing of this, Lord Byng, an old friend of Talbot House since the days when he had commanded first the XVII Corps and then the Canadian Corps in France, and now Governor-General of Canada, urged him to come to Ottawa, and to make his visit profitable by lecturing in the Dominion. Clayton went to Lambeth to consult his old friends, the Archbishop and Mrs Davidson. The Davidsons bade him go to Chelsea and talk things over with Sir George and Lady Parkin, whose daughter, Alice, was the wife of Mr Vincent Massey, the distinguished Canadian statesman. 'I then went up as an entire stranger,' wrote Clayton to Mrs Massey after her father's death some ten years later, 'and found your mother and your father not only kind and welcoming but actually determined that I must go, and go equipped as only they in England could equip me.' So they gave him about thirty letters of introduction to personalities in Canada. 'When I presented these it did not matter that I had come without an invitation. Out of this memory I deduce two things. First, that the Hand of God was in it all; and secondly, that these two lived so truly in the Light of God's own presence that they did not assess trouble as illegitimate or tiresome when something could be done which might in the smallest way assist the Cause of Christ and His Church in Canada.'[2]

Early in the new year Clayton set forth with his many commendations; and by Sunday, 15th January, he was comfortably settled in Government House, whence he wrote to his father: 'My dearest Guv. Here I am . . . happy and welcomed beyond believing . . . a royal welcome from Minnis [who drove Byng on Canadian

[1] *Tubby on Toc H*, No. 49.
[2] Clayton to Mrs Vincent Massey, 8th December, 1931.

Corps H.Q. in the old days], with a large car for my luggage.
So through the city, and past the new Parliament House to this
great place, standing away back. Handed over here to an A.D.C.,
but Mrs Vimy[1] would have none of it, and met me in the Hall, and
the Grand Old Man himself strode out too; so that was that.
Rather a lot of dressing, etc., but that can't be helped, and is
bound to go on . . . I have a week here now for plans, and then
into the thick of it, with Montreal, Toronto, and thence westward
in February, and return here early in March before leaving for
home and Hatchett.'[2] The A.D.C. to whom the padre was
'handed over' was a young French Canadian called Vanier who
thirty-seven years later became Governor-General of Canada
himself. And after that long span, Clayton's visit was still a vivid
memory. 'When Tubby Clayton came to Government House in
January 1922 he was received with open arms by Lord Byng
of Vimy, the Governor General,' Vanier wrote in 1965. 'He en-
deared himself to all the Household by his simplicity and, may
I add, by his deep spirituality, and by his devotion to the men
he had loved and served in war and was continuing to help in
peace.'[3]

Though the Byngs were charming hosts, Clayton's stay at
Government House irked him somewhat, for many Toc H
members were anxious to see him and could not penetrate its
portals: '. . . so I must get freer of state ceremony soon,' he told
his father, 'though no one could be less ceremonious than the
Byngs – e.g. Mrs Vimy took me to her room today to give me a
dose of Fruit Salts, and even the flunkeys and A.D.C.s are very
human. I go out this afternoon in a Ford, calling on all sorts of
folk round about on my own. Clothes are the only pestilential
part of it, and I borrow them from the household generally as the
occasion arises.' What he looked like in his borrowed finery,
history, perhaps fortunately, does not relate! 'I'll never want to
see snow again. Not that it's cold – the houses are only too warm.
But the landscape is eternally blanketed and trying to the eyes. . . .'[4]

[1] Lord Byng's peerage was Byng of Vimy, commemorating his great feat, the
capture of Vimy Ridge in April 1917.
[2] Clayton to Reginald Clayton, Government House, Ottawa, Sunday, 15th
[January 1922].
[3] Vanier to the author, Government House, Ottawa, July 1965.
[4] Clayton to Reginald Clayton, Government House, Ottawa, 17th January, 1922.

The next day he wrote from the Vice Regal train: 'These kind folks are taking me into Montreal for the day to fix up my arrangements there for next week. So I'm travelling on this gorgeous train, and trying to write meanwhile. I'm going to be sick of trains before I've done with Canada. They are stiflingly over-heated; and the landscape in the winter anyhow is deadly. . . . I don't know what your busy spade would find to do here all the winter. The ground is beyond all working for six months on end, during which even interments cannot take place. The coffins are kept in cold storage! All goes well, and I'm thoroughly happy, though a wee bit homesick. But that's as it should be!'[1]

In Montreal he stayed with Sir Frederick William-Taylor, a Director of the Bank of Montreal. 'His wife (thank goodness) is away; so dressing etc. isn't so desperate as usual. He trots off to work like a two year old at 9 a.m. and gets back at 7 p.m. Meanwhile I have my fling on his telephone etc. We've got a big inaugural lecture here tomorrow, from the proceeds of which I hope to cover all costs of the 2 months; and so go forward with some clear profit to bring home. . . . I was admitted yesterday to the highest honour the Veterans in Canada can confer, my only predecessors being the Prince of W., Foch, Byng, Beatty and "General" Booth!'[2] This was Honorary Presidency of the Canadian Regiments. 'It was no doubt conferred at Byngs' request,' wrote Clayton modestly many years later, 'an odd position for a 4th Class Chaplain.'[3]

From Montreal he set out upon his tour of Canada. He has himself amusingly described it.

My plans were *sauve-qui-peut*. Upon the very night, when I left Rideau Hall, I found I had no money for the first train fare. I woke an A.D.C. at 2 a.m. while the sleigh waited to take me to join the west-bound train, and extorted the fare to Winnipeg. I trust this was repaid; I can't remember. The scheme was henceforth simple. My stock in trade was a lantern and some slides. I was to traverse the Dominion, finding what friends I could, what dollars were available. Beside me, as I write, rests the atrocious diary of that journey. It's best left alone: I blush to

[1] Clayton to Reginald Clayton, Vice Regal Train, 18th January, 1922.
[2] Clayton to Reginald Clayton, 68b Mountain Street, Montreal, 21st January, 1922.
[3] Clayton to the author, 17th April, 1963.

turn its pages. For instance, in one place, 132 tickets were marketed at 122 dollars. Only ten persons therefore got the lecture at its true worth; the rest were merely robbed! It says a lot for the long-suffering of the Canadian people that I was not deported out of hand. In the remoter spots, where the cinema was still a novelty, I billed my magic lantern apparatus as a new miracle, enabling a moving picture to stand still! Rotary rolled me forward, 'Lions' leapt at me, Kiwanis took me in and I returned the compliment. In all my wanderings I met no hand which was not out to help a stranger, and only one drunk man in a hotel. He was a delegate, attending a pure milk convention in Vancouver City.

The Canadian tour was a triumph. Wherever the lecturer went he was enthusiastically received by large audiences, and money rolled in. Indeed, so successful was it that at Ottawa on the return journey he found awaiting him an invitation from a well-wisher to visit New York. 'Accepting it. I got aboard a night train southbound. They gave me a great catalogue of past misdeeds upon a form to choose from. I did not think to take it seriously, put Trigonometry in place of Bigamy, and to the searching question whether I would by force or violence attempt to overthrow the Constitution of the United States, replied I had two weeks at their disposal. Armed officers came down the train and were severe with me.' The two weeks in New York were busily spent, and at first his impressions were not happy. He wrote to his father: 'I am wrestling rather fiercely with a city that has never heard of Ypres, but it may turn out profitably.'[1]

Things did turn out profitably. The first unfavourable impression quickly passed; and he could soon write that he 'had found the genuine New York'. He sailed for home in the *Berengaria* on 21st March, 'with no strength left in me, beyond a thankful heart, and 25,000 dollars paid or promised for Toc H anywhere. I spent the voyage in sick bay, sampling the sharpness of the doctor's lancets. My physique had given way. . . .' No wonder the lecturer was exhausted. Thirty-one nights had been spent in trains. He had been the guest of honour at sixteen public lunches, visited four

[1] Clayton to Reginald Clayton, Hotel Belmont, Forty-Second Street and Park Avenue, New York, 9th March, 1922.

universities and eighteen schools and colleges, and had delivered eighteen evening lectures and seventeen sermons. But there was no denying that Lord and Lady Byng's invitation had paid handsome dividends. Twenty-five thousand dollars for the movement was a rich reward for all its founder's efforts. Clayton's Canadian and New York tour in 1922 was the start of Toc H overseas.

The success of the tour, it was soon realized, was largely due to the interest the visitor inspired in young married couples. One result of this was a note which he addressed in May to the Central Executive of Toc H. Hitherto it had been a movement almost entirely devoted to men: the only exceptions were the small body of nurses from Poperinghe who had been admitted as Foundation Members. Was not now the time to rectify this? As Clayton wrote:

All the strongest organizations in the Dominion have, as their substantial support, a Women's Auxiliary. This body functions with real energy and enterprise in a variety of valuable directions. It raises money; brings audiences together; takes the initiative in a great number of social methods of assistance, such as the organization of dances, sales of work, bazaars, etc., and I found again and again that those who had sometimes acted with considerable hesitation in calling such a body into being were on all sides most grateful for the value of the work achieved. My strong conviction is that we shall form a Women's Auxiliary of Toc H. There are, I believe, in England a very large number of unselfish women who would be glad to have within their reach such an avenue of service.

The idea quickly caught on, and in October of that year, Miss A. B. S. Macfie, one of the nurses who had been elected Foundation Members, issued the first of a series of leaflets calling for women volunteers. The response was favourable, and in a very short time there was a band of loyal women members who paid regular visits to the London Marks, inspecting and repairing linen, mending socks and clothes, cleaning and beautifying the House Chapels. Nor must be forgotten or underrated the prayers of these splendid women, with which the movement was constantly sustained. This 'auxiliary movement' has grown out of all recognition in strength and influence since those early days in 1922.

Soon after his return, Philip Clayton was saddened by a tragic event within the Society's inner circle. P.B.C. was staying with Lord and Lady Salisbury, ever good friends of Toc H, at Cranborne in Dorset, whence he wrote to his father: 'The great man took me for a long walk and talk over the downs after tea, with the result that we were too late to dress for dinner, greatly to my comfort. But no pipes in the drawing-room afterwards; so I am having a smoke before bed, while I write to you and Neville Talbot. Beloved Neville! I have heart-rending news today that his young wife (Cecil Mary whom he worshipped), has died suddenly and he is left a widower with a girl of 2 and a nine-month-old boy. Remember him too in your prayers, my dear old guv; for he has been another big brother to me all through.'[1] At about the same time other news of quite a different sort reached him. His cousin, Lord Cavan, had lost his wife in 1920; and now after two years of widowhood, he had married again. Philip wrote to congratulate him. 'Delighted with your note, my dear Cousin,' came the reply. 'You will be proud of your new relation and I am grateful for your prayers. Yours, Cavan.'[2]

One night late in July of this year, Clayton received a momentous summons. He was to repair forthwith to Lambeth Palace to see the Archbishop, who had been suddenly prostrated by a temporary but painful disorder. Clayton sat at the bedside of the man whom he regarded almost as a second father, and they talked of past times, of Talbot House in Flanders, and of Knutsford Prison. The old man enquired after Toc H generally and after the recently opened Mark II. How stood the funds? Was there anything that he could do to help? Then he began to explain what he had in mind. At noon that day he had been to Tower Hill. Did his young friend know Tower Hill and the Port of London? Clayton replied that he had known them as a boy when his father

[1] Clayton to Reginald Clayton, Manor House, Cranborne, Salisbury, Wednesday night.
[2] Cavan to Clayton, Primrose House, Roehampton, S.W.15, Sunday. He had married Lady Joan Mulholland, daughter of the 5th Earl of Strafford and widow of Captain the Hon. Andrew Mulholland who had been killed in the first year of the war.

had business connections there. Did he know the great Authority which regulated the traffic of the Thames? The Archbishop had been there to give a blessing on the completion of the Authority's new building. On his way he had stopped to say a prayer in the ancient Church of All Hallows, but he found it shut and could not gain admittance. This had worried him while he was dedicating the Port of London's vast headquarters. All Hallows, one of the most important benefices in his gift, was deserted. What a sad contrast was the great old Church, shut, cold and neglected, to the busy thriving temple of Commerce so close at hand. On his way home he had once more attacked the doors of All Hallows and beat on them hard. At length, the verger, believing he had to deal with children from the street, angrily flung wide the doors: imagine his astonishment, his consternation, when he saw the Archbishop of Canterbury on the threshold. The visitor had gone sadly in, and knelt to pray amidst the dust and gloom. 'The walls were streaked with grime,' wrote Clayton some years later, 'floor boards agape, the rats were moving to and fro among them; the windows were almost opaque with soot; electric lights in niggardly quantity only rendered visible the darkness and un-relieved decay. The Church had been almost disused for months, and little visited for many years. No restoration and no thorough cleaning had been accomplished since the days of Mason. The eyes of the old Archbishop gleamed. He turned towards me, having thus unfolded in almost stirring tones his grim, intolerable experience. What was there to be done? Whom should he send? When he came back to his room at Lambeth, and was then suddenly thus laid aside, he went on thinking, and he sent for me.'

Gradually, as Randall Davidson talked, Clayton grasped his meaning. He was aghast. He quickly pleaded that Toc H was his life's work with which nothing must interfere. The Archbishop did not contradict him; he merely bade his junior ponder and pray upon this unexpected suggestion. He must consult his Central Executive, then let the Archbishop know how they felt about it. The interview was at an end, and Clayton went away to think over what had been said and to consult his friends. About a fortnight later, he received from his chief a letter confirming the offer he had made:

LAMBETH PALACE, S.E.
11th August, 1922.

My dear Clayton,

After much meditation, much consultation, many criticisms, and I need hardly say earnest prayers, I write to suggest that you should let me nominate you to the Vicarage of All Hallows Barking with the view to your making that historic Church a centre for work among the clerks and others in the City whom you can gather into the company of those for whose deepest welfare you cater, and whom you have shown yourself capable of helping. I do not want you to accept this nomination unless you do, with reasonable clearness, see your way to modes in which you can make the work effective. I do not ask you to let it be all (possibly not even chiefly as the years run on) Toc H work. I want you to have a free hand to use whatever means God seems to show you to be best for winning these young fellows to Christ. If now that you have considered the matter you feel that the difficulties are too great or the place unsuitable or the conditions unworkable, pray let me know now and let us decide on some other tenure of the Vicarage. You know, for I have explained it to you, what strong appeals are being made to me in other directions, urging that All Hallows is the very place either as a centre for our Foreign Missionary work or as a centre for Home Mission work in London. I therefore have no difficulties about finding a good man for a great position. I think, however, that the case you have put before me dominates over the others, and if you are prepared in the Name of God and in reliance on the Holy Spirit's aid to take up this work, I shall rejoice.

Please write to me at Lairg, Sutherland, N.B., where I hope to be from tomorrow for a fortnight. Then we come back to London for a few days before going to Geneva, and during those days – say between Monday the 28th and Wednesday night the 30th – I could see you if you desire it, but you will be able before that to let me hear whether it is Yea or Nay. May I ask you further to say nothing about it to anyone until you hear from me again after I have received your acknowledgement of this letter? I ask this because I do not want the matter to come to the ears of the Bishop of London or the Bishop of Salisbury who are pressing me in other directions until they hear from me that it is definitely settled. May God guide you and all of us to a right judgement in this solemn and difficult matter.

Yours very truly,
(sgd) Randall Cantuar.

The Central Executive Committee of Toc H, duly consulted, were unanimously in favour of their founder accepting the Archbishop's offer of the living of All Hallows. They believed, wrote Clayton later, that he '. . . could perform no greater service than to attempt to build an anchorage wherein the Movement could be tranquillized and re-equipped with peace and consecration. I did not know how all this might be done. I think, indeed, that on both sides there was (most naturally) a certain lack of hope towards All Hallows as a living centre; for there was yet no proof that it could flower. But the proof came, and none can miss its meaning.' 'The decision about All Hallows was, of course, a matter of great difficulty,' Clayton told Lord Salisbury at the time, 'but I feel more and more sure that it's right. . . . The Church – the most beautiful medieval Church in London – stands just opposite Mark Lane Station, close to the Tower of London, and we have every hope that it will serve as a spiritual centre from November onwards for our London Membership.'[1]

What the old Church has come to mean to the young movement, and Toc H to All Hallows, he well expressed some fifteen years later:

> Toc H throughout the world has been enriched, assisted, and safeguarded from All Hallows. No one can estimate the prayerful influence which, from within those walls, has been rendered ceaselessly operative upon the Movement throughout its period of wide expansion. No one who has, throughout these fifteen years, a working knowledge of the divers crises into which the Movement has been plunged and whence it has emerged with added strength, can doubt the contribution of All Hallows. No one who looks among the list of leaders of Toc H, those servants for Christ's sake who do His pleasure, but must acknowledge that these living stones have come to hold the corners of the young structure mainly from the apparently

[1] Clayton to Salisbury, 11th September, 1922.

inexhaustible quarry of fine, true self-denying character which
the grey Church on Tower Hill has hewn with joy, confirming
in them eagerness thus to serve. Without All Hallows, it's more
than likely that Toc H would by now be moribund. . . . The
debt upon the other side is deep. Without Toc H, All Hallows
would have had a scope far more confined, far more conventional. It would have risen to a certain eminence, because the
Church itself is history. It would not however brim to overflowing with water to be turned into good wine; nor would it
have the stewardship of those symbols which, even in among its
marvellously intact inheritance, bring no contrast in their
magnificence and dignity. It was an old man's mind which made
this union. . . . He it was who foresaw that the conjunction of
the then frozen life of this great shrine and of the young, impetuous, ardent stream flowing from Christ's re-wounded side
in Flanders, would bring to both true life in a high measure.

How all this came to pass will emerge as our tale unfolds.

11

The Lamp of Maintenance

'Now let the loving cup of fire
Be lifted over land and sea.
Now may the faith of friends inspire
Our shattered souls with unity.'[1]

During these early years of the movement's re-birth in London, it
became clear to all with the welfare of Toc H at heart that there
must be some method, some peace-time plan for the fellowship
that all felt was essential if the organization was to prosper. The
earliest attempt to work out such a formula was dated from
Cheltenham, 4th February, 1921, and came as a rough memorandum from Lieutenant-Colonel A. Murray-Smith, a London
member who had joined the Toc H 'Cheltenham boys' and had for
some time been discussing such matters with them. His suggestions were thought so constructive that the memorandum was
distributed to local branches.

Murray-Smith's leaflets, headed 'Toc H: Cheltenham Branch,
Some suggestions for what they are worth' had much to say on worthwhile ideals for the youthful movement, together with the need for
fellowship amongst its members, and in two important respects it
had a lasting and noteworthy influence. In the first place, it
stressed the significance of '*the helping of others* – thus doing whatever, little or much, we can to make things a bit happier than they
are at present. In other words, we are out for SERVICE of some
kind or other, thus trying to be Christians in the sense as understood by such padres as Tubby Clayton, Dick Sheppard and scores
of others like them.' This is the guiding principle of what Toc H
now knows as 'Jobmastery', a conception that had scarcely sunk
into the minds of the organizers by the early months of 1921. In
every house, or Mark as they are called, each occupant was
expected to do his share of work, and the Jobmaster was the
supervisor of that work. The Jobmaster has been described by the

[1] P.B.C., *The World Chain of Light.*

Rev. Pryor Grant, a saintly American priest who had been won over to the movement by 'that amazing man' (as he called him) the Founder himself, as:

> the liaison officer between the Group and the Community, or the agencies in the Community. . . . Toc H is interested in much more than the effect of good works on the people who try to do them. It is and must be interested primarily in the quality and effectiveness of the works done. Therefore it can have no more important person in its groups than the Job-master. Upon his wisdom and judgement and teaching capacity depends more than can be described; and this is the grasp of what real service is on the part of those who practise it, and in the development of a real community life.

Murray-Smith's second suggestion, 'rather more serious', was perhaps even more significant. 'Might we remember, in silence *for half a minute*, at each of our gatherings, at supper or afterwards, our old friends whom we have left behind in the Salient or elsewhere?' This suggestion was the germ of an idea from which the Ceremony of 'Light' was developed.

The lamp had not yet been thought of and how it came to pass is interesting. One day in May 1922, Philip Clayton and Barclay Baron, calling upon a rich stockholder in Bristol from whom they hoped for a generous cheque towards their cause, were detained for some time in a dreary waiting-room. 'What a pity', ruminated Clayton, 'that Toc H has no badge, something like the Scouts', which members could recognize each other by.' Then, as he went on talking, apropos of an entirely different subject, he let drop the word 'Aladdin'. In a flash Baron had his inspiration. 'Tubby, you've got it!', he exclaimed excitedly; 'a lamp as a symbol of Toc H!' 'It might do – but what sort of lamp?' The answer was a rough sketch, made on the back of a used envelope, of an ancient Roman lamp. A few weeks later a wooden model had been turned, and from this was designed the bronze Toc H lamp as it exists today. It follows the simple form of such lamps as dimly lit the worship of persecuted Christians in the Catacombs of Rome. On each is engraved *In Lumine Tuo Videbimus Lumen* ('In Thy light shall we see light'). The sacred cipher XP, the first Greek letters of the name of Christ, which often decorated the early Christian lamps – and was later adopted by the women of Toc H for their own 'Lamp of the Magnificat' – they replaced with the double Cross of Calvary, with its superscription forming the shorter arm above the transverse beam. This was part of the coat of arms of Ypres, the use of which had, during the war, been granted to Talbot House by the city's Burgomaster, 'Thus', as Barclay Baron has well said, 'the lesser calvaries of the Ypres Salient, where Toc H was born, are perpetually commemorated in its symbol.'[1] The original Lamp which, once lit, was never suffered to be quenched, was the gift to Toc H of its Patron, the Prince of Wales; the other lamps, replicas of the parent Lamp, were sent out to the branches for use at 'Guest Nights' and like occasions.

The Ceremony of Light is short and simple, but impressive. When the meeting is ready to start the room is darkened and in complete silence the Lamp, the emblem of Toc H and the symbol of the branch's membership in the movement, is lit. Then the following dialogue ensures, closely following, it will be noticed, the suggestion made by Colonel Murray-Smith in 1921.

CHAIRMAN: *With proud thanksgiving let us remember our Elder Brethren:*

> *They shall grow not old as we that are left grow old*
> *Age shall not weary them nor the years condemn.*
> *At the going down of the sun and in the morning*
> *We will remember them.*

THE BRANCH: *We will remember them.*

Then follows one minute's silence.

CHAIRMAN: *Let your light so shine before men that they may see your good works.*

THE BRANCH: *And glorify our Father which is in heaven.*

The Lamp is then extinguished, and the ceremony is at an end. 'The words which precede the Silence constitute an act of Remembrance, those after it a Self-dedication,' as Mr Pryor Grant has pointed out. 'These two ideas belong to the symbolism of the Lamp, which is called and thought of not so much as the Lamp of Remembrance as of Maintenance.'

[1] Baron, *The Birth of a Movement.*

If a new member is to be admitted, he is introduced by the following simple observance.

CHAIRMAN (to sponsors): *Who goes there?*

SPONSORS: *A.B., a friend and a brother to be.*

CHAIRMAN (placing the Lamp into the Candidate's hands): *What is this?*

CANDIDATE: *The Lamp of Maintenance.*

CHAIRMAN: *What first lit it?*

CANDIDATE: *Unselfish Sacrifice.*

CHAIRMAN: *What alone will maintain it?*

CANDIDATE: *Unselfish Service.*

CHAIRMAN: *What is service?*

CANDIDATE: *The rent we pay for our room on earth.*

CHAIRMAN (to the Branch): *A.B. stands before you duly sponsored, and has well answered our questions. Do you pass him?*

THE BRANCH ASSEMBLED: *Pass, friend, all's well.*

This symbol of light caught the imagination of the padre. At the age of thirty he had begun his great work. He had suffered and loved and worked, with all the fervour of a strongly-emotional character, for the men of the Ypres Salient. 'He was knit into the intense passion of World War I', wrote the Rev. John Graham, Father Superior of the House of the Resurrection, Mirfield, 'with a poetic and prophetical endowment of soul and an unrivalled power of dramatizing each casualty, an insight into all the tears and all the glory of death in battle. The peace-time Toc H was the creative expression of this great emotional force; it was not a backward-looking gathering of old sweats; it was the outcome of a determination to build all the agony into a fellowship of renewed hope and purpose.' In accomplishing this task Clayton was positive that he was doing the work that God has commanded him to do. This is reflected in his prayer beginning 'O God, who has so wonderfully made Toc H'. 'The theologian may raise an eyebrow, the friendly critic may find a question mark hovering over the phrase,' comments Father Graham, 'but for Tubby this was the stupendous truth; in that old Talbot House in Poperinghe he had seen with his eyes and heard with his ears and handled and felt and known and been humbled to his knees by the workings of the living God among men. To have doubted that would have been to have deserted the truth burnt into him by an experience which was the reality of his life.'[1]

The living God among men, the reality of God at work in human lives – that was the conviction that he had to impart to others: and one way of conveying this awesome truth was through the Ceremony of the Lamp. The lighting of the lamp in darkness to symbolize the light of the world shining in the darkness of human hatred; the repetition of the pledge to remember, not just the men killed in war, but men in whom the Spirit of God had been at work round the carpenter's bench at Poperinghe. Thus the Ceremony of the Lamp and, to a lesser degree, the work of the 'jobmaster', foreshadowed in Colonel Murray-Smith's memorandum, symbolized the inner spirit of the post-war movement.

It was about this time that the Staff of Toc H was reinforced by an acute Scottish mind – that of Peter Monie. He had had a brilliant career at Glasgow, at Balliol, and in the Indian Civil Service, where he had been under Philip's brother, Sir Hugh Clayton. From Sir Hugh he had learnt much of Toc H and its Founder-Padre; and so profoundly impressed was he with what he heard and, later, saw that he decided to resign from the Service seven years before his time in order to devote himself to the honorary administration of this curious and heartening adventure. On 2nd November, 1922, Peter Monie took over Philip Clayton's shabby desk at Toc H headquarters. Within an hour, it was said, the staff were aware of a new force in their midst. It was soon apparent that a man of first-class administrative ability was at the helm. The Vicar-elect of All Hallows-by-the-Tower could safely leave the business side of the movement in Monie's capable hands. And it was as well that this was so. For Toc H had vastly progressed in the few years since the war, and was by 1922 a movement of national importance.

But Clayton saw clearly the problems that faced him, and these he set out in a letter to his friend and patron, Lord Salisbury.

As you know, my chief anxiety for some time past now has been how to keep the spiritual growth abreast of the material development of the big Society. For November, therefore, my

[1] Graham to the Author, 3rd December, 1964.

chief task will lie in this direction, and P. W. Monie, C.S.I., the Director of Development in Bombay, then takes over from me the main task of administration. His coming is a very great thing indeed for Toc H as a whole. . . . I know him well and love him dearly, and it's a wonderful thing that his great abilities should be thus placed without salary at our service. Meanwhile, in everything except finance, we are going from strength to strength. The visiting campaign of this summer, which has been conducted by some 40 members working in pairs in many parts of England, has produced an extraordinary catena of evidence that the ground is clear and the time ripe for really big developments. I am rather anxious about finance . . . small sums are continually coming in. . . . But that really is not good enough: . . . the movement at this stage must secure a series of large gifts, if it is not to be hampered during the tremendous period of developments now before it.[1]

Already plans were afoot for a great rally to celebrate the seventh birthday of Toc H, at which the newly-conceived symbol, the Lamp, was to be used for the first time. Already hopes had been raised high by the granting to the movement by King George V of a Royal Charter of Incorporation, and by the many prominent men associated with it, who were lending their powerful aid. And amongst them was the new Patron, the Prince of Wales, the young officer in the Salient who had come many times to Talbot House, and who now in post-war years recognized its value. 'Toc H', declared the Prince enthusiastically, 'is plainly one of the best things of its kind emerging from the years of sacrifice. . . .';[2] and he demonstrated his anxiety to see it flourish by the gift of the Central Lamp of Maintenance, the symbol of the movement, the Lamp that ever shines, from which all other Lamps are derived. Already money began to flow in, so that by the end of the year Clayton could report to Sir Godfrey Thomas, the Prince of Wales' Private Secretary, with somewhat exaggerated optimism, that 'Toc H is really not only afoot, but aflame. Thanks to various folk, we have now climbed our first big financial foothill and have £20,000 in the Bank which isn't so dusty, in addition to an income

[1] Clayton to Salisbury, 11th September, 1922.
[2] October 25th, 1921.

from membership etc. of about £3,000 p.a.; so we can really take courage and go forward.'[1] That was all very well; but such sums were totally inadequate for the ambitious projects that Clayton and his supporters cherished for the new movement. How could they secure the far larger sums needed if these plans were to be realized? That was the most pressing problem of the hour.

Now, strange as it may seem today, in those early times the one thing the organization lacked was the support of the City of London. This shortcoming the Prince was quick to see, and he determined to spare no effort to remedy this defect. In the autumn of 1922, therefore, he sought for Toc H the powerful support of Lord Revelstoke, head of the great House of Baring, and an old and trusted friend of the Prince and his family. His letter sets out very clearly what Clayton had achieved and what was yet to be done.

> St. James's Palace, S.W.
> 30th October, 1922.

Dear Lord Revelstoke,

As you probably know I am extremely interested in the work and development of a movement known as 'Toc H' (or Talbot House) which originated in the Ypres Salient in 1915 at a time when all class prejudices were at best temporarily forgotten. Since the war, owing largely to the energy of the Reverend P. B. Clayton, M.C., who was its Chaplain and now acts as General Secretary, it has grown in the most amazing manner and is regarded by many people as the best thing in England that has come out of the war.

It aims at forming rallying centres for the hundreds of young men who each year come to the big cities, generally away from their homes, to take up the business of life and evoking in them the spirit of mutual service and self-sacrifice that was revealed during the years of the war.

Three years ago, 'Toc H' had less than £50 as its total assets. Today, as shewn in its Royal Charter, it has over £20,000 in investments and nearly £30,000 worth of house property, freeholds, furniture, etc. Three houses are open in London which are crowded to overflowing every night, with big

[1] Clayton to Thomas, 12th December, 1921, Duke of Windsor's Toc H Papers, Windsor Castle.

waiting lists, and houses have been established in Manchester and elsewhere in the provinces.

'Toc H' in London is directly serving some 2,000 members most of them juniors in the City, and through them is making a great contribution to the social service of London as a whole, but it is almost unknown to senior people in the City itself. It is, however, holding an Anniversary Celebration at the Guildhall on December 15th next, at which I, as Patron, am presiding, and it is in connection with this that I should be more than grateful if you could spare a moment in the near future to see Clayton and give him your advice as to the best way of using the Guildhall Ceremony to make the City of London take notice.

I am sure you will like Clayton, he is an extraordinary good little fellow, who lives entirely for 'Toc H' and will explain to you better than I can the amazing growth of the movement which is almost more than its leaders can cope with.

It would be of the greatest assistance to us all if you could see Clayton and advise him about the City side of things. 'Toc H' has many friends, but, owing to the nature of its origin, few among the big businesses; and as the majority of its members work in the City it is only right that an attempt should be made to establish some form of liaison.

Yours sincerely,
Edward P.

As a result of this appeal Philip Clayton had a useful meeting with Lord Revelstoke, and by his instrumentality Toc H became known to, and in due course supported by, many of the leaders of the country's big business.

In the Royal Charter of Incorporation granted at this time the objects of the Association were thus formally expressed:

1. To preserve among ex-service men and to implant and preserve in others and transmit to future generations the traditions of Christian fellowship and service manifested by all ranks of the British Army on Active Service during the war.[1]

---

[1] In 1925 this was amended by omitting 'of the British Army' and adding 'thereby encouraging its members through the common Christian life of the Association, to seek God, and helping them to find His work and to do it'.

2. To encourage amongst the members of the Association the desire to perform, and to facilitate the performance of, all kinds of social service as between and for the benefit of all ranks of society.

3. To promote among all people a wide human interest in the lives and needs of their fellows and to foster in every man a sense of responsibility for the well-being of his fellow men.

4. To mitigate by habit of mind and word and deed the evils of class-consciousness and to endeavour to create a body of public opinion free of all social antagonisms.

Such were the cold, formal, somewhat stilted words in which the Charter enumerated the objects of Toc H. But many members were not entirely satisfied with what Mr Baron described as 'the undemonstrative precision of legal phraseology'. Accordingly, at a meeting gathered at Grosvenor House during the Birthday Festival, a *rider*, since known as the *Main Resolution* of Toc H, was passed with one accord:

Remembering with gratitude how God used the Old House to bring home to multitudes of men that behind the ebb and flow of things temporal stand the eternal realities, and to send them forth strengthened to fight at all costs for the setting up of His Kingdom upon Earth: we pledge ourselves to listen now and always for the Voice of God, to strive to know His Will revealed in Christ and to do it fearlessly. Reckoning nothing of the world's opinion or its successes, for ourselves or this our family, we will endeavour to think fairly, to love widely, to witness humbly, and to build bravely.

On 14th December, the eve of the birthday, the Royal Charter received the King's signature. Toc H had grown to years of discretion; it had become a recognized national institution. And it was just seven years old.

The Birthday Festival at Guildhall was preceded by an Induction and Thanksgiving service at All Hallows-by-the-Tower. At the first, attended by the Bishops of Winchester and Pretoria, Lord Salisbury, the Lord Mayor and Lady Mayoress of London, the Burgomasters of Poperinghe and Ypres, and a host of notabilities, and before a great congregation of young people who filled to overflowing the ancient Church, Philip Clayton was inducted to the benefice by Dr Winnington-Ingram, the Bishop of London. Following the Induction, Christmas Carols and Blake's splendid hymn 'Jerusalem' were sung, and the Family Thanksgiving Service, at which the Prince of Wales was present, started at about 7 o'clock. After the service, the new vicar took his Royal Highness round his Church and showed him the place where the Prince's Lamp was to stand – and has stood ever since.[1] – on top of the tomb of Alderman John Croke, 'Citizen and skinner, who lies below the altar tomb in the north-east chapel of the church . . .[2] the spiritual ancestor of Toc H'.

The ceremony at Guildhall that evening was presided over by the Prince clad in Toc H blazer and tie and wearing flannel trousers. The great gathering of two thousand people in the ancient hall that Richard Whittington, five times Lord Mayor of London, had helped to build some five hundred years before, witnessed their Patron light the Prince's Lamp, that from that day forwards has never been allowed to be extinguished. From this Lamp, given by him in memory of his own fallen friends, he then lit forty similar bronze Lamps, each the symbol and the proud possession of one of the earliest branches of Toc H. This act, carried out with stately ceremony, was the central item of the Guildhall programme: it brought a splendid day to a glorious close.

[1] Except during the Second World War, when the Lamp was moved to the Crypt for safety.
[2] *Survey of London*, Vol. XII (Part 1), The Parish of All Hallows Barking, p. 27.

12

World Tour

'The Lamp, lit round the world.'[1]

During the next five years the main tasks of the founder of Toc H were to extend its rapidly growing influence, and to rescue All Hallows, its Guild Church, from the neglect from which it had for so long suffered. Toc H, it was now agreed, must make its appeal to the younger brothers of those who had been left behind in Flanders. 'Give them a home and a friend right on the spot where their working lives are spent,' was the appeal; and the various Marks were designed to forward that very object. But Clayton was anxious that the ancient Church, so long without any *raison d'être*, should play its full part in the new post-war life of the district. A place was wanted where city workers who could not afford restaurant prices could eat in comfort their frugal midday meal brought from home in a sandwich-tin or paper bag. The Vicar threw open the doors of his Church to meet this very human need. The elderly, the bigoted, shook their heads; but Clayton did not care. In due course suitable quarters were found elsewhere, and the All Hallows 'Lunch Club' came to an end. But he had achieved his two-fold object. The Church had been put to good use; and large numbers of workers who had previously been scarcely aware of its existence had found their way into the unknown building. Some of these no doubt would stay for spiritual refreshment. And so it was to prove. The historic Church – swept, garnished and revitalized – became an acknowledged centre for the hungry for God's word. Services were regularly held; at first they were sparsely attended, but in time, as more and more young city workers learnt of the remarkable work of its Vicar and fell under the spell of his magic personality, they came to sing with him, to pray with him, and (under his guidance) to rejoice and give thanks to God for the blessings of their lives. 'I

[1] *Tubby on Toc H*, No. 22.

want to thank you so much for letting me come to you last night,' wrote Clayton's cousin, Dick Sheppard, in October 1923. 'It was a wonderful service and I was enormously impressed by the youth and keenness. Also, you have done a most remarkable thing in altering the whole of your Church without upsetting your simple parishioners. We are learning a lot from you. God bless you, old boy.'[1] This delighted the recipient – 'so undeserved', as he modestly told his father.

Side by side with the renovating of All Hallows the work of Toc H progressed apace. New Marks were opened in many centres where their need was keenly felt, and regular donations began to flow in. This success encouraged its leaders to hold a second Birthday Festival on 15th December, 1923. At the second gathering, as at the first, the Prince of Wales lit the Lamp in the Ceremony of Light: on this occasion he was assisted by General Sir Charles Harington and Sir J. M. Barrie, the playwright and novelist, while the Duke of Devonshire read the lessons. On such an important occasion all must be appropriately attired, Clayton wrote to General Harington:

> Part of your wedding garment for 15th is now on its way to you by post, a Toc H blazer and tie. The third requirement is grey flannel bags and a soft collar. The Prince turns up thus habited and so do all the delegates, so if you can bring yourself to do ditto it will be splendid. I am attacking your fellow Lamplighter, J. M. Barrie, this afternoon with the same proposition, but a smaller size in blazers. Two impromptu committees met at Mark II last night. One of the big-made men to find you an appropriate size blazer. The other exclusively composed of small Scotsmen to find one for J.M.B. . . . Barclay Baron has drawn up a complete operation order for your information concerning the Guildhall. If you see any need for, or have any time for previous collaboration, Sir James Barrie's address is Adelphi Terrace House, Strand, W.C.2. May I add that, while not on the programme, it's only fair to warn you that a tabloid speech will be clamorously demanded from you. . . .[1]

[1] Sheppard to Clayton, 6 St Martin's Place, Trafalgar Square, W.C.2, 19th October, 1923.
[2] Clayton to Harington, 7th December, 1923.

This second birthday celebration was an unqualified success, in spite of one discordant note – in the musical sense but in no other. The evening was to terminate on a high tone, the singing of 'Rogerum', the song that meant so very much to Philip Clayton. 'The first time, I think, I heard it sung', he recorded, 'was by thirty-five survivors of the Queen's Westminster Rifles who had left one hundred of their friends behind them that night; and swung down into Poperinghe, many of them wounded and gassed, to billet in the great store next to Talbot House. It was a new song set in their mouths that ordered their going and behind the roughness of the words there was more than a little shy thanksgiving. . . .' Its use must be the privilege of Toc H members only; it must not be sung or taught to Scout Troops, Boys' Clubs or other such organizations. 'I am strongly opposed to it being sung publicly to audiences who knew nothing of its origin, or its sacred associations with the ordeal of Flanders. . . . Moreover, I think I can conscientiously say that I have never sung it myself without an explanation beforehand of the reason why. I do not deny that it is dangerous, like strong meat; but it is strong meat for men, and if properly explained and understood will continue to lead them on. Surely we must revolt from the conception that our Lord prefers the musical modulations of a Minor Canon to the clean free marching song of men who were learning to laugh at fear, and to move together to their duty.'[1] But on this second anniversary occasion there was a slight – indeed a somewhat amusing – hitch in the singing of his beloved song. The Band of the Coldstream Guards had been prevailed upon to play for the Festival, but unfortunately the music for 'Rogerum' had only been written out at the very last minute, and the players found it by no means easy to read the manuscript and play from sight. Accordingly, they started very slowly on the opening verse. This was far too tranquil a rendering for Clayton who was singing in his immense bass voice and beating time for all to follow; hence the singers under his conductorship reached the end of the first verse by the time that the band had got halfway through it. The result was chaos. Amidst the laughter that greeted the confusion, Clayton bellowed: 'It's the old story: the singers go before, the minstrels follow after.'

[1] *Tubby on Toc H*, No. 72.

Though donations were flowing in to Toc H fairly satisfactorily, they were far from sufficient to support the rapidly expanding movement. It was, therefore, decided that early in 1925 Clayton should make a world-wide tour, and that he should be accompanied by Pat Leonard, whose success in Manchester had been quite phenomenal. Clayton's trip to Canada and New York in 1922 had been a huge success. This was to be a far more ambitious enterprise. But one thing greatly worried him. His beloved sister Belle was ill – 'very gravely ill', as he told his cousin, Isobel Armstrong,[1] and both his brothers, Hugh and Jack, were abroad. With Philip's departure, there would be no one at hand in a crisis.

Before he left, Clayton was summoned to York Cottage, to preach before King George V and Queen Mary, whose regard for him had survived the abruptly-ended sermon of his Knutsford days. From Sandringham he wrote to his father:

My dearest Guv. I'm just waiting for lunch, and probably shan't get this finished before the bell rings. If not, I'll do it tonight. The job here is ever so much more homely and happy than at Buckingham Pal. I got here yesterday evening, and had dinner (no other guests) at 8.30 (their clocks here are kept $\frac{1}{2}$ hour fast for early shooting!). They were both extraordinarily nice and simple and kindly; many inquiries about my throat, and about the journey ahead; they ask about you at home. The cottage is really little more than a cottage. . . . After dinner, we did cross-words, with between-whiles conversation till 11 p.m. I'm afraid I didn't get up for early Church this morning, as I'm not very full of vigour yet. But the service at 11.30 was quite jolly, much less stiff than at B.P., and my voice just held out. This afternoon we've been walking round the village, looking at Clubs, Institutes, etc. and moving about in a very homely way among barking dogs and apple-cheeked children. At one stage the Queen literally ran back to an old village woman she had just passed, and said, 'I've done that for you. It will be all right.' I don't know what it was, but it was just a little glimpse of her thoughtfulness that greatly pleased me. Tonight I am to dine with them again, and don't feel half so shy about it.[2]

[1] Clayton to Isobel Armstrong, 29th January, 1925.
[2] Clayton to Reginald Clayton, York Cottage, Sandringham, Norfolk, Sunday [January 18th, 1925].

K

Many years later Clayton wrote to a friend on the same subject:

> During their residence the King himself becomes the village Squire, deeply concerned with any local problems and thankful to be free of State affairs – although he never could be wholly free; but none the less he and his wife and children could when at Sandringham be at their ease. King George V was, so I understood, one of the finest country squires in England. At Sandringham on Sunday afternoons the entire family went for a long walk round the farms and through the village street, greeted respectfully by all concerned. Behind all this there was the utmost pride and genuine regard displayed towards them without the formal tone that is adopted in Court affairs. The visitors received not only every kind consideration, but a new insight into a regime which has no awkward side to it whatever. The King and Queen would always do their best to make the week-end preacher feel at home. The sermon did not matter in the least, provided it was short and to the point. On Monday morning all anxieties which he brought with him would have been removed.[1]

The parting from his father was painful. Reginald Clayton was eighty; a few years previously he had lost his beloved wife; and now, with his daughter Belle gravely ill and all his three sons abroad, life was hard for the old man to face. But he bore the ordeal bravely. 'I did just want to send a word of utter admiration for your courage today, which was greater than my own,' wrote his son from on board R.M.S. *Antonia* before sailing, 'and I have all the excitement and experience ahead, while you have just your sweet old life – garden and prayer and patience (in both senses!) I never loved you so much as I did today, and tonight it's a deeper chord than ever. God bless and guard you and uphold you, who have ever been to all your children the true example and pattern of earthly Fatherhood, thus teaching us the truth of the first words of the Lord's Prayer, as few sons today may learn it in their homes.'[2] The *Antonia* sailed that night, and thus the Rev. P. B. Clayton and the Rev. Pat. Leonard set out on their world tour, after having

---

[1] Clayton to Colonel B. Hubert Cooper, 8th April, 1952.
[2] Clayton to Reginald Clayton, on board R.M.S. *Antonia*, 9 p.m. Thursday [February 5th, 1925].

received what Leonard noted as 'a great send-off' at Southampton.

The crossing was rough, Clayton reported to his father, so that '. . . the passengers have mostly remained horizontal, and we are two days behind time already. Pat and I however, survived; myself gloriously immune, Pat more questionably so. Besides plethoric meals, we are getting a solid nine hours' sleep night after night, and feeling ready for anything in N.Y.'[1] Five days later he announced 'a joyous visit to Halifax', and that they were steaming for New York, which they reached on 17th. 'I'm really rested and refreshed', Philip told his father, 'and eagerly ready for the great task ahead.'[2] Their reception in the States was friendly. 'Pat and I are sitting in the Board Room of the Cunard Company, surrounded by masses of letters, mainly unanswered, and phone messages galore, and all the impedimenta of an arduous campaign,' he wrote a few days after their arrival in New York. 'However, the Cunard folk are kindness and help personified, from Ashley Sparks down. . . . The job is very confusing, but amusingly so; and we are both in the best of health and spirits. We have ten more days here – not much money, I fear, but that remains to be seen. It's best of all if Toc H starts in earnest in U.S.A.; as please God, it will.'[3] He returned to this theme on the eve of departure for Boston. 'We've had a good time in New York, not large sums of money, but – what is better – real deep keenness, which will I trust issue in Toc H being really formed as a native U.S.A. movement.'[4]

In Boston Clayton held a half-hour service in the Cathedral at 12.10 each day on '. . . the Christianity of sacrifice and service illustrated by Toc H; It's a fine sight and atmosphere – the best yet – and quite wonderful to see 1,000 people each weekday thus gathered; and the congregation has grown steadily through the week. We are both very happy here – much more so than at New York. . . .'[5] They stayed a few days in Toronto, and so to Ottawa where once again the hospitable Byngs welcomed them: 'Here we both are for 3 days real respite and refreshment, which I think we

---

[1] Clayton to Reginald Clayton, on board R.M.S. *Antonia*, 19th February, 1925.

[2] Clayton to Reginald Clayton, on board R.M.S. *Antonia*, 15th February, 1925.

[3] Clayton to Reginald Clayton, 25th February, 1925. Sir Ashley Sparks was Resident Director of the Cunard Steamship Company in 1925.

[4] Clayton to Reginald Clayton, 6th March, 1925.

[5] Clayton to Reginald Clayton, The Cathedral Church of St Paul Boston, Friday, 12th March [1925].

have earned honestly,' he wrote to his father from Government House, '. . . the Byngs are perfectly charming to us, and we could not ask for a sweeter haven (apart from Hatchett itself) for these spring days. . . . I was commanded by their Excellencies to have breakfast in bed this morning, and did so obediently. Next year is their last in Canada, and they will be a great loss everywhere; for they have won the love they deserve by their wisdom and sincerity. It's especially good to find Religion has the deepest hold upon Byng himself, who speaks of it with the faith of a true Toc H man, and prays and reads as devoutly as my own father. . . .'[1]

In Toronto the travellers reported hopefully to Peter Monie in London, that they had met a certain Jack Price, whose wealthy father Sir William Price had recently died. Jack had promised $5,000 to help start Toc H in Toronto, and to consider with his family Clayton's suggestion that he should found Toc H in Montreal with a gift of $25,000 in memory of his father.[2] A copy of this letter to Monie, Philip sent to his father. '. . . the wonderful help of Jack Price etc.', he wrote, 'will I think give you a glimpse of what we've been through, and of the joyful fruit thereof.'[3]

But though he might write home cheerfully and optimistically there is no doubt that the strain of the journey was beginning to tell. Perhaps it was partly the heat that was afflicting him; but, whatever the cause, Philip Clayton, though only in his fortieth year was already beginning to call himself old and to consider who should succeed him. And even then, in 1925, his thoughts were turning towards two promising young men, who had already shown their attachment and their value to the movement, Tom Savage, aged twenty-five and John Daly, twenty-two. This may amuse us as we look back on the past after more than forty years. But so it was; and we find Clayton whilst at sea *en route* from Vancouver to Auckland, New Zealand, writing to Tom Savage:

North America was full of emptiness geographically, and a deal of spiritual vacuity as well. The Romans found their power on force, and tend to terrorize rather than persuade. The limited

[1] Clayton to Reginald Clayton, Government House, Ottawa, 31st March, 1925.
[2] Clayton to Monie, 180 Simcoe Street, Toronto, Easter Tuesday [May 5th, 1925].
[3] Clayton to Reginald Clayton, King George Hotel, Saskatoon, Saturday, St Mark's Day [April 25th, 1925].

(and disunited!) Protestants massage the middle-classes with much oratorical energy; and the little pitcher of the C. of E. between them is in the position of poor Alice (in Wonderland) with both Queens bent on making her uncomfortable. *Mais, nous verrons*: or rather *vous verrez,* for I don't expect to go to Canada again. Toc H is a high-mettled horse, but its present rider isn't fair on it. Clowns don't make good jockeys; nor even good clowns, when they grow old. So the next act is to get ready; and that's what I'm writing about to John [Daly] and you. Mind you love one another like blazes; or you will both go below. This is a queer letter; if it's too difficult to read, try reading between the lines.[1]

To Daly, then at Mirfield, he wrote on the same day and in similar strain. '. . . But you, my very dear Sir, and a bunch of others whom God is calling, have got to get ready to take Toc H over, perhaps by 1930, certainly a few years later; and it will be a big thing by then, if God's Will continues to urge it forward. You and Tom Savage are likely to be the Pat and Tubby (not in shape, I trust) of the situation at home. . . . That's what's in store for you. I'm thinking; and it's not too soon to tell you so. You can't contradict me promptly across 10,000 miles . . .'[2] – and much more in that strain.

By the end of May Clayton was comfortably established in Government House, Wellington, for Whitsun week-end; thence to Christchurch – '. . . the most English place possible – more English than England. The stream by the school is called the Avon.'[3] At both these places branches of Toc H were successfully launched. Thence he crossed to Australia, and stayed with Lord Forster at Admiralty House, in Sydney, where he received a wonderful welcome: 'Today a civic Reception by the Labour Lord Mayor; and the whole of the chieftains of Sydney struggling to get into the lunch, at which the Gov. General proposed our healths, and I talked hard and fast. Since then a meeting of the Provisional Executive, a first go at the office in Hamilton Street, and an inaugural meeting of two groups tonight.'

Here Philip received alarming news from his father; his sister

[1] Clayton to Tom Savage, 17th May, 1925.
[2] Clayton to John Daly, 17th May, 1925.
[3] Clayton to Reginald Clayton, 4th June, 1924 [mistake for 1925].

Belle had had a dangerous relapse. '. . . I am cabling this week-end to the office, to save you the anxiety of a cable', he telegraphed, 'and shall hear from them early next week of her recovery or her passing over. I am more distressed for your anxiety than for the dear sufferer herself. She is safe in God's hands. Goodnight my loved father, your spirit is a daily inspiration to me.'[1] Within a few days 'the dear sufferer' had passed over. Less than eighteen months later the loved father followed his daughter into the unknown. On Saturday, 22nd October, 1927, Reginald Clayton died in his eighty-third year after the first illness he had ever experienced.

From Sydney, Clayton went to Brisbane in his native State of Queensland; and as he approached home, the welcome became even warmer. At Brisbane he was surrounded by relatives and old friends of his parents, including his kinsman, Harry Clayton, and his family still living at Maryborough. Harry whisked him off to the old home. 'We pulled up stumps in Brisbane at 9 p.m. last night,' he wrote to his father, 'and Harry met us at the train and travelled with us through the night. I didn't find sleep easy for once, as the line is in a pretty rocky condition. At 5.30 a.m. we alighted at Maryborough Station, and trotted round briskly to the garage where H.C. keeps his Ford while on Legislative duties at Brisbane. We climbed aboard with our kit, and through a cold white mist crept out to the old home. Here the family was all up to receive us with a warm-hearted welcome, and hot buttered toast and tea. . . .' The family were Harry and his wife Emily and their children, and Harry's younger brother. . . . 'Then we sat about and thawed and chatted until the sun conquered the mist, and the landscape became visible. Then we had breakfast proper, and soon after started off for a triumphant career around Maryborough. It gave me a glimpse of what no amount of books on Queensland could have made real to me; and at every step I was picturing you and Mother in the happy life which has left so true and deep a memory among the older folk here.'[2]

A few weeks later Clayton was at Broken Hill, so full of memories of his beloved father's early life. 'In the old days of

---

[1] Clayton to Reginald Clayton, Admiralty House, North Sydney, 17th June, 1925.

[2] Clayton to Reginald Clayton, Gonora, St. Swithin's Day, '25. [July 15th].

"half a halfpenny bun" at 88 Bishopsgate Within I little thought that I should ever find myself writing home from Broken Hill!. . . . Today I am preaching to the miners – the best paid in the world – and looking out across the dust-swept mining town which gathers round the great shafts.' From Broken Hill he had good news to send the old man at home. About £500 had been subscribed to start Toc H in Adelaide, and an anonymous gift of £5,000 had been received to endow a Memorial Chaplaincy. So, as he joyfully wrote, '. . . we feel at last that Toc H in Australia is really on a substantial footing. *Laus Deo !*'[1]

In the following month Clayton reached Perth, Western Australia, and stayed at Government House. 'Here I am at last, with a week's work before the boat to Jack (*S.S. Malatian*) then from Penang by the Suva Maru to Colombo, then Calcutta, till about Nov. 20th, when I join Hugh in Bombay, so the homeward journey is begun. I'm very happy and well – happy because Toc H is coming true, well, because God's good to us both.'[2] The voyage home was put out of schedule by the slowness of the *Malatian*, and everything in consequence was very much rushed. But the travellers left the ship at Surabaya '. . . and did a tremendous road race across Java to Batavia – 630 miles in 16½ hours! There we caught a Dutch boat to Singapore, and saved a week. Since then, it's been a long round of journeying and speech making night after night; but the very best of fun.'[3]

In late November he was in Calcutta, telling his father that at the end of the week he was to go *via* Delhi to Bombay, thence home, except for forty-eight hours in Jerusalem, where he stayed with his old Army Commander, General Plumer, who earlier in the year had been appointed High Commissioner in Palestine.[4] 'This will reach you, I hope, on Dec. 14th', he wrote whilst crossing the Red Sea, 'and I shall creep into Hatchett on Thursday or Friday, Dec. 17th, 18th, I hope. I shan't be officially in England until Saturday, so deny all knowledge of me till I turn up! I expect to reach Paris on 16th from Trieste, and cross to Dover,

[1] Clayton to Reginald Clayton, Broken Hill, 8th S. aft. Trin. [August 2nd, 1925].
[2] Clayton to Reginald Clayton, Government House, Perth, 11th September, 1925.
[3] Clayton to Reginald Clayton, British Residency, Perak, 14th October, 1925.
[4] Clayton to Reginald Clayton, Bishop's Cottage, Calcutta, 16th November, 1925.

and thence HOME. Then up for the Festival, and HOME again for Christmas. *Laus Deo!*[1]

In the event he did not quite keep to those dates. He reached England on the Saturday, the very day of the Festival. The magnitude of his services to Toc H were eagerly recognized that night by the tumultuous welcome he received from the great company that packed the Albert Hall. He had been away for almost twelve months, and in that time he had circled the globe. By his travels he had given an international significance to the movement that was his life and of which he was the soul.

[1] Clayton to Reginald Clayton, Red Sea, 3rd December [1925].

13

Tower Hill

'May it become the treasured possession of all
Londoners, nay of the whole Empire from far
and near, that Britons from all climes may
visit this hallowed ground with reverence for
the past and with hope for the future.'[1]

'Once upon a time, an unattractive boy, nine years of age, inky and
predisposed to curiosity, stood gazing at Tower Hill through iron
bars. The seas and the waves were roaring in a Dock Strike; and
his father, then a merchant in Bishopsgate Within, brought him
down in the dinner-hour to get a glimpse of a mass meeting under
John Burns himself. The Dockers were led magnificently, and
followed with old-fashioned loyalty. . . .'[2] Thus Clayton described
what was presumably his first visit to that part of London which
was to be his home from about 1923, when he moved into the
Porchroom of All Hallows' Church, until his life's end. After a
few years in these somewhat cramped conditions, which he shared
with his curate, George Moore, Clayton moved first to No. 7
Tower Hill and then to 42 Trinity Square. But whether he was at
No. 7 or No. 42 it was all the same to him; they were both on 'The
Hill', the place for which he had an abiding passion.

He saw beyond the mean streets, the huge, ugly warehouses
and offices. His mind's eye dwelt not on the drabness, but on the
drama of the place: the great Roman wall which crosses Tower
Hill from north to south, the building of the Tower in 1078 by the
saintly Gundulf Bishop of Rochester under the command of
Norman William, its intimate links with every Norman, Plan-
tagenet and Tudor Sovereign. His thoughts dwelt much on the
illustrious blood that had for centuries drenched Tower Hill.
There the assassin Felton purchased the knife that cut short the
life of mighty Buckingham. Near by in The Bull died, in extreme

[1] Clayton and Leftwich, *The Pageant of Tower Hill*, p. 262.
[2] ibid., p. 1.

poverty, Thomas Otway, author of *Venice Preserv'd*. In Great Tower Street dwelt the profligate Earl of Rochester, who for some weeks posed as an Italian physician and fortune-teller and did good business. At the Czar's Head on the South side of Great Tower Street, Peter the Great – during his visit to England in 1697 and 1698 – displayed his prowess in drinking brandy and beer.[1] On Tower Hill William Penn was born. In Little Tower Street, the poet Thomson lived and here in 1728 he composed his *Summer*. In Seething Lane for many years lived Samuel Pepys. Off Seething Lane is Crutched Friars, called after the Crossed Friars of *Fratres Sanctae Crucis*, who had a house here. To the east is the Minories, taking its name from the Minoresses or Nuns of the Order of St Clare. Farther eastward we find ourselves in Goodman's Fields, site of a Roman burial-place, named after a local farmer of Queen Elizabeth's time. Here stood the famous Goodman's Fields Theatre whither all the fashionable world flocked to witness the great Garrick in the role of Richard III. In Royal Mint Street, once called Rosemary Lane, died Richard Brandon, the executioner said to have beheaded Charles I. In East Smithfield the poet Spenser was born. Near by was the ancient village of Ratcliffe Highway, made of ill-repute in December 1811 by the barbarous massacres of two families for which no one was ever brought to book. Not far from the former Ratcliffe Highway is Wapping, where, at the Red Cow in Anchor & Hope Alley, the monstrous Jeffreys was apprehended dressed as a sailor. Dragged to the Tower he shortly died there, partly from drink, and partly from injuries received from the infuriated mob.

Such events of the days of long ago were constantly before the eyes of this historically minded cleric; and he longed to see his beloved Hill restored to something like what it has once been, an ancient 'Park or Pleasaunce' unsullied by the hideous buildings of modern times.

In point of fact, Clayton had already prepared some plans which showed how his day-dreams might come true. These he had discussed with some devoted friends and admirers, such as Lord Goschen, Sir Ion Hamilton Benn (his Churchwarden at All Hallows), Sir Follett Holt, Sir Kenyon Vaughan-Morgan and

---

[1] Peter the Great occupied John Evelyn's house, Seyes Court, Deptford. The Czar's Head public house in Great Tower Street was destroyed in the Blitz.

others; but it was not until he had a fortuitous meeting with a man of wealth and vision that his plans made any real progress. It chanced that in June 1926 some members of the Corn Exchange begged the clergy of All Hallows to hold a commemoration service in memory of their fellow Londoners who had fallen on the Somme on that awful summer's day, 1st July, 1916, which had cost the Capital in one morning more lives than on any other day of the two thousand years of London's history. Invitations were hurriedly despatched, and – at the last moment, and quite as an afterthought – a 'timid telegram' was sent to Sir Charles Wakefield, head of the great firm of C. C. Wakefield & Co., which dealt in lubricating oils and appliances, asking him to attend. Rather unexpectedly he came, and Clayton seized the opportunity of disclosing his plans. Wakefield, who was, like Clayton, a Londoner by adoption, was caught by the imagination of the scheme, and pledged his support. 'Thus', recorded Clayton, 'began our friendship in All Hallows.'

The trouble had really started in 1864, though its origin was earlier. In 1465 a certain Robert Denton, at that time Chaplain of All Hallows, had bestowed the freehold site and a series of small houses to the east of All Hallows Alley on the Royal Hospital of St Katharine by the Tower, to build an extension providing beds and treatment for poor priests 'who had lost their wits'. The extension never materialized; and almost exactly four centuries later the trustees of the Royal Hospital leased the whole site to a speculative builder called George Myers for a term of eighty-four years. Without delay Myers put up an immense building of monstrous proportions, popularly though incorrectly known to our grand-fathers as the 'Mazawattee Building'. It was in the words of Cecil Thomas, the distinguished sculptor, '. . . the largest oblong box that would go into the site, with as many flat holes in it as possible. . . . It fails by size, colour, monotony, proportions, and architectural trimmings which do not trim. *It earns for us the amused contempt of foreigners.* No other race would tolerate this nightmare.' As this 'nightmare warehouse', as Clayton called it, rose, the Vicar of All Hallows of the time called on Mr Myers to protest that this ghastly erection excluded light and air from his Church and from all around it. In response to this plea Mr Myers made a gift to the Church of a Chancel window, 'the colours of which', as Clayton has unkindly recorded, 'ran in the first rain-storm'. This was hardly fair, for the fault was probably due to the builders having fixed the window back to front, for which blunder Myers can scarcely be blamed. Be that as it may, the window was removed, and the object which should have been screened by it remained to 'shut out light and air from having a free course, and flooded every pair of eyes with misery'. After the war the offending building was 'old, half-empty and inflammable. A strong east wind and All Hallows could scarcely be saved. The "dark Satanic mills" of William Blake need no more illustration.'[1]

The first of Clayton's objects for the improvement of Tower Hill, which he discussed with Sir Charles Wakefield, was the demolition of this monstrosity by 1948 (when the lease was due to expire) or sooner if possible. This was fundamental. But Clayton had other aims in mind which, though subordinate to the first, were also important. The second was the removal of a small misshapen building erected in 1911 on the pavement of Byward Street by the Underground Railway. The third and fourth steps concerned the Tower of London, and would therefore require the consent of the Constable. One of these was the creation of a children's tidal playground upon the long shingle beach in front of Tower Walk and the provision of a constant guard at low tide to render it safe; the other that the public should be admitted on those midday occasions when the band played on the Western Moat. Two final aims related to the eastern side of Trinity Square. The first concerned the authorities of the Underground who, in constructing their railway, had pulled down a section of the Roman Wall leaving a gaping cavity. Clayton's object was to roof over this open cutting, to lay turf upon the roof, and to create a new square giving public access to a fine surviving section of London's ancient wall. The sixth and last suggestion for improvement was, that the Commissioners of Crown Lands, who owned the freeholds of 22 and 23 Tower Hill and let them on a yearly term, should reclaim this lease and create here an Eastern City Garage, thus stopping the abominable misuse of Trinity Square (itself the true Tower Hill) as a mere parking place. This proposed garage, it was claimed, would pay its way handsomely, and would greatly simplify the whole traffic problem in the neighbourhood.

[1] Clayton and Leftwich, *The Pageant of Tower Hill*, pp. 283–4.

Beyond these six vital proposals the planners envisaged one further proposition that would require legislation. This important step was thus set out in their Agenda:

> ...that the City of London should re-open negotiations conducted by the Corporation when Tower Bridge was built. The proposition then was that Great Tower Hill should be handed over to the City. These negotiations should soon be renewed upon the basis that the City should reclaim its ancient and most reasonable control up to its ancient Wall. This step would bring Great Tower Hill as a whole within the City Boundary once more; thus preventing the Hill from being ill-lit, ill-paved, disreputable. This famous site is now an ugly No Man's Land, between the boundaries of the City and the Metropolitan Police. The City Corporation would thus protect effectively those dangers to good order and to decency which afflict Great Tower Hill; which would thus be restored to its true use for the health and happiness of working citizens.[1]

Wakefield was anxious to do all in his power to forward these highly practical proposals; but at first difficulties were encountered. City etiquette required that the Alderman of Tower Ward should consent before Wakefield could take a part in Tower Hill Improvement; and for a time this consent was withheld. But happily in 1932 a more enlightened Alderman in the person of Sir Howard Button was elected, and he readily gave his consent. In consequence, the Tower Hill Improvement Scheme was officially opened with Queen Mary as its Patron; Sir Charles, recently created Lord Wakefield of Hythe, as its President; and with Sir John Anderson, later Lord Waverley, Lord Blackford, Sir Douglas Ritchie (Solicitor to the Port of London Authority) and Mr Edward Holland-Martin as members. This influential Trust soon got to work with startlingly successful results. St Katharine's Rents, the site of Myers' odious warehouse, was re-purchased for £50,000; near-by buildings were acquired and demolished; and the paddling-beach and playground for the city children was in due course achieved. Much had already been done by the outbreak of war in 1939; much of what was still to do was accomplished by the German air raids. Myers' 'Nightmare Warehouse', for

[1] Clayton and Leftwich, *The Pageant of Tower Hill*, pp. 286–8.

instance, and an ugly little building, 18 Byward Street, were demolished partly by enemy action and partly by the instigation of the Trust. These sites were handed over to the Corporation of the City of London as an open space to be maintained in perpetuity for the benefit of those who visit Tower Hill whether on business or pleasure bent. Thus, through the vision of the priest and the generosity of the benefactor, 'The Hill' was greatly improved.

While all these things were being done, other anxieties faced both Clayton and Lord Wakefield. Clayton felt strongly that the house in the Rue de l'Hôpital at Poperinghe 'which has such sacred associations for thousands of us', should not be entirely closed to Toc H, and that its owner, who had returned to the house, should at least allow a tablet to be affixed to its walls. Apparently M. Camerlynck was completely unco-operative: he would not permit pilgrims to enter the house, nor would he allow a plaque to be set up on its walls. In consequence, we find Clayton as far back as 1924 writing anxiously to the Prince of Wales's secretary, Sir Godfrey Thomas: 'It is a great hope among many of us that we may ultimately be able to purchase at a fair price the old house in Poperinghe and keep it for our pilgrimages and re-establish its chapel, which would in many ways be the most perfect Church for the Salient, as suggested by Lord French, Meanwhile, we would earnestly ask that Monsieur Coevort Camerlynck should not be so inhospitable to pilgrims who desire the privilege of entrance.'[1]

At first the owner of Talbot House was adamant. But at last in 1926 a body of pilgrims led by Clayton himself went out armed with a personal introduction from Prince de Croye of the Belgian Embassy in London to the Burgomaster of Poperinghe. The Burgomaster pleaded the cause of the pilgrims so effectively that the owner at last consented to admit them to his house in relays of twenty. The whole visit was a triumphant success. 'Tubby celebrated next morning on the Great Stone of Remembrance in the Reservoir Cemetery at Ypres,' wrote Jock Gillespie, one of the pilgrims.

Most of the main body went to Poperinghe by train and the women by bus. This time the doors were open and Tubby went

[1] Clayton to Thomas, 12th August, 1924.

in with the first twenty people to the Chapel. The rest of us, awaiting our turn, went around the garden with the 'Gen'. The brick wall on the left was still pockmarked by shell-fire. 'Gen' took us across the garden and showed us the spot where the Carpenter's bench was found. Finally it was our turn to go upstairs. As we mounted the narrow stairway we met the first party coming down and we saw by their faces that they had not only seen, but also had understood their vision. The loft had retained its use as an attic but at one end still stood the dais that had supported the Carpenter's bench and there, in front of this, stood Tubby with bowed head; a disused pram stood in one corner and some onions were laid out on the floor. We all instinctively knelt as we entered for we knew that the ground whereon we stood was holy.

This was destined to be the first of many pilgrimages to the well-loved shrine.

Some three years later, in the summer of 1929, ugly rumours began to circulate. 'I hear now that the dear old place is sold to be a Bank,' wrote Clayton sadly to General Sir Fabian Ware, of the Imperial War Graves Commission, 'and I should be most grateful if the good offices of the C.R.C. could be enlisted to discover whether the Bank in question will allow us to rent, or (failing that) to revisit from time to time the Upper Room, so sacred to us all. Would you be so kind as to cause enquiries to be made on our behalf?'[1] Four months later it was reported that M. Coevoet Camerlynck was asking £4,000 for the house, 'which is probably in excess of its value', as Clayton wrote to Sir Godfrey Thomas,[2] and that a Belgian bank was considering making an offer. But within a few weeks of this, the generous Wakefield stepped in, purchased the property himself, and presented it to Toc H.

Thus at last at the crucial moment the Old House was saved, and the light which had shone so brightly in the black darkness of war was re-lit in the Upper Room at Poperinghe. Very shortly afterwards it travelled round the world, forming a Chain of Lamps and Rushlights steadily maintained by members, to complete its mammoth journey at the great annual gathering of the

---

[1] Clayton to Ware, 10th July, 1929.
[2] Clayton to Thomas, 16th November 1929.

movement in the Albert Hall on 6th December, 1930. 'When at the Albert Hall tonight this Chain of Light is completed', declared the Prince of Wales, 'I would have every member realize that to be worthy of it he must put duty first. There is much the younger men can do to help the world, if only they will do it, and do it now. Many years after a great war, one shortage at least still continues, that is the loss of leadership. It is to help in finding and inspiring leadership that Toc H seems to me so significant; and those who would be leaders must learn through fellowship and service.' This need to inspire the young with the spirit of service was uppermost in Clayton's mind; and it was his earnest hope that the re-acquisition of Talbot House would prove an inspiration to all those visiting the beloved and hallowed spot in the years ahead. 'It seems to me quite beyond estimate what the Old House may do in the immediate future, and for generations yet unborn,' he wrote to Major Paul Slessor of Toc H headquarters. 'I feel this opening year is highly critical. That is to say, it matters quite intensely that every man and boy who goes to Poperinghe should come back energized by his experiences. If by God's Grace we can achieve this thing, it means that we shall be building up sons of the Old House everywhere quite steadily; and it will subsequently become a seal upon keen membership to know the whole great story intimately.'[1]

But the acquisition of the Old House presented problems both financial and administrative, as Clayton explained to Mr Hurst of the Car & General Insurance Company, who ever since his first encounter with the founder had been an active member of the movement. 'The Old House is now ours by his [Lord Wakefield's] great kindness; but its re-birth will only bring full blessing if it is made available for Toc H universally.' There must be no class distinction; therefore a subsidy would be necessary, or only the well-to-do would be able to visit it. At least £250 a year was needed for that alone. Then there was the question of running the House. It was estimated that about 3,000 Toc H members might be expected to visit the shrine during this summer of 1931, and of course many of the general public would come as well. A house-keeper was therefore obviously necessary, for the whole responsibility could not be allowed to rest on the Belgian caretakers. A

[1] Clayton to Slessor, 20th April, 1931.

dormitory with at least twenty cubicles must be built, and one room must be set aside for a small war museum to teach the younger generation what the Salient stood for. 'All this is an immense task which may be of the finest widest influence on English life and character,' Clayton told Hurst. 'There are now, as you know, nearly two hundred schools in touch with Toc H, and these boys must have facts presented to them in every way that is wise and serviceable. Through my experience already of introducing parties of schoolboys to the Old House and the surrounding country, I am quite certain that the kind of plan which I have sketched above is virtually essential to the full use of this inheritance.'[1]

When the two men presented their problems to the generous donor of the house, Lord Wakefield promptly agreed to pay for whatever repairs were needed and to endow the building with the sum of £10,000 for its upkeep. With what joy did Padre Clayton conduct that Easter's pilgrimage to the Salient! 'It was a truly great experience,' as the Rev. J. R. Lewis recorded from Stony Stratford shortly afterwards. He had joined the party at St Pancras Station a complete stranger, yet was soon made to feel that he was amongst friends. He wrote to Clayton afterwards:

I find it very difficult to describe in any way the impression that the Old House gave to me, save only that it was something unique. I learned for the first time how a place can be peopled with Spirits of the Past. Throughout the house, but especially in the Upper Room, I was just aware of the presence of the Elder Brethren – a strange, quite unique, but very real experience. And if this was what I felt, who am new to Toc H and never fought in the war, I can but dimly guess what the House means to Toc H as a whole and to you especially who knew it in the war years. The glimpse that I was able to catch of the spirit that is at the heart of Toc H in the gatherings we had together is something that I prize immensely, not only because it helped me to a knowledge of the movement which I am entering, but because it sounded again to me personally that

[1] Clayton to Hurst, 11th May, 1931.

L

note of devotion to service to our Lord which is the way of my Ministry.[1]

Also in the company of pilgrims that day was Ex-Sapper Will Leonard, the carpenter, who had known the Salient well in the war years. Hard times and a sick child had recently claimed most of his attention; but now at last after a long interval he was revisiting the place he had loved. Shortly afterwards he set down for Clayton his remarkable experience:

> On arrival at Talbot House, Poperinghe, I took the first opportunity possible, and kneeled down in the Upper Room. I don't remember praying or using any words, I may have done; but I remember (as I had some weeks previously) asking God for an answer to some problem which was worrying me at Easter time 1917. Then, all unbidden, there came into my mind the lines from *The Ancient Mariner* (which I had not read for years).
>
> > The many men, so beautiful!
> > And they all dead did lie.
> > And a thousand thousand slimy things
> > Lived on, and so did I.

I remembered what you wrote just after the war, about the best men having died and left us second-raters to carry on the jobs and do the things they would have tried to do had they lived. I felt greatly abashed. . . . My mind didn't wander as much as usual, and I became more absorbed in the service than any time for some years. I can remember kneeling down again after the reception, so what happened must have been after that. I think then my mind was as near passive as ever I get in church. I don't usually think in pictures; but then, there came into my mind a vision, as if I stood on high ground looking back from the Line, over a long stretch of desolate, muddy, rain-swept country, dimly seeing figures moving. In short, just such a scene as we were familiar enough with in the war years; but with this difference, that much more poignantly than I ever did in the war years I felt something of the almost intolerable and seemingly interminable agony of it. . . . [And then suddenly the

[1] Rev. J. R. Lewis to Clayton, the Manse, Calverton Road, Stony Stratford, 6th May, 1931.

vision vanished.] I then found it hard to remain kneeling. I
think I half rose and kneeled again; but I felt impelled to stand
up and, when I did (though I saw no vision and was fully
conscious of where I was and what I was doing), I felt that I was
standing in the presence of a great company of free men, free
through Christ, and in some way their agony linked up with
His. . . . I think I remained standing, conscious of their presence,
all the time to the end of the service, when for a few seconds I
knelt down . . . There was the sense of being uplifted in that
Great Company, my unworthiness to be of their company
eliminated; but what, I think, shook me was the realization, in
some measure, of the agony they had known.

That shows something of what the Old House at Poperinghe
meant to one old soldier on his visit that Eastertide in 1931. From
that time forward it has been the shrine to which pilgrims from
many parts of the world come year after year to renew their vows
to God and to recall their comrades whom they left behind in
Flanders. 'Every movement with a religious basis has found
inspiration in a pilgrimage,' wrote Sir Alec Paterson at this time.
'We go back to our beginnings to understand our growth and see
our objective. The lad who was a baby in the war gains more by
going to the Old House in Poperinghe and imagining the refreshment of the tired soldier than by listening to many poor
reminiscences of mine or any other. The Old House is more than
a place of sentiment – it is a fact of history. I know fellows of
straight and simple mind who have found the depths of Toc H in
no crowded Guest Nights but in the strange simplicity of a
Belgian house where it all began.'

14

Some Post-War Problems

O Christ, who lovest all men well,
What now is marred in us remould,
What now is weak in us dispel,
Add the new truth. Confirm the old.
All stale embitterment make sweet,
Cool heads, firm hands, and ardent feet.[1]

In the years following the First World War, Toc H was faced with many problems, not the least of which was the question whether it should include Christians of all denominations or should confine itself to members of the Established Church; and in this controversy a distinguished Scottish theologian, a devoted member of the movement, became involved. To Dr George MacLeod, later to become Lord MacLeod of Fuinary the problem was this. In the war years the Table in the Upper Room had been the home of all denominations; but, when the movement acquired for the first time in All Hallows an ecclesiastical 'home', it was announced that there would be Holy Communion for Confirmed Anglicans in the Guild Church, and that others would go to a 'Free Church Communion' at some other shrine. That, MacLeod argued, was all wrong. Either Holy Communion was, as it was said to be, the very core of the movement, in which case the altar at All Hallows, as had been the Carpenter's bench in the Upper Room, must be the home for them all; or, alternatively, if Church Law forbade the whole family from meeting together round one Communion Table, then in that case the Sacrament should be separated from the movement, each individual member communicating in his own Church, and the family should meet in one place where the members could pray and read the Bible together. In short, Dr MacLeod was accusing Toc H of being too narrowly Anglican and not sufficiently all-embracing. On the other hand, this lack of eclecticism was the very thing that Peter Monie, the Honorary

[1] P.B.C., 'For Strength', *The Vineyard*.

Administrator of the movement, was complaining of in MacLeod.
Monie wrote to Clayton early in 1926:

> George MacLeod and I have quite different ideas of Toc H.
> I regard it as fundamental that Toc H should include 'all sorts
> of Christians' and I am certain that this *cannot* be realized unless
> Toc H stands clear of ecclesiastical disputes, is scrupulously
> careful to leave such matters to the Churches, and avoids
> attempting to help the cause of unity by 'gestures' etc. of its own
> devising. The people who talk most about unity aren't neces-
> sarily the people who do most for it. Some of us believe that for
> the present prayer is the straightforward and only effective way
> of helping. However, the point is that 'all sorts of Christians'
> will not agree about the gestures and interference and con-
> trivances and disobediences which some of us are suggesting.
> And what *you* have to choose between is a Toc H which does
> include 'all sorts' and a Toc H which is out to back a particular
> 'solution'. George and some of the people in and out of Toc H,
> who agree with him, are quite openly in favour, not of excluding
> 'Anglo-Catholics', but of making Toc H impossible for them.
> They are working openly for a sort of Pan-Protestant Toc H.[1]

Incidentally, it appears that at the time of this embroglio Peter
Monie was contemplating entering the Roman Catholic Church
and hoping that he might continue as Administrator. 'So,'
commented MacLeod, 'you might say that Tubby, having failed
to strike a fish, cast the fly backwards and caught the ear of a
rabbit;' adding hastily in a note: 'I am not speaking personally!
I loved Peter M.'[2]

That was the Rubicon to be crossed or not to be crossed, and
the founder must decide. Ecclesiasticism was the great danger.
'The advanced section of what is called "High Church"',
recorded one Toc H padre from Australia, 'are trying to capture
us and are rather upsetting the non-conformist or free churches
which out here are non-con,' and he pleaded for what he called
'. . . some sort of Freedom of the Altar'. He continued: 'We cannot
be an interdenominational society without allowing at least as a
principle the value of inter-communion. Toc H cannot be purely

[1] Monie to Clayton, 124 St George's Square, W.1. 5th January, 1926.
[2] MacLeod to the author, 7th January, 1964.

Anglican any more than it can be purely any other denomination. . . . We have a great deal to learn for Toc H is bigger than any one Church or one Communion. The pain of the last few years has given me a new conception of the Cruelty of Pharisaism, the age-long crucifying influence which antagonizes Love. We want breadth as well as depth if our scope is to be catholic as the Christ. I see Toc H as a mighty power transforming the narrow exclusiveness of dogmatic ecclesiasticism into the freedom of the happiness of the Kingdom of God.'[1]

Another difficulty that faced the founder of Toc H was the problem of the Unitarians, and in this he was distressed to find himself for a time at variance with his friend and cousin, Dick Sheppard. The Toc H rules provided that their padres might be 'Ministers of any Christian Denomination'; and in face of that, Clayton had at a meeting of the Central Council submitted a resolution to the effect that this provision excluded Unitarian ministers. The logic of this cannot be gainsaid, and indeed Unitarian congregations make no claim to be Christians. As Mr J. L. Hines, a Unitarian minister of Halifax, clearly stated, his congregation was 'dedicated to the worship of God'; and that this excluded neither Jew nor a devotee of most of the great Eastern religions. 'A Unitarian Church', he frankly admitted, 'is not necessarily a Christian Church, and Toc H with its orthodox Christian foundation cannot, in my opinion, be blamed for its assumption that Unitarian Ministers are not necessarily Christian.' However, a Toc H member wrote to Sheppard, who was on the Central Council of the movement, inviting him to lead the attack against this resolution. This, partly because of his affection for his cousin, Sheppard declined to do: but he did promise to come to the meeting and protest in person, and – 'unless there are other reasons than the mere stressing of denominationalism at the expense of the Unitarians' – to resign from the Council. Sheppard's letter was marked 'Confidential': nevertheless the news of his opposition soon spread, and Clayton wrote indignantly that this pronouncement, which he was not permitted to see, was to be used in opposition to his resolution at the Council meeting. In the event logic won the day and warm tempers soon cooled. 'The rather hot-headed advocates of "reunion all round"', as Sheppard's

[1] Rev. H. E. E. Hayes to Monie, 16th July, 1926.

biographer admirably put it, 'could not fail to be mollified by the
Council's gentle and unanswerable argument that it was absurd to
claim for any group of people characteristics they do not profess
to be theirs; and there was little opposition to the decision that,
in future, the rule confining the title of Toc H Padre to men who
represented bodies professedly Christian must be observed.'[1]
The breach between the cousins, though sharp, was soon healed;
and Sheppard, most generous of men, came to see the justice of
Clayton's reasoning.

Yet, in spite of this resolution it must not be thought that
Clayton had anything but respect for the people whom his
motion excluded from being Toc H ministers. A Unitarian once
wrote that it was his fate to have been brought up as a Congre-
gationalist and never to have derived any help from that faith – 'I
am unable to realize God or the present personality of Jesus,' he
explained, 'my position being an acceptance of the idea of God
vaguely as the "Cause of all" and of Jesus as an expression of
Himself in terms of Man, an admission of the life of Jesus as the
perfect ideal for man to copy.'[2] To him Dr Clayton replied that
'Unitarianism is in many churches in England, and in some of
America, a work of highly spiritual character which we must all
respect. My earnest hope is that as your co-operation in Toc H
goes forward, your own first hand spiritual experience will bring
you to the one tremendous truth that Christ is our contemporary;
not only a teacher whose death two thousand years ago left a
fragrant but pathetic example, but Himself now high and lifted up,
the very King of Kings and Lord of Lords; the living Leader, the
abiding Saviour, the unfailing source of strength in trouble and
temptation, the Fountain of all Sacrificial love within men's
hearts today.'[3]

Faith in the Incarnation was, it seemed, at the root of the
problem. Toc H had grown and been nourished upon that tenet:
could it be right, as some urged, to regard that belief as not
essential, and to give equal sanction to the work within Toc H
churches which taught the Incarnation and to those which deny
that such a thing took place? The trustees of the movement had

[1] Ellis Roberts, *H. R. L. Sheppard: Life and Letters*, pp. 178–9.
[2] P. P. Perry to Clayton, 20 Hazelwood Road, Northampton, 18th March, 1928.
[3] Clayton to Perry, 22nd March, 1928.

made a stand, and rightly so; 'otherwise', as Clayton wrote: 'we should have slipped into being a society without distinctive tenets, and disowning its origin and Divine allegiance, to the bitter deprivation and impoverishment of men needing Christ, as indeed they do. To go to them with an uncertainty upon this fundamental fact of His Divinity, to leave it as a mere matter of debate, in which the padres appointed by Toc H would provide the pros and cons, is to me unthinkable; and while I have made no endeavour to organize a party – I trust Toc H too well to dream of doing so – I am, however, certain that the leaders, old and new, of Toc H at Home and Overseas, will agree that we cannot compromise upon the Incarnation, or leave the Divinity of our Lord in doubt.'[1] And again a few days later to the Bishop in Korea: 'The Unitarian issue is most sorrowful, but it is quite clear that Toc H must stand on its teaching upon the Incarnation. . . . It is of vital importance that the Branch should stand firm. The one good result of the controversy is that it does give a real opportunity of teaching the Incarnation. Please go ahead and do it.'[2]

The disagreements with the Rev. George MacLeod led the latter to give up his paid Chaplaincy in 1925, though he continued to attend meetings of the movement in a non-executive capacity: and he is reported as having said on one occasion that Toc H was the only thing he knew which was capable of making the inferior Englishman into a fairly reasonable imitation of a genuine Scot![3] So it is good to know that less than two years later Clayton was writing in the friendliest spirit to 'My dear George' that: 'It is plainer to me day by day that you cannot ultimately stand apart from the work to which you were indubitably called in 1922.' He had followed the correspondence between MacLeod and Peter Monie, and it was clear that oil must be poured upon the troubled waters. 'Foolish as I am,' wrote Clayton tactfully, 'I am too wise to meddle with a thrust in tierce exchanged between two terrible Scots minds, both lambent with the love of God.'[4] He had done his best to build a bridge across the dividing gulf on which the two sides could meet; and in the following year we find

[1] Clayton to Rev. A. R. Grimes, 7th March, 1928.
[2] Clayton to Rev. John Daly, 13th March, 1928.
[3] Clayton to Colonel F. R. S. Balfour, 6th January, 1939.
[4] Clayton to MacLeod, 14th January, 1927.

him asking the Bishop of London's permission for MacLeod to preach in All Hallows. 'As you know Toc H in England is mainly Anglican', wrote Clayton to Dr Winnington-Ingram in 1928, 'though the Methodists are making an increasingly notable contribution of Padres, men and money: Baptists, Congregationalists, and so on, are strong in some areas. In Scotland, however, Toc H is quite naturally chiefly Presbyterian, and my opposite number in Scotland is the Rev. G. F. MacLeod, M.C., Assistant Minister of St Cuthbert's, Edinburgh. He is a most remarkable figure, the grandson of old Dr Norman MacLeod, and himself destined to be Moderator before many years are passed.[1] He is deeply devoted to Toc H, and the debt is mutual and lifelong. In 1925 he made proposals for inter-Communion, which we rejected, rightly. The cost of that rejection was his resignation of his post as whole-time Padre, and the cessation for the time being of his work for Toc H in Scotland. He has now, however, slowly regained his confidence in the movement and renewed his remarkable activity.'[2] Most unfortunately, as Clayton told the Bishop, these events had created a widespread feeling within the Church of Scotland that Toc H had affronted this Ministry, a feeling that was shared by no less a person than Lord Haig; so it is much to be hoped that the Bishop's permission was forthcoming on this occasion for the distinguished Presbyterian to preach in the wonderul old Church of All Hallows.

A Baptist Minister wrote at this time:

> Whenever I enter its doors, I forget that I am a Baptist (and I'm a Baptist to the backbone) and that All Hallows is of the Anglican faith and order – I look upon it as the Soul of Toc H. I feel a very unworthy being as I walk round; the very atmosphere soothes the soul and quietens the mind. Somehow, I can't explain, I even come out uplifted, and feel as though I have come into contact with that Divine and eminently spiritual power that lifts the heart and soul far above those things that would tend to drag down. I wanted to show my friend, a lady who knows but little of wonderful Toc H, our Church, its Lamp, and if possible its Founder Padre, who is known by sight to

[1] In fact Dr MacLeod was Moderator of the General Assembly of the Church of Scotland from May 1957 to May 1958.
[2] Clayton to the Bishop of London, 14th March, 1928.

her father, who is a highly placed Customs engineer. I hardly expected to find you at home – you are as illusive as the Pimpernel.[1]

On the other hand were the Noncomformists, worried lest Toc H Societies in general and All Hallows in particular were becoming centres of Romanizing propaganda, one of whom pointed to an unfortunate article in the *Church Times* to support this view.[2] To this Clayton replied that he knew nothing of the article, that he was not responsible for what the press saw fit to print, but that his correspondent seemed strangely ignorant of Toc H and what it stands for.

Meanwhile of course All Hallows must retain its Laudian traditions, previously held by Lancelot Andrewes, and many of them very deep and dear to John Wesley. There's no need to discuss them here; for your letter makes it very clear indeed that you regard ritual of any sort as contrary to the whole teaching and life of our Lord, Jesus Christ, and that historic links in the way of ordination or continuous worship obscure the whole purpose of His Life (these are your own words). Since these are your convictions, it's not relevant that I should do more than honour your sincerity; for it would be quite useless to expect you to share what I regard as a real heritage of Church life down the years. . . .[3]

There was another Low Churchman also who feared that Toc H was too High Church. 'There's a widespread impression that more and more Toc H is being taken over and controlled by very high churchmen,' he wrote: 'Will you very kindly tell me how far these ideas are true?'[4] Pat Leonard replied on Clayton's behalf:

Toc H is neither High Church nor Low Church, I can most solemnly assure you that Toc H has no ulterior motive but is what it professes to be, a Christianizing society basing its methods on the belief that for most men the surest way to learn to love God with heart and soul and strength is to learn to love your neighbour as yourself. The first great Commandment stands pre-eminent, but cannot truly be divorced from the

[1] Rev. T. J. Pettman to Clayton, Aldershot Baptist Tabernacle, 21st December, 1928.
[2] *Church Times*, 24th December, 1930. V. A. Rattenbury to Clayton, 68 Grosvenor Road, Muswell Hill, N.10, 16th May, 1931.
[3] Clayton to Rattenbury, 21st May, 1931.
[4] Captain G. Bush to Clayton, 13th December, 1931.

Second, hence Toc H's insistence upon fellowship; but profiting by the experience of the War Toc H believes that human fellowship can only be built on the foundation of service, hence the prominence given to the Jobmaster. In a nutshell I would say that Toc H believes whole-heartedly that if it can make men set their feet upon the Way and can encourage them to keep moving along it in the right direction they will sooner or later meet the Lord of the Way. It has no other purpose than to introduce men to God and to help them to find their true happiness in working in harmony with His Will for the building of His Kingdom upon Earth.[1]

On the other side there were the Roman Catholic members of Toc H faced by the very real difficulty of corporate communion. 'We had our initiation on Thursday last, and the first joint Corporate Communion is to take place on Sunday next,' wrote one of them, Miss Vera M. Green of Worthing: 'I, and one other member of our group, are Catholics. Is there any way we can find out what part our co-religionists are taking in the family life of Toc H?.... Please don't think I'm trying to worry you with purely frivolous questions. Toc H being pre-eminently a Christian family I know you will understand how important the question seems to us ... We can't go to that first Corporate Communion – we can't, not we won't – but we are going to Communicate at the same time. What we want to know is – when Toc H as a body (as for the Birthday Festival) holds any Commemorative Service and Free Church Services are held at the same time, is there any Catholic Padre (R.C.) who holds any service for Catholics, and if so, when and where?'[2] Clayton's reply, it must be admitted, was an inadequate answer to a practical, straight-forward question. Toc H was open to all Christians, he said, since it in no way interfered with religious principles. 'In England there is a steadily increasing lay membership among Roman Catholics, and one or two priests as well,' he wrote. 'In Canada your Archbishop in Manitoba is a President of Toc H, and a priest, under his sanction is a Chaplain to the work in Winnipeg. In India the second group in Bombay is entirely Roman Catholic, and its Chaplain is the Rev. Fr. Dear. My own hope is that the history of scouting will be

[1] Leonard to Bush, 16th December, 1931.
[2] Miss Vera M. Green to Clayton, The Cot, Worthing, Sussex, 17th May, 1928.

repeated, and that in a few years' time, the very natural anxiety with which your Church must view every new movement will be completely allayed in regard to Toc H by the discovery of its true nature, which offends in no particular against the religious principles and practices of its members.'[1] All very true, no doubt, but it does not answer Miss Green's question.

What was really needed was 'a spiritual power-house', a friend, the Rev. A. L. Siderfin, told Clayton: a thing more difficult to create than Toc H itself, as its founder replied. If only the padres of Toc H would more readily put themselves in touch with Mirfield, '. . . but very few have taken my advice, perhaps because my own example is shallow and undisciplined. Mirfield is there with its enormous reserves of just the kind we need. Its birth, its life, its worship, and its work are lifted up in all the joy of stated sacrifice; Gore, Rackham, Frere,[2] and many other men of the highest saintliness and intellectual ability have given their best to it; and I long for nothing more deeply than that the Anglican Padre should agree to make it his spiritual home.'[3]

But the perplexities that faced Clayton at this time were not all connected with the different denominations of the Church. There was also the inevitable conflict between youth and age. Thus in the summer of 1932 he was assailed by his curate, the brilliant Cuthbert Bardsley, who was convinced that if Toc H was to last it must become more spiritual; and who told his Vicar 'if every member is to live the fully surrendered life, living under the guidance of the Holy Spirit, it will mean much suffering at the foot of the Cross for us all. And that suffering will consist mostly of misunderstanding and unpopularity. It is so desperately easy to live the good religious life, so desperately hard to seek the highest; but it is only those who are ready to "go the whole way" who are going to pull the world out of the present terrifying condition. . . . Toc H has a great future only if it contains men who are willing to surrender all in order to follow where He leads. . . .'[4]

Cuthbert Bardsley was aged twenty-five at this time, Philip Clayton fifty-seven: and it was evident that this was a case of a

[1] Clayton to Miss Green, 21st May, 1928.
[2] Walter Howard Frere (1863–1938), Bishop of Truro.
[3] Clayton to Siderfin, 5th November, 1929.
[4] Bardsley to Clayton, n.d., Lunecliffe, Lancaster.

young man in a hurry. The Vicar's reply was at once firm, tolerant and extraordinarily humble:

All I can do is just to carry on, and struggle to be less full of sin and selfishness, so that I may attempt my microscopic fragment for our austere Lord, Who called me out of darkness twenty-four years ago, Whose Heart I have continually re-broken. Who then am I to build a holy thing? Yet build I must. It has been so ordained, and I have been ordained, as you will be. . . . Perfect fraternities do not exist on earth! S. Francis could not build one, far less we; for none of us approaches to his surrender. Ponder his life; it takes away one's breath, and read the Flowers, not as mere literature, but as a real attempt at following Jesus. He walked the way of wounds and nakedness, if any man ever did; and he died broken-hearted, worthy (he said) of being cursed by God. One needs a net, and Toc H serves that purpose. The net needs mending. That may prove the work for your generation. The net must be widespread – that is its nature. It must be in the sea, and not too widely discernible. The fish must not observe its strength too soon; but His Hand must control its casting and its intake. Are you prepared to work with such a net, provided you can quickly repair its obvious rents – which many of us know. We do not ask any to worship it. We do not worship it ourselves, I hope! Our sole concern, as hired and well-fed servants, is with the fish whom the Lord leads towards it. We must not spend too long comparing catches. Angels may know divine arithmetic. Our job is to land fish, and not to quarrel. If I am quarrelsome at any time, you must tell me off. I may improve, and I shall try for your sake, my friend; and because I am very fond of fishing, though a bit clumsy and quite out of date. Alas, I am preparing to be lonely, at least until you come. God bless you.[1]

Another matter that much harassed the founder of Toc H at this time was the wish of many of its members to be re-married in church after their first marriage had been terminated by divorce. On this topic Clayton held rigid – or what he chose to term old-fashioned – views. 'I am, myself, content to be regarded as

[1] Clayton to Bardsley, 24th June, 1932.

completely old-fashioned in my definite views as to the binding character of the marriage Law of the Church,' he replied to Mr Norman Dean who wrote on behalf of a Toc H member and worker overseas who had divorced his wife and wished to re-marry in church. 'I find myself, therefore, bound to decline making exceptions in my fulfilment of what is after all a position of definite obedience to the Church Laws, whereby the sanctity of marriage is upheld. While in a wide experience I realize that these terribly hard cases exist in which the innocent party has to ensure a life-long loneliness, I know that homes re-made in disobedience to the clear teaching of the Gospel can scarcely expect the blessing of the Church upon them. I don't dispute the right of the State to make what laws for Civil Marriages it thinks fit, but I cannot see how the Church can give its blessing to the marriage of divorced persons without contradicting its own Code.'[1] About eight months later he wrote no less uncompromi-singly to the Rev A. C. Dicker, a priest who asked for the use of All Hallows for a quiet wedding of a Colonel whose wife had left him during the war for another man with whom she had since lived, and whom the husband had reluctantly divorced after having made every effort to regain her: 'I'm old-fashioned in my views, and I believe that it is the Church's task to stand firmly to the old conception of marriage. I cannot therefore offer the desired facilities of All Hallows. . . .'[2]

Furthermore, the padre was equally uncompromising in his views on the 'guilty party' to a divorce communicating. Even his consent to the other party was somewhat grudging. 'I can't write a treatise tonight upon the Church Law, which is based on the clear Gospel,' he told an enquirer. 'This forbids divorce. One version only adds a conditional clause. The Church is bound by what the Gospel says. The State is not submissive to the Gospel. "The Innocent Party" who re-marries *may* be the exception, which Our Lord is said (by only one version) to have admitted. If so, you both can come to your Communion. But you must take the responsibility. The Church can't alter the Gospel. "The Guilty Party", having been divorced, is definitely excommunicate.'[3]

[1] Clayton to Norman G. Dean, 28th March, 1929.
[2] Clayton to Rev. A. C. Dicker, 26th November, 1929.
[3] Clayton to ——————— 30th May, 1946.

The Church is probably wise in refusing to adjudicate between the technically 'guilty party' and the so-called 'innocent party' in divorce, for who can fairly maintain that persistent ill-temper or repeated intemperance in a spouse is less reprehensible than an isolated case of adultery? Who can fairly maintain that, where one party to a marriage has for years shown contemptuous indifference or perhaps even active dislike for the other party, that spouse is less responsible for the break-up of the marriage than the one who, under such provocation, has succumbed on occasions to the allurements of the world or to the call of true love? In short, sexual misconduct is not necessarily the gravest marital frailty. The Church therefore declares that neither party may have a religious re-marriage. That seems not unreasonable. But to go further, as Dr Clayton and many of his fellow clerics once went, and to refuse all cases, regardless of the particular circumstances, the blessing of a service in church following a Civil Marriage seems harsh; to condemn both parties to 'life-long loneliness' seems, at any rate to one humble and imperfect Christian, to lack the very spirit of Christianity itself. It is therefore pleasant to be able to record that Clayton, mellowing in later years, found it possible to modify to some extent his earlier and more rigid views on a matter that is often proved one of great hardship and great perplexity.

Another matter that caused Clayton grave concern in the post-war years was the decline of Toc H in military circles. On this we find him early in 1930 anxiously consulting Lord Plumer, the movement's President, under whose command it had flourished in Flanders. Both scouting and Toc H, 'two great movements of our time', had many origins, Clayton told Plumer; but whereas scouting only emerged some years after the South African War, the first four years of Toc H were almost wholly under his command. The Old House was not a civilian, but an entirely military establishment, and its padre was seconded from the 16th I.B. to become its chaplain. Yet, in spite of its Service origin, 'the most sorrowful fact about Toc H in 1930', Clayton told the Field Marshal, 'is that it has, apart from a few senior officers and a few young guardsmen, no membership whatsoever in the present Army; and Gentlemen Cadets at Sandhurst and Woolwich believe themselves by their career of arms cut off from active membership of the movement. . . . At present, therefore, we are faced with the pathetic fact that the Army as a whole is ignorant of Toc H, and, if anything, rather averse to playing its part in what is rapidly becoming the biggest and most wholesome men's Society in the Empire.'[1]

That the movement he loved and of which he was now President had little or no membership in the Army was something that the old Field Marshal could not contemplate with equanimity, and on receiving Dr Clayton's appeal he hastened to put the case before the Army Council. He was well received by that august body, whose members agreed to issue an official directive to remove what misunderstandings there might be and to commend Toc H to the Army. The letter, signed by General Sir Walter Braithwaite, appeared about a month after Clayton's original appeal to Lord Plumer and was in the following terms:

> War Office, Whitehall,
> London, S.W.1.
> 19th February, 1930.

It has been represented to the Army Council by Field Marshal Viscount Plumer and the Revd. P. B. Clayton, in an interview which took place on the 29th January, 1930, between the above-mentioned and the Chief of the Imperial General Staff and the Adjutant-General to the Forces, that an impression has got abroad that officers and men of the Army are, by reason of their profession, cut off from active membership of Toc H. It may be as well, therefore, to state here, quite distinctly, that there is nothing either in the obligations of an Army career or the membership of Toc H which are antagonistic. Quite the reverse. Toc H was born of the Army in war, and there is no reason why officers and men, should not exercise, should they so desire, full membership in peace as they did during the war. Nor is there any more reason why an officer who is a member of Toc H should not meet a private soldier who is also a member of Toc H in the course of their activities in connection with the fellowship, than there is that he should not play football, cricket, or any other game that is, as is well known, played by officers and other ranks in their ordinary everyday regimental life.

[1] Clayton to Plumer, 17th January, 1930.

The Army Council feel that it would be unfortunate indeed if the present ignorance of the aims and objects of Toc H were perpetuated by its parent, the British Army, and wish it to be understood that, for their part, they desire once and for all to state that there is nothing in the constitution of either to prevent officers and other ranks of the Army from becoming members of Toc H. Those members of Toc H who joined that fellowship when at school – as so many do – may carry on their membership throughout their Army career, and others may join without any misgivings.

(Sgd) WALTER BRAITHWAITE.

This ruling was renewed some nine years later, immediately before the Second War, by the following letter from Sir Herbert Creedy, Adjutant-General:

The War Office,
London, S.W.1.
14th July, 1939.

42/General/297 (A.G.3)
Sir,

I am commanded by the Army Council to inform you that they wish to bring to your notice the aims and objects of Toc H.

I am to say that Toc H originated from Talbot House, Poperinghe, where serving soldiers could find the amenities of home life – rest, recreation and friendship.

In February, 1930, the Army Council stated that there is no reason why officers and men should not exercise, should they so desire, full membership in peace as they did during war. The Council wish again to commend the objects of the movement to all soldiers and especially to the newly formed militia. They trust, therefore, that General and other Officers Commanding will give every facility to personnel under their command to associate themselves, if they so desire, with Toc H.

I am, Sir,
Your Obedient Servant,
H. J. CREEDY.

The General Officers Commanding-in-Chief,
The General Officers Commanding All
    Commands and Districts at Home and Abroad.

M

Thus Toc H was authorized and encouraged within the Army, and officers and other ranks were empowered to enjoy full membership in peace-time as in wartime of the movement 'where serving soldiers could find the amenities of home life – rest, recreation and friendship'. They made full use of the opportunities thus presented to them.

Some two years after the meeting with the Army Council, at the War Office, the great soldier who had done so much for the movement died. Lord Plumer's last words to his life-long friend and biographer, General Sir Charles Harington, were 'Build up Toc H in the Army'; and it was just this that Harington tried to do for the rest of his life. As he wrote:

> It is part of our Toc H prayer to be allowed to leap with joy to the service of others. We are really a band of Christian people who do not intend to let the memory and example of those million little white crosses die. Do not they represent the finest example of 'unselfish service'? And so Toc H has been formed to help the younger generation to be unselfish. . . . I am quite sure that Lord Plumer, in his charge to me, felt that the way in which he had been able to attract people of all kinds to him and the way in which he had gained their trust and affection, was in a great measure due to being imbued with the Toc H spirit. By that I mean that such words as jealousy, bitterness, pettiness, etc. never entered into his vocabulary. . . . I ask no one to join Toc H. That is against our principles. I merely say that Lord Plumer believed in it and loved it and it helped him. His last words to me, 'Build up Toc H in the Army' were not said light-heartedly. I pass them on to my readers with this added – 'Come and see for yourselves'.[1]

Many thousands still follow that sensible advice.

[1] Harington, *Plumer of Messines*, pp. 330–4.

15

Between the Wars

O God Who has so wonderfully made Toc H, and set men in it to see their duty as they will, teach us to live together in love and joy and peace; to check all bitterness; to disown discouragement; to practise thanksgiving, and to leap with joy to any task for others. Strengthen the good thing thus begun; that with gallant and high-hearted happiness we may work for Thy Kingdom in the wills of men, through Jesus Christ, our Lord Amen.[1]

In the early years following the First World War, Clayton and his movement were becoming known and appreciated by an ever-wider circle of prominent people in many parts of the world. So one can well imagine the joy with which, in April 1928, Clayton learned from Laurence Binyon that he was to receive the original manuscript of his famous poem *In Lumine Tuo videbimus Lumen*, written 'for the Roll of the Elder Brethren of Toc H'. 'The poem is, as you see, written as if from the Chapel of the Lamp in All Hallows.'[2] It is surely fitting that the poem should be quoted in the biography of the founder of the movement that it so movingly commends.

> The flame upon the Altar lives
> In its own home of Light apart,
> And yet it shines on secret tears
> And in the darkness of the heart.
>
> More real than any world of ours
> Is that still Presence of the Light;
> Happy are they who harbour there,
> Happy, who keeps it whole in sight.
>
> How still, amid our noise and fret,
> It burns and trembles and aspires,
> Drawing our spirits from the Cloud
> And aching of our old desires.

[1] P.B.C., The Toc H Prayer, *A Treasury of Prayers and Praises*.
[2] Clayton to E. Belcher, 3rd April, 1928.

The young-eyed spirits, whom we knew,
  Who smiled, and whom we called by name,
Who went in their own faith to die,
  Are flames within that trembling flame.

Now all the corners of the earth
  Look on them where so clear they shine,
A single glory, radiant fire,
  By day and night a silent sign.

O dear, untroubled, happy Dead,
  Comrades eternal, now and here,
When most we falter in our fight,
  When most we fail you, be you near.

In January, 1931, Mr Henry Gladstone presented to Toc H No.
62 Rodney Street, Liverpool, the house in which his great father
had been born. About £3,350 was available to repair and furnish
'Gladstone House', leaving £5,000 still to be found, to endow a
salary for a whole-time housekeeper. Towards this, Lord Derby
had promised his help. Later in the year Clayton was venturing to
suggest that the tenure of Mark II from the Duke of Westminster
should be converted into a gift, and that No. 121, which had
originally in 1921 been promised merely as a loan, should be
annexed to it in order to provide a Chaplaincy Endowment in
memory of the Duke's mother, Lady Grosvenor, who had recently
died. That was a shrewd suggestion, for, as Clayton himself
admitted, '. . . nothing but his Mother and her love for the Church
of England, and her belief that Toc H was a way whereby the
Church could minister to men, would have led him, either in 1921
or after her death, to make these great endowments.'[1]

In this same year, 1931, the Central Executive of Toc H was
anxious to persuade Lord Irwin, the Viceroy of India, to become a
President of Toc H, and Clayton consulted his old friend, Sir
Maurice Hankey, Secretary of the Cabinet. Hankey discussed the
matter at some length with Mr Baldwin, Irwin's chief, and
himself a President of the movement. 'He was not very encouraging,' Sir Maurice reported, 'It's clear that, if he gets back in office,
he wants Irwin for *big work*. I need not say more. At the same time,

---

[1] Clayton to Peter Monie, 21st November, 1931.

if you are going to write to Irwin, I will write too. I shall tell him frankly of my talk with his old chief and put it to him squarely. It is, of course, quite possible that the Conservatives may be out to office for some time yet – the situation is so uncertain that no man can prophesy – and in that event I don't see why Toc H should not get the benefit of Irwin's help.'[1] In the event Hankey wrote to Irwin on Dr Clayton's behalf, and in March received an encouraging reply. 'He whom I have never met, but nevertheless irreverently called "Tubby" Clayton, is a very persuasive person,' wrote the Viceroy; but he would prefer to leave the matter open until he reached home and had time to look round. 'Will you make my peace with "Tubby"', he asked Hankey, 'and tell him to let us meet when I get back?'[2] 'I expect you will read this letter, as I did, in a very favourable sense,' was Hankey's sensible comment, 'I feel sure that we shall capture him on his return.'[3] After the General Election held that year, a National Government was formed with Ramsey Macdonald as Prime Minister and Baldwin Lord President of the Council. Hence the 'big work' was not immediately available to Lord Irwin, and it was not until the following year that he received the comparatively minor post of President of the Board of Education. In consequence, Irwin on his return from India was free to take up other work, and he was soon a President and devoted member of the Toc H movement.

Another source of encouragement to Clayton in the years following the first world war came from the three Miss Alexanders, wealthy and beneficent sisters living amongst their treasures in stately Aubrey House in Kensington. They had for many years shown their affection and admiration for the rotund and portly cleric whom they habitually and uniquely addressed as Philip; and they were always generously anxious to help Toc H and other causes he had at heart. Late in 1927 they each sent him a cheque for £500 as an endowment of a new Mark XI shortly to be opened. 'My dear "Three Sisters",' replied Clayton gratefully, 'the letter announcing the arrival of the three £500s has come on me at home and is the happiest of New Year's news. . . . Let me say at

[1] Hankey to Clayton, 13th February, 1931.
[2] Irwin to Hankey, 10th March, 1931.
[3] Hankey to Clayton, 30th March, 1931.

least that your united action in this endowment of Mark XI does lift a load from my shoulders and an anxiety from my heart. Whatever happens now, Mark XI will be solidly constructed – a force making for righteousness generation after generation. My prayer for Toc H in 1928 is an old motto from the Psalms – "Stablish the things, O God, that Thou has wrought in us" – and this united gift is a substantial omen of its fulfilment. The National Trust is preserving the Seven Sisters. May God preserve the Three!'[1]

Many other gifts followed from these three sisters, who in 1931 informed their friend that they would henceforth hold themselves responsible for the salary of Miss Coulson, P.B.C.'s principal and invaluable private secretary. Anyone at all acquainted with Miss Coulson – or 'Couly' as she is known by all in the movement – and her work will appreciate what this meant to Clayton and will understand the great gratitude that he showed towards his three benefactors. 'My dear Mary', he wrote to the eldest. 'You make me happy, and you make me penitent. I don't deserve a fraction of all that you have done for me, year after year, all through, unfailingly, from that first day when I was well-nigh desperate. But the whole cause is good, the work is true . . . This is the Lord's own doing. . . .'[2] A few years later he wrote: '"Couly" your gift to me – through all these years – is beyond price in this long Partnership. She soon is going to move into the Church staff flats, new built behind 42. These are the gift of Jean, a year ago. So Aubrey has done everything for me. How can I make him return? God bless you. Philip.'[3] It must be admitted that the Founder Padre of Toc H was generally not a success with women. Yet here was an exception to this rule; and in this connection we might recall the devotion to St Paul – who, like Clayton, had small use for women – of Priscilla and her husband Aquila,[4] the Jewish couple who became his hosts in Corinth, when we consider the generous admiration shown over the years to Clayton by the three devoted women of Aubrey House.

[1] Clayton to Miss Mary Alexander, 2nd January, 1928.
[2] Clayton to Miss Mary Alexander, 2nd June, 1931.
[3] Clayton to Miss Mary Alexander, 28th August, 1938.
[4] 'Give my greetings to Prisca [Priscilla] and Aquila, my fellow workers in Christ,' wrote St Paul. 'They risked their necks to save my life, and not I alone but all the Gentile congregations are grateful to them.' Romans 16, 3–4.

In September of this same year, 1931, Clayton was greatly encouraged to receive a cheque for £200 from an old friend, the distinguished statesman, Mr Vincent Massey, 'Toc H', wrote Massey, 'is one of the things which gives me a "lift" every time I go to England. All power to you!' He and his wife were on their way to China for the Conference of the Institute of Pacific Relations at Hangchow. 'I find it very difficult to concentrate on the Far East', wrote Massey, 'when so much of first importance is happening in our end of the world at the moment, and London in particular. I wish I could see it all at first hand.'[1] 'My dear Benefactor', came the breezy reply, 'it needs a mirage of a wireless photograph for you on the Pacific to perceive the joy and strength your letter brought me.' The money was being put, he told Massey, to the Overseas Department of Toc H Headquarters work. 'This, I feel confident, is what you will approve. It makes just all the difference in this terrific winter work ahead. May God reward you.'[2]

The year was rounded off with a delightful note from that most charming of men, Sir William Hamilton Fyfe, at that time Principal of Queen's University, Kingston, Ontario, but destined to become a few years later Principal and Vice-Chancellor of the University of Aberdeen, addressed to the 'most tubular of saints *or* (with even greater certainty) most saintly of tubs.'[3] 'Very dear Tubby,' he wrote on his 1931 Christmas card, 'I can't let this go without a line of loving greeting from us both – though the Recording Angel alone knows which owes which a letter. I am just back from Winnipeg and other distant places – 81 hours in the train; 6 orations; I mutter a "pleeztameetcha" in my sleep. But, gee, that ain't nuffin to what you're used to, Guv'nor . . . Our love to you is 5,000 miles long. So it'll reach Tower Hill.'[3]

At about this time, Clayton was preparing to leave for Persia. 'I am hoping to leave on Saturday next as the Chaplain and guest of the Anglo-Persian Oil Company and to spend Christmas at their depot at Abadan, Persia,' he informed Dr Winnington-Ingram, the Bishop of London, in mid-December.[4] The proposed visit

[1] Massey to Clayton, Canadian Pacific Railway *en route*, 11th September, 1931.
[2] Clayton to Massey, 3rd October, 1931.
[3] Hamilton Fyfe to Clayton, 23rd January, 1945.
[4] Clayton to Bishop of London, 15th December, 1931.

owed its conception to a certain Charles Sheppard, an under-graduate of New College, who on coming down from Oxford soon after the 1914–1918 war, had joined the Chemical Branch of the Anglo-Persian Oil Company. In due course he was transferred to Abadan for three years and launched there a local branch of Toc H. Sheppard, it seems, had character and ability, and soon many of his colleagues were enthusiastically joining the movement, In consequence, the General Manager in Iran reported its success to his Chairman, Sir John Cadman. Thus Toc H was emboldened to request that a Chaplain might be appointed to the Company. Whilst this was under consideration, Charles Sheppard returned home and died very suddenly at the age of twenty-eight.

Hearing this sad news, Clayton called for the first time at the Company's headquarters, Britannic House, in Finsbury Circus, to tell Sheppard's colleagues that a Memorial Service would be held in All Hallows. Many of them came, including the Chairman himself; thus the Padre first met Sir John, afterwards Lord Cadman, and a firm friendship sprang up between them which lasted until Cadman's death in the summer of 1941. In 1927 Cadman, much impressed with the effects of Toc H in Abadan, asked Clayton to find a Chaplain for what was by then called the Anglo-Iranian Company, to be resident in Abadan. After some delay, Clayton suggested the Rev. Guy Reed, M.C., whom he called 'the patron saint of the Queen's Westminsters'. Within a few months Reed went out to Abadan, where he was an outstanding success, and remained at his post for more than twelve years. A further sphere was made for work in the British Tanker Company, and a third in the Irak Petroleum Company, all under Cadman's control. 'It was a revolutionary experiment,' recorded Clayton, 'but it succeeded marvellously well, and will, I trust, be very long continued.'

So successful was the venture that both Cadman and Clayton were anxious to extend the appointment of industrial chaplaincies to other great concerns. Accordingly on 13th November, 1929, Clayton took his old friend William Temple, then Archbishop of York, to lunch with Sir John Cadman at Britannic House. A thorough review of the situation followed. With the Shell Group and the Underground Railways Sir John thought he could help, in the latter case promising to interest Lord Ashfield, the Chairman. With the Imperial Tobacco Company and Imperial Chemicals, Cadman did not feel that he could achieve anything at the moment, but he was confident that the former at any rate would eventually fall into line. With regard to his own South Wales works, Cadman was willing to consider a development on Toc H lines, with a possible hostel and chaplaincy at a later stage. It was generally agreed that the first step must be the appointment of honorary chaplains with the right to enter big concerns at will, and with the Board's permission to wear upon such visits the uniform and badge of the Company. Cadman promised to see whether the privilege of visiting in Britannic House could not henceforth be extended to a chaplain. Both Archbishop and Padre came away from their lunch feeling that much had been achieved.

Some eighteen months later, Sir John Cadman began to press Clayton to go out to Abadan to see for himself how things were progressing. For some time Clayton could not find the time, but towards the end of 1931 he took up the matter with his friend. 'I scruple to bother you personally,' he wrote to Cadman in October, 'but you suggested some time back that you would like me to do a trip to Abadan. If this is really so – I don't want to intrude – it would be best for me to go right out and be with Reed this Christmas. I could leave London about 14th December, and be away till the beginning of February. If so, I should prefer to take one useful man from here with me, if that were possible....'[1] Cadman joyfully acquiesced in the proposal; so Clayton wrote the letter already quoted asking for the Bishop of London's approval of his plans.

On 19th December, Clayton, accompanied by Stanley Clapham and Henry Chappell, started on his trip. Once arrived at Abadan, they were kept busy. They visited the oilfields whence the pipe-lines ran down for over a hundred miles to Abadan, where of course they toured the refinery. Clayton and Chappell visited Cairo and Alexandria, where they attended local Toc H gatherings, whilst Clapham went on to the Mission for Seamen at Bombay. They sailed for home on a tanker, *British Princess*, and during the voyage of close on three weeks the crew found the padre a lively and persuasive companion. Confirmation classes were held in the master's cabin, the master himself and a number of the men

[1] Clayton to Cadman, 22nd October, 1931.

expressing their wish to be confirmed. When some days out from Avonmouth Clayton sent a wireless message to the Bishop of Bristol; and on landing conducted his pupils to the private chapel of the Bishop's Palace, 'where baptism and confirmation were ministered to those who had decided to come forward'. It was indeed a joyous homecoming.

In view of the immense increase of Toc H in size and influence during these post-war years, it is not surprising that the founder felt it more and more essential to enlist young, active and able assistants to help him carry the burden of his manifold duties. During the twenties and early thirties Clayton was fortunate in acquiring a number of young colleagues of outstanding merit, and ultimately of notable achievement. Some of these acted as his A.D.C.s, some as curates at All Hallows.

One of the earliest of these was a tall young man with a mop of unruly red hair; his name was Tom Savage, he was just down from Peterhouse, Cambridge, and was to become more than thirty years later Bishop of Zululand.[1] But away back in the 1920s young Tom Savage – 'My son Tom', 'My dearly beloved Tom', as Philip Clayton called him – was uncertain of his calling. He was then at Mirfield, which he loved; but perplexity assailed him. He laid his problems before his friend and teacher. 'Two letters – and such letters – stand against me,' wrote Clayton in June 1924, 'and now the longest day is past, I must delay no longer. This is written by day-light after 9 p.m. in a certain bungalow in the New Forest.'

Someone, it seems, had been pressing upon the young man the rival claims of science and economic ideologies as opposed to religion. But Philip Clayton would have none of this old story. Christianity must stand on its own feet; there must be no alliance with any other tenet.

I don't want the Gospel forced into a series of belittling alliances with any economic system, past, present or to come. The analogy of the series of marriages to contemporaneous science is surely a warning. It's the fatal nuptials of the immortal to that which must needs decay. Communism is the latest, but

[1] In November 1960 the Diocese was renamed as Zululand and Swaziland

not the final phase of political thinking. I don't want to see Religion bound up with the ancient regime, nor yet with its self-styled successor. God sitteth above these water floods . . . I'm candidly not prepared to see Christianity getting panic-stricken, and hopping from one piece of economic drift-wood to the next. Do you remember Brother Lawrence – in the noise and clatter of my kitchen, while several persons are at the same time calling for different things, I possess God in as great tranquillity as if I were upon my knees at the Blessed Sacrament. I possess God – it's a terrific phrase. That's what the Church has got to do, getting on with the washing meanwhile, while several persons are calling for different things. I don't pretend that this answers your points. But I think it needs saying. There is no condition of society in which Christianity's impossible to the individual. Conversely, no external facilities will necessarily produce more Christians. The religious Houses were purely communistic, but they were tottering inwardly before Henry sacked them. The vultures gather and swoop down upon the carrion, but the vultures will be carrion in their turn. Only the dove dies not.[1]

Of those who hesitate about taking Orders Clayton wrote a few months later: 'The men who repent taking Orders are very few; but the men who secretly repent *not* taking them are the real and numerous tragedies.'[2]

From 1927 to 1928 Clayton was attended by a tall and attractive young man called Jack Richardson, son of a Derby businessman who bought Graeme House in that city and presented it to Toc H. Richardson was destined to become Archdeacon of Derby a quarter of a century later. To him it seemed that the chief duty of the A.D.C. was, like that of the chaplains to another bachelor cleric, Archbishop Garbett: '. . . to keep him in touch with what the young were thinking, to stand up to him, and in that sense to be a family to whom he could show his affection. . . .' Clayton, like Garbett, was a man's man, and, with a few notable exceptions, had little interest in women. 'He was never easy,' recorded Archdeacon Richardson many years later, 'unpunctual, working to all hours of

[1] Clayton to Savage, 26th June, 1924.
[2] Clayton to Savage, All Hallows Porch Room, 14th November, 1924.

the night, demanding, he wouldn't keep to a programme, never spared himself and wouldn't spare others, but he gave unlimited friendship to those who responded to him.'

In 1927 Richardson and Stanley Clapham accompanied Clayton on a tour of South America, and Richardson has recalled an incident in the Argentine city of Mendoza which illustrates that point. The meeting had been a bad one – the only really bad meeting of the tour – and the outraged lecturer let fly at the inhabitants. 'This place should have been called "Men doze here",' he told them indignantly; and the meeting closed with heated tempers on both sides. The next morning Clayton and his party were to cross the Andes by a train that ran only once a week. Clayton decided to walk to the station with Richardson, whilst Clapham went ahead with the baggage. By an error of judgment Richardson took his chief on the wrong side of a high wall so that they suddenly found themselves three-quarters of a mile from the station with only five minutes in hand before the departure of the weekly train. There was nothing to do but to run for it; so Clayton doffed his overcoat and jacket and went at the double. Thanks to the railway authorities, who held up the train for two minutes, they managed to catch it, but of course it was a very near thing; and Richardson was frightened lest the padre's heart might be strained in that rarefied air. Richardson was entirely to blame; yet never once was he reproached and the matter was never afterwards referred to by Clayton save as a joke to show how well he could sprint. This forbearance was typical and explained the devotion he won from those who worked for him.

Two years later another outsize young man of immense ability joined Clayton as his A.D.C.; this was Cuthbert Bardsley, who in 1932 became his curate at All Hallows and was later to be Bishop of Coventry. Often, Bardsley says, they were up at 4.30 to visit the Fish Market, hand out literature and talk to as many of the fish-porters as possible. Clayton knew them all. Their occupation was often inherited: it was also dangerous, for the careless balance of a heavy burden of fish might break a man's neck. The vicar and his A.D.C. would also visit the vast offices of the Anglo-Persian Oil Company, to which Clayton was honorary chaplain, and the headquarters of the Port of London Authority. The P.L.A.'s main hall, Bardsley has recalled, is reminiscent of the maze at Hampton

Court. Here principal and assistant would take different sides to work their way to the middle. At first many of the men did not seem to relish talking to a parson, but Clayton's exuberant spirits would usually break the ice before long. The task of the A.D.C. was to note how Clayton's talk to the men should be followed up: such reminders as 'wife sick, write to her', 'Husband separated, write to local parson', filled young Bardsley's diary, for he had to be sure that nothing and no one was forgotten. Only once in their tours of local offices was the door almost slammed in their faces: but Clayton promptly put his foot forward to prevent it shutting. 'My dear Sir.' he said, 'You may not be a Christian, but at least you could be courteous.' It was also the A.D.C.'s duty to drive his vicar round in Clayton's very ancient two-seater, which frequently broke down – once at Marble Arch causing a traffic-jam of vast proportions.

One of the outstanding things about Philip Clayton, as Bardsley has recalled, was the fact that he was exactly the same with all ranks, high and low. Once when arrangements for a matinée in aid of Toc H were in the hands of an Organizing Committee of aristocratic ladies, the A.D.C. had to drive Clayton to a meeting of the Committee to be held at the Dowager Duchess of Devonshire's mansion in Park Lane. He was clad as usual, 'in an untidy, patched suit, brown shoes, a ghastly macintosh and a cloth cap'; and Bardsley's well-intentioned efforts to get this state of things rectified before they set out had been met with a blistering rebuff. On arrival at their destination, priest and attendant A.D.C. were met at the door by two flunkeys in knee breeches and silk stockings. To one of these splendid beings Clayton handed his cap, to the other his macintosh. Then he entered into an intimate and prolonged conversation with the two men on the health and state of their families, their work, their leisure, their prospects: only when this cross-examination was complete, and he was satisfied as to the two men's welfare, did Clayton proceed to the drawing-room to be greeted by his hostess. Nor was the Duchess surprised; for Clayton was an old and valued friend of the family and a frequent visitor to Chatsworth, where he always made himself available in the housekeeper's room to any members of the Staff who wished to consult him.

At this time All Hallow's Church was very much alive with

large congregations; and it was one of the duties of the A.D.C. and the senior curate, whatever the weather, to present the Faith on Tower Hill. For Bardsley it was a frightening business. First they would say their prayers in Church. Then they would 'collect a sort of soap-box-cum-pulpit, cart it out on to the Hill and stand thereon'. According to Bardsley 'it was an understood thing that speakers were given ten minutes in which to make their address. After that a group began to gather in for the question time. This was the period I always dreaded: one terrifying old atheist was prone to ask very awkward questions and to make trouble.'

At these outdoor meetings on the Hill Clayton was not at his best for he was impatient, testy, and sometimes lost his temper. But in Church his sermons were remarkable. 'He used to make services live, as nobody I have ever known,' Bardsley has recalled. 'Though unorthodox in certain ways, he would keep meticulously to the Prayer Book, but he would incorporate into his Biddings illuminating and imaginative thoughts about people to pray for. His sermons were quite extraordinary; very seldom prepared, occasionally disastrous, but usually brilliant. He would march up to the pulpit, armed with about eight or ten books: while the hymn was being sung, he would dip into various volumes and then take as his text some thought that appeared to have caught his attention. From there he would move out, striking oil as he went, and usually with great effect.'

When some years later Bardsley was made rector of the large and somewhat moribund church at Woolwich, he invited his old chief to come and preach one Sunday. As the enthusiastic young rector hoped to fill his usually half-empty Church, extensive advertising had preceded the visit. The result was all that could be desired: the Church was filled to overflowing. Then seeming disaster descended upon him: Clayton missed his train, arrived late and in a thoroughly bad temper. And when the preacher mounted the pulpit, things seemed to go from bad to worse. Clayton spent several minutes explaining why he was late, and what he thought of the country's railway system in general and the line to Woolwich in particular. 'I was filled with despair,' wrote Bardsley. Then came a change. The preacher embarked on his sermon, and soon warmed to his work. He preached for forty-four minutes, and kept the congregation spell-bound throughout by the brilliance and eloquence of his address. 'He may not have been a great preacher,' Bardsley conceded, 'but he was usually unforgettable – human, "down-to-earth", with ideas that emerged from a rich store-house of memories.'

Between the summer of 1933 and the summer of 1935 Philip Clayton was attended by a fourth young man of marked ability. His name was John Graham, and he was to become a quarter of a century later Father Superior of the Community of the Resurrection at Mirfield. Graham was typical of the sheltered public school boy with a conventional upbringing by wise and loving parents. His father was for practically his whole life an Uppingham master, and he and his wife were devoted to one another and to their family, into whom they instilled the highest ideals of their genera-tion – the ideals of the Christian English gentleman. Their son John, in his first year at Cambridge, was taken by a fellow under-graduate to a Toc H meeting, consisting of some fifty men, half town, half gown. He was at once won over – by the warmth of his welcome, by the atmosphere of generous-hearted desire to serve, by the uninhibited talk about the standards of Christ, all of which he found refreshing and in marked contrast to the slightly narrow proprieties to which he had been brought up. A visit to All Hallows soon followed; and it was on a trip down the Thames one summer day after Evensong that John Graham first met the founder of the movement. 'He greeted me with that totally dis-arming, open-hearted interest in me as an individual which was the key to so much of his influence,' Graham remembered many years later. 'His entire face appeared to light up at such greetings and he gave one an indescribable feeling of being wanted for some important purpose; one was immediately drawn into a purposeful world and almost awaiting orders. And that spell once cast had an extraordinary persistence and drawing power.' It was through Harry Chappell, a previous A.D.C., that the offer came to Graham of a year with Philip Clayton. Chappell brought the padre to breakfast in John's rooms in Cambridge, and the spell was quickly cast. Clayton was nearly fifty at this time; Graham was twenty-one. 'The incredible adaptability and generosity of the man has never ceased to amaze me,' Father Graham recollected in after years; 'to be prepared to share day-by-day life and activity with a newly-fledged B.A., to trust him utterly, to rely on him, to introduce him everywhere and to everyone, to ask his advice, to take him on holidays, to open his heart and life to him, to have him as a constant travelling companion, when you are a man of fifty, is not only astonishingly generous but cannot fail to bring out something in the youngster so privileged, however slender his qualities.' That all this brought out much in young Graham cannot be doubted. 'Come with me and I will show you where men live,' Clayton declared, and John gratefully accepted the invitation. 'All one's little undergraduate world shrank into nothingness. Without scorn or criticism of it, he had shown one that there were vast worlds of living, suffering, working, earning, to which one was a complete stranger.' John Graham remained at Clayton's side for two fateful years, years of great interest, but also years of much sorrow and anxiety to both master and disciple, years that in Graham's considered view had a greater effect on his life than any other two years of his existence.

16

'Cleanse the Leper'

'We are pernickity on minor points, rigid or lax, straight-laced or lazy Christians; we pride ourselves on being orthodox; we pride ourselves on being heterodox; we are conservative; we are reformers; we will stand stiffly for a principle – which our opponents call a prejudice; we split a hair and think we do God praise. Yet we ignore this plain command of Christ, for which few Churches ever say a prayer, of which most priests are contentedly ignorant.'[1]

Towards the end of 1932, Philip Clayton embarked at Liverpool for West Africa. On departure he was cheered by a message from Sir Hugh Walpole. 'You are building new outposts for the one thing today that has no prejudice, no class, no nation, no dogma; the one force, as I see it, that brings men together and keeps them together because men are brothers, naturally belong to one another, and were made by God to serve one another. You don't need to be told that the world is in pieces. You know this better than I. From what I hear you know men's weaknesses and yet believe in them. You do not expect miracles. You do not think yourself miraculous. But you have a sense of humour; you welcome new things and hard things, you believe in God. Let one who envies you from the bottom of his heart wish you all luck! Hugh Walpole.'[2] 'Most puissant Walpole,' Clayton replied, '. . . we both are knit to Him through that inspiring jest He calls Toc H. I on my side give praise, and go to West Africa. If I come back, I'll bother you, you see. Semper Fidelis. Tubby.'[3]

The purpose of this visit as the guest of the United Africa Company was to study the conditions of life of their junior personnel working up-country and often in isolation, and to report how these conditions could be improved. Clayton stayed

[1] P.B.C., Sermon in St Mary the Virgin, Oxford, 30th May, 1933.
[2] Walpole to Clayton, n.d.
[3] Clayton to Walpole, 21st December, 1932.

with the colonel in command of the battalion stationed near the walls of Kano, a Mohammedan Protectorate some six hundred miles up-country from the mangrove belt which fringes the coast of Nigeria. Here quite by chance he met the District Medical Officer, Dr Turnbull, who casually suggested that he might care to go with him on his first official inspection of the spot outside the South-East gate of Kano, where lepers were compelled to spend the night. Clayton accepted with alacrity; and they set forth in the doctor's car the very next day.

The approach to Kano is imposing. The venerable city, surrounded by a fifteen-mile wall of sunbaked mud, twenty feet thick at the top and far more at the base and reared in parts to a height of about thirty feet, dominates the landscape. This forbidding enclosure is pierced here and there with gateways. Within, all is on an impressive scale. The palace of the Emir of Kano sprawls over several acres, and is said to house a harem of some ten score concubines and several hundred persons of the royal household. There too can be seen the ancient slave market; and, though official slavery has ceased to be, the six decades that have passed since Kano fell without a casualty into British hands have not eliminated the atmosphere generated by long centuries of traffic in human chattels.

The two men marvelled at what they saw as they entered the great city; but as they approached the confines of the leper colony, their mood changed from wonder to horror. They were shattered, nauseated and revolted by the repulsive sight and mephitis that greeted them. 'Here there were human beings without hope,' recorded Clayton some years later, 'some without limbs and many of them blind. I, who had never hitherto beheld a leper in my life, now saw a nightmare laid out before me under the unrelenting menace of the sun. Some of them gasped and cried aloud for water. Others were like the witches in Macbeth stirring their evening meal; women among them clutched enfeebled children close to their breasts. From that time onward leprosy became a nightmare in my mind without redress. . . .'[1] In consequence of this horrible experience the Padre – mindful of the Master's command so little heeded in the modern world: 'Go, cleanse the leper. Freely ye have received; freely give' – vowed

[1] Clayton, *A Fire is Kindled* (Toc H and B.E.L.R.A.).

that, before he left the part of the world where lepers abounded, he would see other colonies that were on or near his route.

Nigeria and the Gold Coast were teeming with leprosy, as he told the Oxford congregation to whom he preached in the University Church on behalf of the British Empire Leprosy Relief Association in the following summer. Around Kumasi in the Gold Coast a considerable proportion of the inhabitants of some fifty villages were lepers; in parts of Uganda, in Abyssinia, right through Rhodesia down to Zululand and Basutoland the foul disease held sway. In Madagascar, throughout the length and breadth of India, up the Burma Road, throughout China, lepers abounded. Indeed, China was worst of all, for there leprosy had its main home, perhaps its origin; and he told his listeners that, though no statistics were available, there were estimated to be a million lepers in that troublous land.

He could do nothing for China, but while in Africa he would see for himself. Accordingly, he travelled eighty miles or so south-west of Kano to visit the leper colony run by the Church Mission-ary Society – a moving contrast to that at Kano. 'There', as Clayton subsequently wrote, 'I found calm and order prevailing; respect for patients, treatment to be had, cleanliness reinforced by explanation, as part and parcel of the whole ideal. One felt that there was here a strong tradition which heightened the morale of every patient – here was the God of Love in operation, touching in tenderness these hideous sores, and lending sanctity to the whole scene.'

In due course, and after having seen more than thirty leper colonies, the padre sailed for home from the port of Lagos. On board by rare good fortune he made the acquaintance of a very remarkable man, Dr A. B. Macdonald, who had gone out to Nigeria many years previously with his wife, before marriage a nursing Sister, had leased some 168 acres of land from the Chiefs at Itu on the Cross River that flows into the Bight of Biafra on the Gulf of Guinea, and had there founded a leper colony. The Superintendent and Mrs Macdonald, who were going on leave, found the padre a sympathetic listener. They informed him of their work, showed him photographs of the colony and of a few of the patients at Itu. They also told him something of the dreadful scourge that they were treating.

In 1871, they informed him, the germ of leprosy, visible under the microscope, was at last identified. The Royal College of Physicians of London had asserted that the disease was hereditary. This, however, was soon found to be completely false. No child has ever been born a leper; indeed, no child has ever contracted leprosy at an earlier age than about six months, and only then if there has been contagion. Leprosy is neither hereditary nor highly infectious. Science knew that leprosy could be ameliorated, if not entirely cured, by a long course of treatment with oil extracted from two peculiar trees indigenous to China. Unfortunately, this Chalmoogra Oil, as it was called, was so nauseous that few patients could retain it. Could it be administered by subcutaneous injection? That was the problem that had faced Major-General Sir Leonard Rogers of the Indian Medical Service and Dr Ernest Muir, Medical Adviser to the British Empire Leprosy Relief Association – two of the greatest British authorities on the disease. These two men worked to such good effect that by 1915 the first injections had been given and were found to yield slow but favourable results. Thenceforth, this treatment, modified slightly by the skill of a group of American doctors, has been increasingly effective, so that it is now reckoned to be, if prescribed in time, permanently curative. Some 90 per cent of cases need not return.

Dr and Mrs Macdonald closed their account by showing the padre three remarkable letters received from patients who had been discharged as cured. 'Each of these letters', recorded Clayton the following year, 'reads like a lost page of the New Testament. Each man ascribed to our Lord's healing hands his liberation from the living death of severe leprosy, and prayed that he would at no stage in life forget the Divine origin of the love and skill so patiently bestowed upon his treatment.' 'I myself owe entirely to your friendship the privilege and joy of my connection with this great task, so dear to our Master,' wrote Clayton to Dr and Mrs Macdonald many years later. 'It was far back in 1932 when I was privileged to travel home and to become your pupil on the voyage. . . . All this began with your inspiration, for you had shown me letters on the ship, written by patients who had been discharged. Each of the letters had a deep effect for they ascribed their rescue directly to our Lord and Saviour.'[1] 'To your friendship

[1] Clayton to Dr and Mrs A. B. Macdonald, 5th May, 1951.

and interest and help', replied Macdonald, 'we, along with the anti-leprosy cause in Nigeria, owe much. It was one of the best things in our lives that, under His leadership, we met you on your voyage home. It is wonderful how comprehensive are your human sympathies – for we know you have many, apart from this – a real "Great Heart". . . . My wife joins in thanks and affectionate homage. Please take care of yourself, and cut some of your activities. There are many padres, but only one "Tubby".'[1]

Thus it can be seen that the seed sown by the Macdonalds on that voyage home in 1933 did not fall on stony ground. On his first night after reaching London Clayton attended a meeting of Toc H in Stepney, where he spoke of the horrors of leprosy. He was so carried away by his subject, that on the spur of the moment he pleaded for volunteers to serve, after a period of training, for five years – first at Itu, and then, if required, in trying to found new leper colonies elsewhere. On that opening night, six men rose from their seats in response to the call. A few months later he was writing enthusiastically to the Archbishop of York: 'Remember Leprosy, if you've a chance, 38 men have given in their names, 2 doctors and 2 nurses for five years' unpaid work in Leper Colonies. This from four meetings only. . . .'[2] Within six months Toc H presented the cause of the British Empire Leprosy Relief Association with £25,000 and fifty names of eager volunteers. When the first body of Paladins sailed on their errand of mercy, the padre, whose burning eloquence had fired them with the needed enthusiasm, thus prayed for their welfare:

Rouse, Lord, the sleeping conscience of the nations at last equipped to rid the world of leprosy. Evoke the warriors' will to volunteer in living and in fruitful sacrifice; strengthen the arm of medicine, lead us forward, supply the Silver and the Gold when needed. Increase our faith; cast out this foul oppression, according to Thy Word and in Thy Name. Teach us Thy courage and Thy love toward the leper, that we may stretch forth eager hands to touch them after Thy example, that hope and not despair may be their portion.

[1] Macdonald to Clayton, The Leper Colony, Itu, Calabar Province, Nigeria, 27th June, 1951.
[2] Clayton to Archbishop of York, 6th December, 1933.

O Lord, Who hearest, make the fortunate hearken and do,
delaying not Thy love, for Thy Name's sake.
                                              Amen.

But that was not the end of the story; for within a few years
contributions to B.E.L.R.A.[1] from rich and poor alike were
coming in apace. 'Publish this on the house tops, for it's the living
Gospel – you'll agree,' wrote the padre enthusiastically from
H.M.S. *Beagle* at Alexandria in February 1936.

> The other night I was in my bridge-cabin working away at
> pressure and rather dreading further interruptions. Being in
> bridge position is strategic, for any man can come, and most
> men do, with all the issues of humanity. Another tap! – who can
> it be this time? A Leading Seaman – whom I scarcely know by
> sight – a recent transfer – so at least I fancy – and an oldish man,
> careworn and reluctant. I said 'What is it?' rather grumpily.
> He said, 'It's not much – something for the lepers, to help
> Toc H help them. I have been reading the Journal in our Mess,
> and heard your talk.' Then he said, simply, 'God's been good
> to me,' and held out a 10/– note, and went almost before I
> could reply. 10/–! And his wages are not £10 a month – and he's
> a married man! His wife will get her usual allotment. But he'll
> have nothing now for weeks and weeks to spend upon himself.

The man was Leading Seaman J. Kirkham of 3 Mess, H.M.S.
Beagle, and his name deserves to be recorded. 'Write him a letter.
He deserves to hear,' Clayton told Colonel Mynors Farmar, to
whom he was writing. 'Replace the 10/– note from my Current
Account. I'm keeping it. It's sacred.'[2]

Within eighteen months Toc H had raised a large sum for the
cause of the lepers, yet more was needed. 'Two million lepers
under our own Flag,' Clayton told a fellow parson, '... no
crusade can have a clearer blessing than that in which Toc H is
now involved. The men chosen to go out unpaid as welfare
workers in the Leper Colonies deserve to be regarded as our best,
and every district which is worth its salt should (in my view)
rouse the whole countryside to see that they are honoured and

---

[1] British Empire Leprosy Relief Association.
[2] Clayton to Farmar, H.M.S. *Beagle* at Alexandria, 6th February, 1936.

supported. . . . Volunteers are readily forthcoming and are needed. The one big problem is support for them: five years of work, with travelling expenses, necessitates some £1,300. Toc H has raised in all more than ten thousand pounds towards this work and I thank God for it. . . .'[1]

But that was to prove only a beginning, and in due course the total Toc H contribution to B.E.L.R.A. reached the sum of £100,000 together with a flow of volunteers eager and anxious to play their part in the wonderful work which (they firmly believed) they were undertaking at the bidding of their Heavenly Father. In a few years the Medical Secretary of B.E.L.R.A. was reporting enthusiastically on the work of these lay workers.[2] At Katsina and Maiduguri, two settlements in Northern Nigeria each sheltering between 200 and 250 lepers, mostly in a helpless condition, he reported on the 'selfless enthusiasm' of the two volunteers, Crayford and Pedrick, who rallied round them a few patients not too maimed in body or crippled in mind to clean up the settlements, erect new buildings, and tend the sores of their less fortunate fellow-sufferers. At Somalia in Kano Province, conditions were much better, and here, largely due to the splendid work of William Lambert, the Toc H representative, was found an atmosphere of cheerfulness and hope. 'I have had some difficult times and it has been hard work,' Lambert told Clayton, 'but thank God instead of the lepers running away as I was told they would, they are coming in ever-increasing numbers and we are extending to the extent of another forty houses, and even then we shall be full. It is sad to think that next to nothing has been done until now. This place is a God-send to those with ulcers and wounds, and it is worth while if only to cure these poor souls and send them back home. Yours in the service of our Lord.'[3] At Itu, Calabar Province, the great colony housing some 1,500 patients, the volunteers Norman Crayford and Hamish Macgregor reported the lepers to be wonderfully brave and cheerful, under the remarkable influence of Dr and Mrs Macdonald. Crayford reported seeing in one afternoon first a toe removed and then a perforating ulcer

---

[1] Clayton to the Rev. R. J. Davies, 25th August, 1937.
[2] Notes & Report on Toc H workers engaged on leprosy work in Nigeria, by Dr E. Muir, July 1936.
[3] Lambert to Clayton, c/o The Resident, Kano, 4th June, 1936.

opened and a drain tube inserted – all without anaesthetics; the patients just sat quietly, often in pain, but without complaint. Indeed, a remarkable spirit of cheerfulness prevailed, as Macgregor himself reported to Clayton. 'The first impression of the colony is a rather surprising one – that of happiness,' he told him. 'One usually associates leprosy and despair together – such is not the case – the prevailing things are hope – and happiness. The general cheerfulness is amazing and infectious too – so that everybody is taken in to it – wherever you go you are greeted with a cheerful word – and it is good that it is so. The colony is amazingly well organized – and it seems to me to be a splendid circle, the treatment, the work, the church and the school – all bearing on one limb, the betterment of these people – physically and spiritually. . . .'[1] At the new and most modern settlement at Oji River in Onitsha Province, the volunteer Parker working under Dr Money was considered sufficiently reliable to be left in charge of the fifty or sixty patients during the doctor's absence in India, where he had gone to study the most advanced methods of anti-leprosy work.

As can be imagined, the life of these volunteers was hard. One of them described how they rose at 6.30 a.m., breakfasted between 7.30 and 8 o'clock. Then they had a variety of duties to perform, such as treating the patients medically, supervising the labour gangs, working in the out-patients' department, cleaning the hospital, or doing office or dispensary work. After lunch they rested for half an hour, and at 2.30 p.m. until tea time they operated or supervised more labour gangs.

William Densham wrote to Clayton:

> I have learnt to give treatment at the Leper Hospital and to give injections for yaws. Whilst I've been here I've repaired about a mile of colony road and planted $\frac{1}{2}$ mile of rubber trees, but heavy rains have washed away the road again and it will have to be done afresh. We have had such heavy rains that we have been cut off from the neighbouring towns several times. . .
> A fortnight ago we all went some 30 miles (of which we had to walk ten through the bush, and hard going it was – poured all

---

[1] Macgregor to Clayton, The Leper Colony, Itu, Cross River, via Port Harcourt, Nigeria, n.d. [late August, 1935].

the time and we were soaked) to visit some lepers who have been turned out of their villages into the bush and left to fend for themselves. They have built their own homes and have land to farm, but having no treatment when they become ill, as they do pretty soon – they're just shut up in their houses and left to die. In some places round here the percentage of leprosy has been proved to be 30 and probably higher. Any thinking person can work out for himself the fact that the work that all the missions and B.E.L.R.A. with Toc H are doing is just pecking at the problem. Nigeria will still become a country composed *entirely* of lepers in the future if money is not put forward to stamp out in several generations this scourge. . . . Undoubtedly Toc H has taken up one of the finest pieces of work since the abolition of slavery. . . .[1]

'I am settling down to the work here and shall never regret the step I have taken,' Celyn Evans, another volunteer, reported; 'these poor people need all the love that we can give them. . . . Of the 150 odd patients we have here only about 20 men and the same number of women are able bodied! Some are in a very bad way. One came in the other day who had crawled 5 miles on her hands and knees and one came in only yesterday with her legs all raw flesh; how she managed is more than we can make out. I thank God for the strength to serve them and pray that I may be privileged to serve them for a long time to come.'[2]

Faced with these horrible conditions, it is not surprising that Clayton and the Toc H authorities in London were promising to send out further volunteers and extra funds to forward the great labour of mercy to which they had set their hands. Only anticipation of the coming war held Clayton back from attempting to start an international crusade for leprosy relief. That, he saw, was impossible in the immediate pre-war years, but they must not be deterred from doing everything possible for the stricken: 'Meanwhile it would be perilous and wrong that any member of Toc H should think himself absolved from helping lepers by passing resolutions about peace,' he declared. 'God is not mocked; and

[1] Densham to Clayton, The Native Administration Leper Colony, Uzuakoli, via Port Harcourt, S. Nigeria, 19th October, 1937.
[2] Evans to Clayton, C.M.S. Leper Colony, Zaria, Northern Nigeria, 1st December, 1938.

our Lord would not take much heed of such a lame excuse as this for any disobedience to His direct command that lepers have, in His most sacred Name, a special claim for help from every Christian. Deferring help until the world gets straight is to post-pone obedience indefinitely to a direct command of Jesus Christ – for this the individual will be judged.'[1]

But we have advanced beyond the year 1933 which was a notable one in Clayton's life. In the Birthday Honours he was created a Companion of Honour, a high distinction ranking only second to the Order of Merit. Three years later he was to be appointed a chaplain to the King. So the state was appreciative of the remarkable services rendered by perhaps the best known, respected and loved Anglican parson of his generation.

During the years immediately preceding the second world war, Philip Clayton, like the Apostle to the Gentiles before him, travelled far and wide – to the Middle East, India. In 1934, at the urgent plea of Sir Herbert Stanley, the High Commissioner and the local President of Toc H, he visited for the first time the Union of South Africa. 'Sir Herbert Stanley thinks Toc H South Africa is strong enough to stand a visit from me,' he told Sir Godfrey Thomas, the Prince of Wales's Private Secretary, early in the new year. 'So I am proposing to go this year, June to October. . . .' He was to take with him John Graham, the young Cambridge man whom the padre had so vividly impressed at their first meeting; and as he had work to do also for the Iraq Petroleum Company, he must go first to Haifa on the coast of Palestine, thence to the oil field of Kurkuk in Iraq, and so on by tankers down the East Coast.[2]

During an October week-end in the previous year Philip Clayton had stayed at Sandringham to preach the Sunday Sermon. '. . . about 20 minutes sermon is the normal thing,' warned the Rev. Arthur R. Fuller, Rector of Sandringham, adding 'it is a tiny building but as H.M. is rather deaf, it is wise not to drop one's voice too low'.[3] The preacher had thus had an ideal opportunity of regaling members of the Royal Family with details of his pro-jected travels; and we may be sure that he made full use of it.

[1] Clayton to Ringwald, 25th April, 1938.
[2] Clayton to Thomas, 27th January, 1934.
[3] Fuller to Clayton, 17th October [1933].

Thus shortly before his departure he was cheered to receive from the Duchess of York, Patroness of the League of Women Helpers of his movement, a farewell letter written in her own hand.

145 Piccadilly, W.1.
July 6th, 1934.

Dear Founder Padre,

As Patroness of the League of Women Helpers of Toc H, I hope most earnestly that your visit to South Africa may be productive of a great advance, not only in the many groups and Branches, but also in securing for the movement the keen goodwill of those who have influence and the desire to help.

At home we know the value of Toc H, the members of whom are trying in various ways to live up to the aims of the Family and giving good service to the Community.

I hope that many in South Africa who are not yet members of the League, but are in sympathy with its ideals will show their goodwill, as friends have shown it here, by helping in practical ways to further its work.

Already overseas the growth is wonderful. I send my greetings to all members in South Africa, and shall look forward to hearing a good account of the League on your return home.

Yours very sincerely,
Elizabeth.[1]

A few days later Clayton and his A.D.C. set out on their travels – travels which were to shatter the padre's health and bring him near to death or madness. Only the devotion of a small body of his closest friends saved him for the further work that he was destined to fulfil.

---

[1] H. M. Queen Elizabeth the Queen Mother's Clarence House Papers.

17

De Profundis

'The real truth is that everything which is really living is really in danger.'[1]

When Philip Clayton and John Graham left England in April 1934, the padre was a very tired man, quite unfit, though he did not know or would not recognize it, for the laborious duties that lay ahead.

Several years earlier, on the occasion of the Toc H birthday celebrations at Kimberley, Clayton had in a trenchant letter set forth for South Africa his views on the colour question. Modern science tells us, he had written, that all life is one, 'stretching from the mollusc and the protoplasm up the steep stairs which lead to the saint, the mystic and the poet. . . . In Christ all faithful men are indeed already one. In Him all ethnic variance is but the divers facets of His radiant glory. The extremes of culture and ignorance, of ownership and service, of liberty and law, of sex and age, are solemnly surrendered. There is neither Jew nor Greek, nor bond nor free, nor male nor female; all are one.'

Studied within this vast compass, the colour question gets rather cut down to size. Yet it is very much with us and it would be indeed foolish to ignore divergencies of creed and caste, to pretend that things are not where they plainly are, to deny the evidence of our senses. What then must Toc H do? At first it must 'embrace by sympathy races akin to our own in instinct and tradition; thence it can again go forward and find forerunners in other minds eager for what it brings, yet widely aloof from much in English England'. Intelligence is, as Clayton rightly pointed out, a far greater barrier than colour; for example in Colombo Toc H could include the Ceylonese, the Cingalese, and of course the Ceylon Burgher; but it would be many a day before it could include the coolie who would not be able to comprehend the

[1] P.B.C., 'Toc H and the Colour Question' in *Earthquake Love*.

instincts which make happy freedom possible. Faced with these problems it is the task of Toc H, Clayton told his South African followers, to offer to the 'child races' a 'working example' of European civilization 'expressing Christianity in acts of tolerance and unselfishness which need no gift of tongues'. How far had they acted on his precepts?

In Rhodesia he was disgusted at what he found, and in harsh terms he expressed his disappointment to Peter Monie in London.

> I celebrated at Salisbury Cathedral, and am now going to bed at 8.30 p.m. All in! I've never had a more exhausting or depressing time with Toc H than in the Rhodesias. If things go on like this down in the Union, I shall cut short my stay and put to sea. The thing has been a nightmare for the present, and I have no hope it can be improved without a whole-time staff, layman and padre. Left as it is, the thing is futile parody and, dangerous to Toc H through frequent scandals. It simply turns my stomach to discover what has grown up under the Toc H name. . . . If things do not improve . . . it will but wear me out to no good purpose to go round bleating to these mis-taught teams, which don't contain (so far) more than a handful of men who are worth their salt in faith or practice. Yours de profundis. T.[1]

A few days later, fearing that this was 'rather pessimistic', he wrote in the train on his way south to Johannesburg that he had showed his pencilled note to John Graham, '. . . and he passed it as no mis-statement of Toc H Rhodesia. . . . Whether my patience stands the wear and tear of all the tours arranged I don't quite know. I was not made for Southern Africa, and this whole show may be my Waterloo; unless most unexpected gifts emerge . . . The Church throughout South Africa seems to blame me for Toc H being secular although I have an alibi so far. My function is therefore not too pleasant; the rod v. honey is my contribution. If they don't like it, I shall sail away. . . .'[2] Bitter words indeed and were they justified? They had certainly been passed by John Graham, who assuredly was no fool. Yet it is hard to avoid the reflection

[1] Clayton to Monie, 29th June, 1934.
[2] Clayton to Monie, train to J'burg, Somme Day, 1st July, 1934.

that there is not much of the familiar Clayton in all this. In fact, he
was on the verge of a nervous breakdown.[1]

Later in the month we find the travellers comfortably lodged
with Lord Clarendon, the Governor General in Durban. 'I'm
here in gilded comfort for a fortnight, since I crocked up on
coming from Rhodesia,' he told Miss Jean Alexander; 'the old
job – insufficient circulation! But things are getting better daily
now; and I shall hope to go through with South Africa though it
must be a modified programme.'[2] In point of fact things were far
more serious with him than this letter showed. But for the
moment at any rate the worst had been, not cured, but staved off;
and the next day he wrote a slightly less pessimistic letter to Pat
Leonard:

> The situation here is still chaotic on the side of organization,
> but there are signs of hope and solid virtues. At present I am
> technically resting under the orders of a solemn doctor, who
> has discovered that my circulation has once more fallen below
> par considerably. I am, however, getting better rapidly,
> although harassed by innumerable letters. Toc H is not
> immune from lunatics anywhere in His Majesty's Dominions,
> but here no post fails to bring me autograph books, Biblical
> prophesies and scripture texts with a serrated side intended to
> convey stern admonitions. Most of these are Toc H in origin.
> This morning someone writes that they are packing up and
> bringing over 'An Altar' for me 'to dedicate' at Maritsburg, the
> thing to bear a subsequent inscription in brass upon its front
> that 'Tubby' did it! I trust my answer will not hurt their
> feelings.

Meanwhile Toc H South Africa needed funds to endow three
chaplains – Dutch Reformed, Methodist and Anglican – three
lay workers and a headquarters. Poor Sir Herbert Stanley, the
High Commissioner, had been slaving away at the Toc H post-bag
which each week got more unmanageable, and still there were no

---

[1] It is difficult to know how far Dr Clayton's dissatisfaction with Toc H in South
Africa was due to their attitude to the colour question and how much to their
general inefficiency. Father Graham read the whole of this chapter and passed it as a
true record of the sad events of 1934 and 1935; but his sudden and unexpected death
deprived me of the opportunity of discussing this point with him.

[2] Clayton to Miss Jean Alexander, King's House, Durban, 17th July, 1934.

headquarters, no printed balance sheet, no annual report, no finance committee, no lawyers, no bankers. 'The Maze at Hampton Court, or the wood in *Alice in Wonderland* are child's play to this thing; which has, however, some good in it.'[1] One asset was his A.D.C., a tower of strength in adversity: 'John Graham – who's so good that I just fear him –' he told Barkis three days later, 'is talking Tower Hill to Rotary tomorrow: his first big public speech. God bless the man. He won't let me attend and listen to him. . . .'[2]

Meanwhile, there were troubles at home to worry him. Cuthbert Bardsley, his curate at All Hallows, was leaving to become rector of Woolwich; and at the same time his other curate, Tom Savage, was also anxious to leave the Hill and to work once again in South Africa. The loss of two curates at once would be intolerable and must at all costs be prevented. 'My dear Tom', their vicar wrote anxiously from Johannesburg to Savage, 'I have written to Cuthbert for 2 agonizing hours, saying goodbye.' He did not expect to be home by Christmas: all depended on tankers to Mauritius, Abadan and Cairo. 'The lesson of this trip is "don't half build",' he told his young curate. 'I humbly beg that you will not make plans to leave Tower Hill at Easter '35. That doesn't mean you shall not be sent forth upon a trek for which your soul is pining. But you must face it. You are in Toc H; and if you left within six months of Cuthbert, the loss would be beyond our sustenance . . . You have more hold than Pat and I combined upon the situation for the future. If Toc H is to be what it can be, the grandparents must not be left to mind the baby. . . . Toc H is the most troublous task conceived. That is why you of all men must not leave. Six months out here would do a world of good, or longer if you feel that this is right. But you must NOT GO OUT. I reassert it, certain – for once – that here is Christ's command. It may be grievous, but it is the truth.'[3]

In spite of ever-failing health and strength, the indomitable padre concluded his merciless tour; and the result was gratifyingly successful. 'In spite of being rather under the weather, we can thank God for marvellous great kindness in the strong city of

[1] Clayton to Leonard, King's House, Durban, 18th July, 1934.
[2] Clayton to Baron, King's House, Durban, 21st July, 1934.
[3] Clayton to Savage, Johannesburg, Transfiguration [6th August, 1934].

Jo'burg,' he told Sir Godfrey Thomas. 'I think we can now definitely reckon that Toc H Jo'burg will now have an income of £2,000 p.a. for 5 years anyhow. By that time it should be thoroughly established. . . .'[1] In fact this was an under-estimate for some £3,000 a year had been promised to finance a whole-time staff of padres and lay-men to set Toc H on its feet in South Africa; and in all this Clayton paid eloquent tribute to the splendid work of his gifted and enthusiastic A.D.C. 'We're almost at the end of this strange programme, which, without John, would have been one long nightmare,' wrote Clayton to the Rev. F. E. Ford. 'Indeed, I wouldn't have attempted it. For my immediate chastening, I have now a brutal boil doing a week's eruption behind my ear, which sours my tempers further. But by God's grace, Toc H South Africa has now got something solid in the Bank, and can proceed less like a house of cards. . . .'[2] And a week later to Peter Monie: 'I come home very slowly by your leave. I'm badly over-strained and very old. Please God, I'll never again have such a show to tackle; and yet it looks as if Australia, N.Z. and all the rest need the same process!'[3]

He was clearly near the end of his tether. 'We sail tomorrow by tanker from Abadan – three weeks of bliss and quiet badly needed,' he wrote to the Alexander sisterhood at Aubrey House. 'This cannot be a letter, but it brings a Compass[4] you may care for; and my love to Aubrey, my dear home where it all began.'[5] And a fortnight later: '. . . Meanwhile, we are at sea, crossing the line upon a tanker bound for Abadan. Then we shall take it easy for a time, or may just go across to my Bombay Brother . . . I dread the English winter and the work! . . . Let this scrawl bring home love to my home, more now at Aubrey than just anywhere. . . .'[6]

Before the year was out he was with his brother Hugh, who was living at Belgaum in the Bombay province of India. There he learnt that satisfactory arrangements had been made for All

---

[1] Clayton to Thomas, Johannesburg, 9th August, 1934.

[2] Clayton to Ford, Victoria Hotel, Cradock, C.P. 21st September, 1934.

[3] Clayton to Monie, c/o Graham Mackeurtan, Inchmahome House, Prospect, Durban North, 28th September, 1934.

[4] The journal of Toc H South Africa.

[5] Clayton to Miss Jean Alexander, Rand Club, Johannesburg, 3rd October, 1934.

[6] Clayton to Miss Jean Alexander, 21 Loveday Street, Johannesburg, St. Luke's Day, 18th October, 1934.

Hallows so as to allow Tom Savage to go to South Africa as he so ardently wished. It was a sorry blow for the Vicar. 'Each selfish prop is thus withdrawn from me,' he wrote pathetically to his curate, 'and I can't argue for the long retention of the best friend and the most strengthening character All Hallows has had *twice* since its revival. I shall not feel that '42' is real without you, but you will come back! . . . Go then, dear Tom, we shall be lost without you. But only when we're lost by being heartbroken, can men be found for God. So get thee hence. It is absurd to say I'll pray for you. I don't know how to; but I love you, Tom. Tubby.' The letter ended with a postscript, a true *crie de coeur*: 'You've known me well. Weigh up my *faults*, and write them down and send them out to me. How can I frame my life on fitting lines? NO SOFT SOAP. T.'[1] And he followed this up a few weeks later with verses addressed to 'Tom Savage, priest and pal, soon outward-bound to Toc H Headquarters, Johannesburg'.

Wherever you go, Tom, whenever it haps
That you tuck up your cassock and pack up your traps,
You may reckon on one thing – a thing you will dream
Worth counting on always – the Trust of the Team.

Am I never to see you again, my great Tom,
Playing Simon Stylites with perfect aplomb,
Doubling Gore and Isaiah, till doubters desist;
While you do in the Devil, no glove on your fist.

Build Jo'burg her Mark, and surround it with steel;
Till the Rand in your hand is the Land of the Leal:[2]
Drill solid foundations! These only will keep
All the men, who *are* men, down your Robinson Deep.

God bless you and keep you whatever you do,
God give you good luck with your Mark and your crew,

---

[1] Clayton to Savage, Hulme Park, Belgaum, 25th November, 1934.

[2] Land of the Leal–the Realm of the Blessed Departed, Heaven. See the Song by Lady Nairne (1766–1845) *The Land of the Leal*. 'I'm wearin' awa' John, . . . to the land o' the leal.' This song 'has not been improved by the traditional substitution of "Jean" for "John" as the person addressed – a change perpetuated partly because of the quite mistaken supposition that the song was meant to express the dying words of Burns – for the sentiment of the song is essentially that of a woman'. *Cambridge History of English Literature*, XI, p. 233.

o

Then – when you have done what you know is God's Will, –
Don't trek the Sahara! Make straight for 'The Hill'.

P.B.C.

Beneath the verses on the original manuscripts appear these
words: 'P.S. I wrote this today, 5/1/35, in a bit of sunshine, in my
joy in you. It ran right out like this with no corrections beyond
one line! I thought you'd like MSS. T.' The corrected line is the
second of verse three.

But though the padre kept reassuring his friends that he was
much better and gradually recovering, John Graham, the man on
the spot, had taken fright at his condition long before they reached
Belgaum. Clayton's general deportment, his exaggerated talk, his
constant testiness – all proclaimed that there was something
seriously, even alarmingly, wrong with him; and in late June and
July the A.D.C. despatched to Pat Leonard several letters 'written
no doubt without balance or moderation', as he freely and
generously admitted many years later.[1] These urgently begged
Leonard to exert his own influence and mobilize that of his
friends to persuade Clayton to retire for six months to Mirfield, to
give himself a chance to recover from the devastating effects of the
South African tour. Graham's letters may well have been a trifle
over-charged; but it must be remembered that they were written
by an inexperienced young man of twenty-two who (though
undoubtedly wise beyond his years) had become seriously and
justifiably alarmed at what he was witnessing.

Be that as it may, the effect of his letters was unfortunate.
Leonard had a long confabulation with the Archbishop of
Canterbury (Lang) who, hearing only Pat's side of the story, was
naturally sympathetic towards his view. Lang, accordingly, wrote
in his own hand a kind and persuasive letter urging the invalid to
drop everything for six months and return home, and at the same
time absolutely refusing to accept his tendered resignation.
Leonard also enlisted the services of the Archbishop of York,
Clayton's life-long friend William Temple; the Superior of the
Community of the Resurrection (E. K. Talbot); Lord Wakefield;
and Colonel Medlicott of the Anglo-Persian Oil Company – and
they all wrote to India in the same sense. Simultaneously he urged

---

[1] Graham to the Author, 3rd December, 1964.

Neville Talbot, who had recently returned to England, from being Bishop of Pretoria, to become vicar of a Nottingham parish, to join forces with them in a united effort to control their stricken friend. In consequence, each wrote his views; and all their letters, either by accident or design, arrived by the same post.

'This was very great unwisdom, I have always thought,' recorded Father Graham thirty years later, 'and Tubby was shocked and horrified and very, very angry. He broke down mentally and physically, seeing himself in the hands of enemies hitting him in the back, his life a failure, his future in ruins. This was a very dark night for him indeed, and he took a long time, almost a year, to recover poise and a sense of proportion.'[1] Nor is this surprising. With no evidence before them save Graham's report, Philip Clayton's dearest friends failed to recognize that he was dangerously ill, and attributed the malady to a combination of spiritual dryness and Philistine gaucherie. 'Personally I am not really worried about his physical health, though the Doctor at Durban, after examining him, said that he was suffering from low blood pressure,' Leonard had written to Talbot. 'My real concern is that all these big schemes – Tower Hill Improvement; Oil Company; Leprosy Campaign, etc. etc. – are jeopardizing his soul's health. His undoubted influence and power with the upper ten in state and commerce has rather gone to his head. Certain it is that he has lost all that whimsical, child-like delight in the simple man, and, except in flashes, he gives people the impression of being a bad-tempered and difficult little genius, instead of the inspired visionary and man of God. The fact is that his life is thoroughly undisciplined, and I am convinced that our only chance of preserving the treasure that God has enshrined in him is to compel him to submit for six months at least to the discipline and power of a place like Mirfield.'[2]

Faced with this clarion call from Pat Leonard, Neville Talbot had set about composing his missive, and tactless is the kindest word that can be used for it.[3] Referring to information received from a 'letter from a friend in South Africa' and without men-

[1] Graham to the author, 3rd December, 1964.
[2] Leonard to Talbot, 24th September, 1934.
[3] It is unfortunate that the letter was destroyed with many other of Dr Clayton's documents in the blitz, but the comments of others upon it are sufficient to reveal its tenor.

tioning John Graham by name, he sprinkled his letter with such phrases as 'at the clear risk of pushing you under', 'unfaithful to the will of God', 'violent self-will', 'no longer a bearer of a message from God', 'the sacrifice of your prayers and your priesthood': and all this without any consultation whatsoever with Clayton's personal doctor and friend of Poperinghe days, Leonard Browne, at this time in private practice in Harley Street.

Amidst all this concatenation of insensibility, one voice of reason was heard loud and clear. At a meeting of the Central Executive of Toc H at which these melancholy matters were being debated, the Rev. Frederick Baggallay, the companion of Philip Clayton's Oxford days, 'Bags' to all his friends, rose to declare bluntly that, whatever others might say, he intended to sail for India forthwith at his own expense and to bring the invalid home. Whilst others wrangled, Baggallay acted; and before the year was out he had joined the Clayton household at Belgaum. By the time he arrived the patient was showing some signs of improvement, though hardly as much perhaps as he bravely told the anxious sisters Alexander. 'In point of fact I am very fit in body, taking my walks and playing lots of tennis,' he reported to Miss Jean Alexander on New Year's Day, 'but sleep is very difficult to get and till this mends, as it is slowly mending, I cannot very wisely start for Home. Easter, I think, will see me in London, but I shall not be at work until the Autumn. All this has been a bit of rough time but I am very thankful to be here. My brother and his wife have been most marvellous. . . . You know Aubrey is most dear to me and you and Mary my best friends on earth. Give her my constant love. I am going to rest in for a few months, relying on your prayers which can now be without anxiety for I am now definitely convalescent after the two worst months I have ever had'.[1]

Later in the month he reported to his good friend the Duchess of Devonshire, at that time President of the Women's Section of his movement. 'South Africa Toc H required of me far more than I, already sick, could give. The Clarendons are wonderfully kind; but from July–September I had a modified (!) programme of 7,000 miles of Train – 25 sleepless nights, and 178 public speeches! However, Toc H S.A. has now got a real start, some £15,000, and a strong staff can now be appointed and afforded. No more

[1] Clayton to Miss Jean Alexander, Hulme Park, Belgaum, 1st January, 1935.

begging in England for Johannesburg! In October, I came up by Tanker to Abadan, and nearly went West. But the Grace of God and the good doctor saved me. So I'm now here, and very much progressing. I've lost two stone, which is a sound affair. . . .'[1]

In fact it was some time before he could leave Hugh Clayton's hospitable roof; but by the early spring Baggallay had brought him home. He was promptly put under the care of Leonard Browne, the doctor whose long and intimate knowledge of him was an outstanding asset; and he stayed for many weeks with Mr Lancelot Prideaux-Brune and his wife in their Surrey home. Prideaux-Brune had been associated with Toc H since 1920 and had known the padre and the Old House in Poperinghe during the 1914–1918 War. To the Prideaux-Brunes, whose recently-born child Kenneth, one day to play a prominent part in the running of Toc H, Philip Clayton was anxious to christen, and to Frederick Baggallay he owed much for their sympathetic help in his hour of need, a debt that he was always anxious to recognize.

Nor did Baggallay mince his words with those whose lack of judgment had had such unhappy results. '. . . I for one am convinced that nine-tenths of what John Graham wrote and Neville quoted was moonshine . . .',[2] he wrote to Dr Browne from India; and to Talbot, who begged him to be frank, he was brutally outspoken. Pat Leonard, he averred, '. . . was prepared to accept the verdict of a boy of 22 on the spiritual condition of, to put it mildly, a Priest of unquestioned spiritual power and achievement. . . . You ask me to be critical: I don't think you ought to have been quite so ready to accept the verdict of this boy (whom I do not fancy you had ever even met!) against your best friend, without more exhaustive enquiry . . . You did envisage a possible crash from your words "at the clear risk of pushing you under"; I don't know exactly what you meant by this phrase, but you obviously contemplated something pretty big in the way of a mental and spiritual crisis. Was it a justifiable risk to take with a man of Tubby's emotional make-up?'[3]

Faced with this barrage, Neville Talbot grievously regretted his precipitate action. 'However, Leonard, I hope very much that no

[1] Clayton to Duchess of Devonshire, Hulme Park, Belgaum, 22nd January, 1935.
[2] Baggallay to Browne, Hulme Park, Belgaum, 23rd January, 1935.
[3] Baggallay to Talbot, 76a Rochester Row, Westminster, S.W.1. 26th June, 1935.

irretrievable harm has been done,' he wrote to Dr Browne. 'If I
had seen you before', he freely and generously admitted, 'I would
have written quite differently to Tubby, and I feel the force of
what you say about our having mainly weighed in on him as
though he were just naughty, and left out the fact of sickness.'[1]
'I do feel very bad at having made Tubby suffer so through what
was blundering and ignorant on my part, and have told him so,'
he told Frederick Baggallay; and again to Dr Browne some time
later: 'O that I had been put in the way of consultation with you!
But that is spilt milk.'[2] The milk had been spilt indeed. Neville
Talbot was Philip Clayton's most valued friend. Though Talbot's
work in the Salient during the war did not compare with that of
his co-founder of Toc H, Clayton had always placed his friend
on a pedestal. This was the admired colleague, this the respected
bishop who, after little real thought and investigation, had re-
proved his ailing friend and fellow priest. Folly could scarcely
be carried further.

With so many broken bottles it was hard indeed to pick up the
pieces. But in time good will and good sense prevailed. With the
coming of summer Clayton gradually responded to the ministra-
tions of doctors and to the affectionate solicitude of his host and
hostess in Surrey: and with returning health and sanity he was
prepared to look with greater charity upon the clumsy inter-
ventions of his well-meaning friends: 'his generosity and mag-
nanimity were as ever stupendous,' recorded Graham. 'He
forgave completely and saw, of course, that criticism of him
was not a pack of ill-informed lies but contained an element of
truth.'[3]

In April of this year, 1935, Clayton was overjoyed to hear that
his friend and helper John Daly had been appointed the first
Bishop of Gambia. 'My dear first Bishop', he wrote delightedly,
'I tried to pray in your cathedral church; but little did I dream
on that occasion that the first bishop would be an early jobmaster of Toc H Cambridge, my helper for a year on Tower Hill,
and ever afterwards my faithful friend whose priesthood has

---

[1] Talbot to Browne, St Mary's Vicarage, Nottingham, 7th December, 1934.
[2] Talbot to Browne, St Mary's Vicarage, Nottingham, 1st May, 1935.
[3] Graham to the author, 3rd December, 1964.

brought joy without a shadow, in every recollection of you, John. . . .'[1]

In August Clayton was sufficiently recovered to travel to Malta. At that moment the Abyssinian crisis broke; and his old friend Admiral Sir W. W. Fisher, Commander-in-Chief of the Mediterranean Fleet, invited the padre to spend some months with his men. As chaplain of H.M.S. *Codrington* he went to Malta, and thence to Alexandria, a city, he remarked, 'which lost St. Mark and broke St Catherine, and has not since been reimbursed in holiness'. There he transferred to H.M.S. *Beagle*, whence he wrote to John Graham, who was studying theology at the College of the Resurrection at Mirfield: 'I feel I ought to be extremely happy, for here I am with free tea, cheap tobacco, a slot to sleep in with two ports permitted to be open at most times, a lot of pals full of domestic problems . . . and sea all round, noisy guns and trouble in the wind. If this were all, deprived of past and future, released from memories of recent date and from the misery of coming home to four months more of Harley Street attendances, I should be happier than I deserve. . . .'[2] But the thought of the work ahead weighed him down. The spirit was willing enough, but the flesh was still weak. He knew well what his work with the Navy must be. 'My dear Cuthbert,' he wrote to Bardsley on St. Bartholomew's Day, 'our job ahead is the old fashioned one of making friends with all and singular, finding some points of contact, and developing it into the realm of mutual confidence. This isn't much to do, but it's worth trying. It is the pitface of all work for Christ to find men where they are, on their own ground, and to attempt to undergird their lives with a human friendship leading to recognition of the light within them. . . .'[3] Some three months later he wrote to Charlotte Tetley, who in 1929 had given him the home in Trinity Square soon to be famed as 'Forty Two': 'It is plainly right that I should still be here, for were I not, some 27 ships would be without a friend for services. They have no chaplain otherwise afloat, and it is good for me and serviceable to spend this prolonged period afloat. Hence I am not hurrying home as I intended, but sticking to 5,000 men for Christmas and perhaps

[1] Clayton to Daly, 23rd April, 1935.
[2] Clayton to Graham, H.M.S. *Beagle*, 13th September, 1935.
[3] Clayton to Bardsley, 'St Bart's Day' [24th August], 1935.

another month. It all depends on Signor Mussolini, who must soon see that he can't get much further. I'm wonderfully better in health and spirits. I haven't been so fit for many years: so that this break may prove a real blessing. . . .'[1]

In January of the New Year, King George V died. 'Indeed, the old order changeth very sadly,' wrote Clayton to the Duchess of Devonshire. 'How great has been this universe of sorrow. All through the Fleet men mourn a friend and father. Yours devotedly, Tubby.'[2] In February the traveller sailed for home on board H.M.S. *Queen Elizabeth*, flagship of Admiral Fisher. '. . . There is plenty for you to do,' the Admiral wrote to him, 'but *it's all done* by your mere presence in the Fleet, and *I want you to remember that* and not tire yourself out or worry about anything – just stop with us – and throw a word here and there and I may be able from time to time to indicate special places where they are most required. I believe the Fleet at the moment to be the most important part of the Empire and to have you in it of supreme value.'[3] No wonder that, with the administration of such healing draughts and with the fresh tang about him of the sea he dearly loved, Clayton rapidly regained his physical and mental vigour; and came at last to look upon the agonies that he had endured as little more than a frenzied dream.

---

[1] Clayton to Mrs Tetley, 2nd December, 1935.
[2] Clayton to Duchess of Devonshire, H.M.S. *Acasta*, 3rd Destroyer Flotilla, Mediterranean Fleet, 25th January, 1936.
[3] Fisher to Clayton, Queen Elizabeth, 10th February, 1936.

18

Last Years of Peace

'The world is dark; seldom has it been darker.
The more need therefore of the light you bear.'[1]

When Philip Clayton returned home early in 1935 he still had to undergo a period of convalesence under the supervision of Dr Browne. Not all who saw him at this time agreed on his future capabilities. His old friend Sir Reginald Wingate, indeed, found him in the early summer looking extraordinarily fit, and wrote to him: 'It was a real joy to see you yesterday after all those months during which you have been "going up and down on the face of the earth" striving for the welfare of your wonderful Toc H Movement, and, in consequence, have had to suffer from the overstrain – but I was indeed glad to see how much your health had improved – and – provided you give yourself a proper chance to refrain from all work for a few months longer – I firmly believe you will be better and stronger than ever and good for many more years of splendid service.'[2] His colleagues in Toc H, on the other hand, were, it seems, somewhat dubious about the founder's future. 'Toc H H.Q. discourage any independent action on my part . . .', he told Tom Savage a shade sadly; 'they still permit me to assist in money raising; but when it comes to Toc H principles and methods, I am far behind the times. However I am busy on the Hill and happy in the work upon the whole, so that you needn't worry over me . . .' And he added in a postscript: 'This sounds bad-tempered, but it is not so. I dare say they are right to put the brake on, but it is odd to feel Toc H remote.'[3]

Later that year came the shock of the abdication, inevitably a great blow to Clayton. '. . . I have hardly seen you except for a few minutes at the Hyde Park Hotel and just for a second at the

---

[1] P.B.C at Staff Conference, Digswell, September 1938.
[2] Wingate to Clayton, Queen Anne's Mansions, St. James's Park, 2nd May, 1935.
[3] Clayton to Savage, All Hallows Porchroom, E.C.3, 26th July, 1936.

House of Lords on that tragic day,' wrote Lord Salisbury. 'And it is this which has reminded me that you must have felt in a special degree the bitterness of the Crisis. For we in Toc H have a great debt of gratitude to the former Prince of Wales, and you probably have been almost in despair at the blow. . . .'[1] 'Nothing could be kinder or of more comfort to myself than yours of 26.12.36,' Clayton replied a week later; but his chief concern was for the friend who had so faithfully served the Prince. 'My principal distress is Godfrey Thomas,' he told Salisbury, 'whose 17 years of noble-hearted influence are wasted and unrecognized apparently, even by the Archbishop in his words denouncing the bad influence of others . . . Now he goes for a month to c/o H.M.S. *Rodney*, and Tim Harington at Gib. will comfort him, I pray. Send him a word of generous recognition. If any man deserves it, it is Godfrey.'[2] And to General Harington, the Governor of Gibraltar, he wrote on the same theme the very next day.

> For seventeen years he stood by Ex-H.M. and has been his good angel and his guardian, his best friend and his wisest influence. What has occurred has broken his whole spirit, and yet he is too brave to let it show. The future may be difficult for him, since it is most uncertain what will happen, and whether he will be retained or not, since the new King has brought his own staff. . . . If ever all the facts are pieced together and all the lies taken out and burnt, the work, example, and quiet influence of Godfrey exercised for good upon the man who was King of England, whom we all love and miss, will then be known to have been nobly given. Godfrey has been the hero through it all, and heroes suffer most when things go wrong. So I shall think of you and him together; and be content and thankful that he is received into your friendship from the first.[3]

To Thomas himself he wrote in comforting strain. '. . . You really made the Prince in all things good; and you must never think that this was wasted, for God will surely find a way of using

[1] Salisbury to Clayton, Hatfield House, 26th December, 1936.
[2] Clayton to Salisbury, 3rd January, 1937.
[3] Clayton to Harington, 4th January, 1937.

your creation of that character. Comfort yourself with this in your affliction, the like of which is beyond all analogy – the guardian friend, who has given every energy and been defeated by an ugly episode – this must not haunt your days. Life stands still undefeated; and God will use you, as He has all through.'[1]

In fact, Clayton's worst fears were not realized, for Sir Godfrey Thomas was first nominated Assistant Private Secretary to King George VI and then Private Secretary to the Duke of Gloucester, a post he held for twenty years.

In March the new King and Queen held a Reception at Buckingham Palace, and Philip Clayton wrote an amusing account of this to a young man, Ray Beck, who some years previously had accompanied the padre when he called to see the Duke and Duchess of York at their house in Piccadilly. On that occasion the company had adjourned to the nursery where Clayton's inseparable companion, his cocker spaniel 'Smuts', had played the piano to the young princesses. The children had been further mystified by two pieces of cloth material produced by the padre: in daylight both looked brown, but in artificial light one brown piece turned green! Clayton now wrote to Beck, in 1937 a student at Cuddeston Theological College, and later to become vicar of a west-country parish:

I thought you would be amused to have a record of yesterday afternoon, since you came with me to Piccadilly. I put on my blue suit, selected by Gen. for the occasion, and went down rather late by Underground to Victoria, where I picked up a cab, and passed the policeman and drove right in the last of the bunch. By 4.15 the red plush central staircase had been ascended by all other persons. Yesterday the Royal Family were suitably disposed for the reception, and nothing could be said as we moved past. . . . The reception being over, a series of encounters then took place. The Household staff, including Mrs Bowlby and Lady Spencer had the thing in hand, and I was told that I was on the list of persons to be seen especially, and stationed by a furious open grate to roast myself until my turn came round. While I was waiting, I had the good fortune to see the Wakefields, both of them, hand in hand. I cut them out of

---

[1] Clayton to Thomas, 29th December, 1936.

the general mêlée, told Lady Spencer and Mrs Bowlby, and finally was summoned to the Queen. She was as nice as ever, and affirmed her determination to retain all her friends on Tower Hill. . . . The point which would amuse you most of all was that the two Princesses asked for you and asked for Smuts, and wanted him to come. The Queen turned round at this stage in the conversation, and said that Smuts in future must be brought to liven up the Court; but Princess Elizabeth informed her Mother that nobody could find a piano! As for the little shreds of coloured stuff, they had been left behind at Piccadilly. Some other friends you know were present, including the Headmaster of Eton and his wife. . . .[1]

Later that year the Devonshires invited Philip Clayton to view the Coronation procession from their house in Carlton Gardens. 'It is a bird's eye view only, and, if the trees burst into leaf, it will hardly be that,' wrote the Duchess's Secretary, Miss Elsie Saunders, 'but the Duchess would like to send you tickets if you could come.'[2] However, the padre had been allotted a seat in Westminster Abbey: 'It is grand that you have a seat in the Abbey, no one could fit it better,' wrote Miss Saunders, adding gaily, 'Now *you'll* say I mean the 18 inches allowed, but of course I mean "more worthily".'[3] In the end the padre was invited by the Queen to occupy a seat in her private box in the Abbey, an honour that he greatly appreciated.

A few months later Clayton was saddened by the sudden death of his cousin, Dick Sheppard. He was only fifty-seven, and for the past eight years had been Dean of Canterbury. He was buried in the Cathedral; but a previous service was held at his old church, St Martin-in-the-Fields, and at this Clayton preached the funeral sermon. It was a touching tribute '. . . not to a great social servant, not to a prophet whose golden cord is broken, but to a hand and heart which mirrored clearly among mankind the hand and heart of Christ'.

In 1938, Clayton, General Sir Charles Harington and others connected with Toc H were anxious to send a greeting to their old chief, the Duke of Windsor. In their message they, perhaps

[1] Miss Saunders to Clayton, 2 Carlton Gardens, S.W.1, 8th May, 1937.
[2] Clayton to Beck, All Hallows Porchroom, E.C.3. 17th March, 1937.
[3] Miss Saunders to Clayton, 2 Carlton Gardens, S.W.1, 4th May, 1937.

tactlessly, mentioned the possibility of his return to England and bade him have patience. Their appeal evoked a somewhat dusty answer. The Duke wrote from Cap D'Antibes:

Dear Tubby,

Many thanks for your letter of September 1st, and for the good wishes you send from yourself and on behalf of Tim Harington and others in England. I am glad you mention the subject of our return. It's not necessary for me to tell you that the Duchess and I look forward to visiting our country again, and, later on, possibly, to resume some of the activities with which I was primarily interested. It would, however, interest me to know how long, in your opinion, the patience to which you refer is expected to last, as having been away close on two years, it would be difficult for me to judge! . . . Our plans for the winter are still somewhat uncertain, but I expect we shall be in Paris most of November and December when there might be an opportunity of meeting if you were coming over.

Yours sincerely,
Edward.[1]

Two months later Clayton thus telegraphed to the Duke, who was then back in Paris: 'Tim Harington and I and many thousands throughout Toc H would send our gratitude for all that you have done to build Toc H from the first days. The Birthday Festival is to be held on Saturday, 10th in Albert Hall. May we give them your Greetings and God-speed. Clayton'.[2] No doubt the desired message was returned; but all else was in vain. The Duke of Windsor was not suffered to aid Toc H or any other cause in Britain from that day forwards.

In January 1937 the new Queen, who was already Patroness of the League of Women Helpers subsequently renamed first Toc H (Women's Section) and more recently Toc H Women's Association, consented to become Patroness of Tower Hill Improvement. Meanwhile, the finances of Toc H, in spite of the splendid efforts of Clayton and his body of helpers, were causing anxiety; and in the autumn of 1937 the Bursar told Her Majesty's Lady-in-Waiting,

[1] Duke of Windsor to Clayton, La Croe, Cap D'Antibes, A. M., 4th October, 1938.
[2] Clayton to Duke of Windsor, Hotel Meurice, Paris. The message was telegraphed at midnight on 8th–9th December, 1938.

Lady Helen Graham, that the movement's overdraft was £20,000, its income £25,000 and expenditure £30,000. This state of things was also worrying the Duchess of Devonshire, who felt that not enough was being done within the movement itself to face up to the position. 'If it is intimated that Her Majesty cannot do anything to bolster up the very unsound finances unless the whole position is cleared up', she wrote to Lady Helen, 'it would force them to set their house in order.' Their house was to a considerable extent set in order by a Garden Party on behalf of Toc H held at Hampton Court with the Queen present, that raised a net sum of £11,000. So the movement's finances may be said to have improved considerably in the immediate pre-war years.

About this time to his great delight the padre received a letter of warm congratulations on his achievement from the Canadian Prime Minister. 'My heartiest congratulations upon the magnificent work you are doing and your vision for the future of your "colony",' wrote Mr R. B. Bennett. 'And my very sincere, but much belated thanks for the delightful hour you gave me on my Sunday visit to the Headquarters of Toc H – I shall always remember the historic Church: the ancient walls: the splendid and patriotic lectures and the fine atmosphere of happiness and contentment everywhere apparent. What a truly splendid bit of work you have done and are doing. You were very kind to me but I feel I will be able to tell our Canadian friends something of what you have done on Tower Hill and of the far-seeing plans for the future. I send you my best wishes and, if I may, my affectionate regards with high esteem.'[1] 'Your letter will be treasured on Tower Hill', replied Clayton, 'many a year after my harvest-home. If anyone should write a life of me, I hope that this may come into his hands; although it is an over-generous statement.'[2] This hope has been fulfilled, and Bennett was as good as his word: he sang the praises of Toc H and its founder in Canada, and he himself became a generous benefactor.

Early in 1939, P.B.C., accompanied by a young cousin, Peter Le Mesurier, set out on a tour of India and the Middle East. The trip, the whole cost of which was met by Lord Wakefield, was arranged

[1] Bennett to Clayton, The Mayfair Hotel, Berkeley Square, W.1., 19th October, 1938.
[2] Clayton to Bennett, Trafalgar Day [21st October], 1938.

by the First Sea Lord, Sir Roger Backhouse. They travelled by
way of Gibraltar and Malta to Alexandria, where – such was the
reputation of Toc H in Egypt – they were permitted to land
without visas and with some twenty pieces of luggage. But Egypt
had not, it seems, such a good reputation with the padre. 'Behold
us in this modern Noah's Ark proceeding to Bombay in our best
suitings. . .', he wrote gaily to Donald Cochrane in London from
on board P. & O. *Strathallan,* 'we have now finished with the land
of the Pharaoh and flies and unwashed nondescripts. Toc H in
R.A.F. is going soundly. It is the civvy stuff which doesn't
grip. . . . This big barn's expensive, and getting out to India via
Egypt will have cost us at least £200! But we have done some good
by the detour, Gib., Malta, Aboukir, Ismailia, are all of them most
genuine affairs.'[1] A week later they arrived at Bombay, to be
greeted by Sir Hugh and Lady Clayton. Thence they travelled to
Calcutta; and as they came up the Hooghly, they learned of the
premature death of Lord Brabourne, the popular Governor of
Bengal. 'Thus', wrote Le Mesurier, 'it was beneath a cloud of
universal sorrow that we landed.' The next day, Friday, 24th
February, he represented Clayton at the funeral service in the
Cathedral. 'A more impressive service I have seldom attended,'
he recorded. 'The Cathedral was filled with every sort of person,
of all colours, races and religions. I was very fortunate to have a
seat from where I missed nothing.'

Early in the following month the travellers were at Lahore,
where they were guests at Government House. From there Le
Mesurier reported that the padre was very well though working at
high pressure; that his labours had already borne fruit, and would
surely continue to do so. At Calcutta much was achieved. At
Agra the padre dealt with local problems 'with marvellous
patience and understanding.'[2] They travelled by car to Delhi
where Clayton was lodged by Vice-Admiral Fitzherbert, thence to
Lahore, whence a fortnight later the padre sent one of his characteristically breezy messages.

Dear Every One on Board Tower Hill, You may be wondering why a stream of letters in answer to your own do not

---

[1] Clayton to Cochrane, P. & O. *Strathallan,* 2nd February, 1939.
[2] Le Mesurier to Miss Macfie, Government House, Lahore, 7th March, 1939.

emerge. The truth is that the Indian trains prohibit all penman-
ship; but Peter and your pensioner are no less thankful for your
prayers and love. We know, of late acutely, that Near Home
Troubles have come, and linger or augment. Your prayers for
us are answered day by day. Our prayers for you are equally
sincere. You will forgive our silence. It is now the Silence of
fulfilment. By God's grace we have completed much of what
we hoped, and are both well; and on our Homeward way. If
there is need to hasten, we shall hasten. If not, it's wisest not to
disappoint those who expect us overland at Abadan and at
Kirkuk. Thence we shall not delay. God watch between us
ever, Tubby.[1]

Though the clouds were dark and lowering they did not hurry
home; and six weeks later they were at Habbaniyah by the
Euphrates in Iraq. Thence Clayton wrote to 'My dear Godparents,
Lord and Lady Wakefield', a graceful allusion to the fact that they
were meeting the expenses of the tour:

At last, we are within two weeks of Home, even by train,
which is the cheapest route. We ought to reach Paris on May
9th, and there we halt to pay a private visit to two old friends,
Maurice Hankey (whose views upon the present situation are
worth fine gold) and on to the Duke of Windsor, who wrote to
ask me to look in on them. We mean to reach Tower Hill on
May 12th or 13th; possibly before that date. It will be great to
be at Home again, more fit and healthy than I've been for years,
and ready to do anything for England. . . . This journey has
been fruitful for Toc H and far beyond has spread a sound
morale. We have met thousands and have been much impressed
with Godliness and honesty and humour. The race is still the
best there is on earth, under the hand of God. It meets bad times
with an abundance of patience. . . . I see ahead a big development of Toc H work in the three services, and the necessity of
cheerful centres of Christian influence among the training
camps, where every force making for righteousness will be
required. We must – as I suggested to Toc H a year ago – try to
obtain a building at Scapa Flow, also at Devonport for R.N.

[1] Lahore, 3rd March, 1939.

All Hallows destroyed in the blitz, 1940

Talbot House, Poperinge, and the chapel as they are today

membership, which is most promising. Here R.A.F. – as elsewhere on our trip – are in good fettle, and have put some of
their best into the work of Toc H. Your servant and godson,
Tubby.[1]

In September, 1938 – eighteen months earlier, and in the very
month that Chamberlain signed his famous agreement with Hitler
in Munich – Clayton had written ominously to William Lambert,
who was contemplating abandoning his work for the lepers and
coming home to face the war that he felt sure was imminent,
begging him to put all such thoughts out of his mind. 'You and
your mates, in my convinced belief, have chosen God's own way
of Active Service. . . . Your duty is most plainly to remain deep in
the work to which you are devoted, and not to volunteer for service
of the destructive kind.' But he had '. . . small sympathy with
pacificism':

> I regard [pacificism] as a dangerous delusion too loudly
> trumpeted in recent years. The noise which it has made has
> been responsible, to some extent, for making Europe think that
> the British will stand anything. We had a clear cut case in '35,
> when Italy was gassing Abyssinia. Had we then been prepared,
> we should have led the world at large in an unmistakable
> crusade, based on the firmest grounds of human evidence. We
> were, however, palsied at the time; our ships were obsolete, our
> Air Force tiny. We missed our chance, because we were too
> weak worthily to sustain a cause in which some fifty nations
> were in sympathy. Today we are beginning to repair our lack
> of strength; not more than a beginning. If we were strong, we
> could not now be menaced. Much of the blame for this sad state
> of things is, in my view, due to the fatal error of those who
> would not let this country arm, regardless of the world and its
> state.[2]

So much for the policy of appeasement; and the padre had no
doubts as to how things were going. In this month of September
1938 he gave an address entitled 'Pioneers' at the Staff Conference

---

[1] Clayton to Wakefield and Lady Wakefield, Air House, Habbaniyah, 26th April,
1939.
[2] Clayton to Lambert, 27th September, 1938.

at Digswell in Hertfordshire. 'Next year or 1940,' he told his audience, 'Toc H (according to its origin) will take its small but most distinguished part in a vast tragedy. The date alone is doubtful. The conflagration cannot be gainsaid. Our whole remaining hope is here and now to recognize the danger, not to hide our gaze or turn away, appalled, but to face facts – and facts are stubborn things. Within a few months now, most of our men and a large number of our staff will be engaged in war. . . .'

Clayton arrived home from his Indian tour in the middle of May 1939. Within a few months of his return, for the second time in a quarter of a century England was at war with Germany.

19

The Second War

'The army turned me down for the time being on grounds of age. I shall get younger later! Then we must try for Talbot House in France.'[1]

In July 1939 Dr Clayton spent three days at the headquarters of General Wavell, then C.-in-C. Southern Command but on the point of going out to form the new command of the Middle East, and was impressed with what he saw. 'It is good to see the army going strong. . . .'[2] he told a friend. Thence he went to pass the few weeks immediately preceding the outbreak of war with his colleague George MacLeod on the tiny island of Iona off the west coast of Scotland.

This remote spot had in the sixth century been made a centre of light for northern Britain by St Columba. Here he had built his monastery, where the Christian virtues of humility and meekness were rated above orthodoxy of religious observance. On Iona it was the personal relation of the soul to God the Father, the humility of Jesus, the brotherhood of man, the fellowship of the saints, that Columba and his fellow monks taught to the unlettered people of the north.[3] And when in 597 'the proud, gentle, humble, impulsive old saint'[4] died at the advanced age of seventy-six, he left behind him faithful followers to carry on his work both in the barren north and southwards to the fertile plains of England.[5] The Celtic saint's monastery on the surf-beaten shores of the Atlantic, sacked by the Vikings in 802, was succeeded by the abbey raised by the Benedictines in the thirteenth century. In the twentieth, this building, after many years of neglect, was in ruins; and it was the aspiration of MacLeod and Clayton to restore it to

---

[1] P.B.C. to H.M. The Queen, Rothes, Markinch, 1st October, 1939.
[2] Clayton to Brigadier R. G. Cherry, 24th July, 1939.
[3] *The Cambridge History of English Literature*, Vol. 1, p. 42.
[4] Arthur Bryant, *History of England, Makers of the Realm*, p. 81.
[5] Stenton, *Anglo-Saxon England (Oxford History of England)*, pp. 86, 118–19, 122–3.

its former glory. It was also their object to instil into the aimless intellects of their fellow countrymen something of the spiritual teaching infused into the minds and hearts of the northerners by Columba and his apostles one thousand three hundred years ago.

But war was imminent and Clayton must play his part. He reported to Scottish Command, Edinburgh, only to be told that he was far too old to be sent to France. He then sought out the Admiral and begged for employment. This application met with rather more success, and he was sent to Orkney, where the Archdeacon was ill, to take charge of the welfare of naval personnel in the far north. 'I am to act throughout the coming winter as Archdeacon of the Orkney Islands, with my headquarters in the little town of Kirkwall, where already we have built a Toc H hall for troops in various duties connected with the Fleet and the R.A.F.,'[1] he reported to Captain Euan Wallace, the Minister of Transport. And he asked the Lady-in-waiting to tell the Queen of his absence in the north, where he was '. . . trying to help a bit with ships and men, especially the trawlers and small craft. We are building temporary huts and one big hall against the winter weather. . . .'[2] He asked for a signed photograph for the main hall, a request that was readily granted. Other gifts followed; and, when timber was needed for a small chapel, the Queen gave instructions for this to be supplied from Glamis. 'I have handed over Tower Hill (in sandbags now) to the most cheerful hands of Michael Coleman and his garrison,' he told a friend. 'For these months I am north with ships and men, and then (if not again turned down on age) I'll get to France, for Talbot House the Second. God save the King and watch between us, Tubby.'[3] A gallant but vain hope, for his age was fifty-four!

From the far north he wrote to his devoted friends, the Alexander sisters. 'Faith is now at a premium in our lives, and every time I get a word from you, my faith is helped to fresh stability,' he told Jean in July 1940.

It cannot be that the immortal cause, for which we have been privileged to stand alongside others and now stand alone, is to

[1] Clayton to Wallace, 26th September, 1939.
[2] Clayton to Lady Katharine Seymour, Rothes, Markinch, 1st October, 1939.
[3] Clayton to 'Nunk', North, 2nd October, 1939.

be lost. It fails but to succeed, under the hand of God in His due time. . . . I often turn aside from things in hand to let my spirit move in your direction and walk in Mary's garden with you both, hearing wise words with little scraps of fun; then I come back again to what I'm doing, refreshed at heart for having been with you. I should be south again during October, but who can say what comes? To trust in God is the one thing we all can do at present; and trust in Him is never unfulfilled. This letter therefore simply seeks to bring my human love and blessing, if it may. So I commend you to His Holy keeping. Yours ever, Philip.[1]

To Mary Alexander a few weeks later he wrote: 'The world indeed is spinning down in darkness; yet there is light, but not yet signs of dawn beyond the glimmer on the far horizon. But in the men and women there is light that has no source on Earth; and that remains uninfluenced by its horrible surroundings: a smiling face within a sombre frame . . .'[2] 'What a wonderful man you are!', wrote Mr R. B. Bennett from the Ministry of Aircraft Production in September. 'Every time I see your signature I am grateful that kindly Providence gave us such a man at this time in our Empire's history. The Lord be with you.'[3] High praise from the austere, autocratic Canadian.

Clayton was accompanied to Orkney by his batman, Pettifer; by a young South African, Peter Le Mesurier; and by Donald Cochrane, then recovering from a double hernia. These three, before they had been north for more than a few weeks, shared the duty of reporting sad news to their chief. As everybody who knew Philip Clayton is aware, he was inordinately fond of dogs; and he had had for several years a cocker spaniel, known to all by the engaging name of 'Smuts'. This dog, which bore his name by special permission of the General himself, had been brought back from South Africa by Lord Hugh Beresford, naval A.D.C. to Lord Clarendon: and, when his owner was ordered to sea, he gave his pet to the padre, whose devoted companion he had been

---

[1] Clayton to Miss Jean Alexander, Thurso, 9th July, 1940.

[2] Clayton to Miss Mary Alexander, Toc H on Active Service, 29th August, 1940.

[3] Bennett to Clayton, Ministry of Aircraft Production, Millbank, 9th September, 1940.

ever since. Now in December 1939, Pettifer, Le Mesurier and Cochrane had the painful duty of breaking the news that 'Smuts' had been killed by a lorry in the blackout in Kirkwall. Within minutes of this information having been telephoned to Clayton, who was in the south at the time, the Field Security Police were on the telephone to Cochrane demanding to know who had murdered General Smuts! News of the sad death of 'Smuts' soon reached Queen Mary; and, when Philip Clayton was on leave, she summoned him to Badminton, the Gloucestershire home of the Duke of Beaufort to which she had been exiled for the duration. There she insisted on presenting him with a golden cocker with aristocratic connections. This gift Clayton reported to the Duke of Windsor, then Governor of the Bahamas: 'My dear old Chief while I was south, I had the joy of going to Badminton in order to receive a cocker spaniel of the name of 'Bill' who had a pedigree beyond compare. I got there on a Sunday afternoon and had the joy of seeing your Mother together with the Beauforts. She was well and very understanding over Orkney: so Bill and I came back to this big job, which is more pleasant in the summer weather, and to many friends on land and sea . . .'[1]

A year later news far graver than the death of a greatly-loved little dog greeted the Vicar of All Hallows during one of his visits to London. In the small hours of the morning of Monday, 9th December, 1940, a bomb, presumably intended for the Tower of London, crashed on the east vestry of All Hallows, wrecking the great east wall and window, and shattering with blast the inner Church. 'There was nothing that could be done', recorded Michael Coleman, the Acting Vicar, later to become Bishop of Qu'Appelle, 'for the place was in complete darkness and no light could be shown. I saw the pulpit and the whole of the High Altar had gone. It was too dark to see what the full damage was. . . . I returned to "42" and told Tubby the sad news. He seemed at once quite dazed, and I was rather fearful, but we said our prayers together and he at once wished to go and see the damage for himself. Planes were overhead and more bombs were dropping, and I persuaded him that it would be useless, particularly as he cannot see at all in the dark.' So they waited until early light. Soon after 6 o'clock Clayton and Coleman returned to the scene. The fires

---

[1] Clayton to Duke of Windsor, 5th August, 1940.

were now completely extinguished; and they mournfully surveyed the devastation. Then something riveted their attention. In the little garden built by Pettifer next to the East End of the Church, the fountain was still playing and the goldfish were still peacefully swimming in the pool. The bomb had landed less than ten feet away!

From London Clayton went for a few days of rest and comfort to his old friends Lord and Lady Bledisloe at Lydney in Gloucestershire. From Lydney he was summoned to Buckingham Palace: the Queen wished to hear first-hand the extent of the damage to the old Church. A few days later Clayton returned to duty on Orkney. At Christmas he gave Communion to some three hundred servicemen at posts of duty round Scapa Flow. And then, four days after Christmas, the second blow fell. '... All Hallows Church had now been gutted clean on Sunday night,' wrote Clayton to Cuthbert Bardsley. 'Wounded on 2nd Sunday night in Advent, she is consumed on Sunday night that follows Christmas Day. Forgive them, for they know not what they do. I have no altar now, save in my heart ... That one man's heart is broken matters little. More hearts than mine, and saints of every sort – those inexpensive, unimportant folk who form the aristocracy of Christ – will mourn the blackened walls, the outraged relics. ...'[1]

Michael Coleman has told what happened.

Thousands of incendiaries fell and the Church itself was not hit, but the whole of Great Tower Street, the whole of Hay's Wharf block, Mazawattee & Johnsons' caught and burnt right out, and with the great wind the Church was soon in flames. The Thames was at low tide and no water pressure could be got, and there were hundreds of fires everywhere. The roof fell in, and the inside pillars on the South side are gone, but the North ones still stand. The bare walls stand, but that is all, for the Tower, though it now stands, will probably have to be pulled down. The Porch Room above and below is completely gutted, but the great North door and all that North wall will probably be fully preserved and can be built on to when the new All Hallows rises. Thank God the Undercroft stands. ...[2]

[1] Clayton to Bardsley, 31st December, 1940.
[2] Coleman to Clayton, 42 Trinity Square, E.C.3, 6th January, 1941.

'When the new All Hallows rises.' Faith indeed amidst the holocaust! After the first attack, perhaps, there was a hope that the skill and enterprise of architects might effect a repair. But now that the Church had been completely gutted how could this be possible? After some eight centuries of life, Richard Coeur-de-Lion's splendid foundation was no more. Or so it seemed. Yet before many years were passed, thanks almost entirely to the faith and boundless energy of one man, a phoenix was to rise from the ashes on Tower Hill.

Faced with this news, Clayton started south; and when he was sitting in an hotel in Inverness a further shattering blow struck him. The wireless was turned on for the news, and the padre was shocked to hear that his great friend and benefactor, Lord Wakefield – the Old Chief, as he affectionately called him – had died that morning. This was totally unexpected, and it was indeed a sad man who reached London the following day.

But this was no time for grief. The war must be won and Philip Clayton must play his part. His work on Orkney was done; so later in the year he succeeded in getting himself appointed Chaplain to the Anglo-Saxon Line, which formed a portion of the Tanker Fleet. Their Chaplain had joined the R.A.F. and no substitute had been forthcoming. He wrote to his old Oxford friend Geoffrey Fisher, the Bishop of London, for his sanction;[1] and to an unknown correspondent: 'We have now put a rain-proof film of concrete over the ruins of the dear old Church. Our little war-time Church is in the Porchroom. . . . I am now shortly handing over here and doing three months' seatime for a change as Chaplain to the Anglo-Saxon Line, which forms a portion of the Tanker Fleet. . . . I hope to be with them till Easter next; so if you have a Tanker in the Convoy, and see upon a bridge a small squat figure, looking like Father Brown, without the brains, I shall be honoured if you make a signal.'

The bracing air of the sea, the companionship of sailors, the sense of doing his duty and of work well and bravely done soon restored his spirits, and so on St Thomas's Day[2] of this year, 1941, on board *M.V. Diplodon* he composed these charming lines.

[1] Clayton to Bishop of London, 6th October, 1941.
[2] 21st December.

PASS FRIEND, ALL'S WELL

Mercy and truth go with you, friend!
It is not in our hands to bless:
We stand beside you to amend
Our future, our faintheartedness.

The old, the young, the weak sustain
More sorrow than surrounds our lot.
Until He makes His purpose plain,
Can we bring hope, where hope is not?

What He permits, defeats the mind;
But, when we silently share 'Light',
Grief is discovered countersigned;
The sculptor's tool was plied aright.

Yon lonely outpost few defend
With tortured brain and aching eyes,
On the main chart, may co-extend
With others of like enterprise.

Ere men, whom you relieve, depart,
Let Light and silence re-instil
The homage of a thankful heart,
The ardour of a quickened will.

With the Anglo-Saxon Line the padre soon found himself in various parts of America. They put in at San Francisco, where he presented several of the crew to the late Bishop Karl Morgan Black for confirmation. He also found a hearty invitation from the Ambassador, Lord Halifax, to visit him in Washington.[1] From the West coast he crossed to Chicago, and then worked his way southwards to the ports of Texas. Wherever he stayed he managed to build up groups of sympathetic people ready and willing to welcome sailors from the British tankers when they called in to pick up their cargoes. Finally he returned northwards and sailed for home in the *Eulima* shortly before she was sunk by torpedo with almost total loss of passengers and crew.

Soon afterwards, in 1943, he sailed to Gibraltar in a small naval

---

[1] Halifax to Clayton, British Embassy, Washington, 24th February, 1942.

craft, and there boarded a frigate bound for Bombay. From Bombay he travelled to Ceylon and thence to the Hooghli. Here he found awaiting him instructions to report to Delhi, where he was the guest of his old friend, General Wavell, recently appointed supreme commander of the South-West Pacific. From Wavell's headquarters he went to stay with his brother, Sir Hugh Clayton, and then made a tour covering Karachi, Abadan, Teheran, Basra, Bagdad and Haifa. From Haifa he sailed for Alexandria to Malta, and so to Gibraltar which he reached in late October 1944.

The years 1943 and 1944 were sad ones for the Founder Padre. In April 1943 Neville Talbot died, and Clayton preached the sermon at the Memorial Service in St. Margaret's, Westminster. Nearly ten years had passed since the unhappy events that had for a time clouded their friendship; and now, all passion spent, Clayton paid eloquent tribute to his dead friend. Neville's ashes had been placed in the crypt of All Hallows, and no spot could be more fitting. 'For Neville was in very truth and purpose', declared the preacher, 'the Kingly foster-father of Toc H. His strength was never spared from its inception. He endured hardness, agony of mind, despisings from the doubtful, hindrances from unexpected quarters, misunderstandings, grief, ingratitude, to fortify the House which he set up. . . . He never tolerated compromise as to the goal. Toc H was nothing worth if it should fail to base its work on worship. . . .' As a Chaplain in the war his work had been noble. 'Chaplains on Dunkirk Beach, chaplains in Libya, chaplains in Ships, chaplains upon Air Stations have in these latter days done their white magic. But has there ever been another padre for whom his old battalion, weary from the line, have put their caps upon their bayonets, with three unprompted cheers on meeting him?' His work had been in the front line. In the early autumn of 1914 Talbot had been ordered to remain behind with a rear section of the Brigade Field Ambulance. But such regulations were not for him. 'Neville broke through this obsolete confinement,' the preacher told his congregation, 'and rejoined as the first chaplain in the line itself, with the 3rd Battalion of the Rifle Brigade; he had been with them in South Africa. To that deliberate indiscipline, all chaplains owe their freedom to accompany troops into the fighting. Over one hundred chaplains paid for this privilege, gladly, with their lives.'

Some years before, Talbot had lost his young wife after a short married life of remarkable happiness, and ever since had been a lonely man. But now all was well. 'The lover is united to his bride,' and 'now the Passionate Pilgrim is no more a lonely figure, as he was at heart; for all the love of kindred and of children. There are indeed no sexes and no races nor any Church within those shining walls. But there is love, and Christ will bless the water, making it wine, as at the marriage feast. The Passionate Pilgrim will obtain reward.' Then he quoted the noble lines called *The Passionate Man's Pilgrimage*, composed by Sir Walter Raleigh during his first imprisonment in the Tower.

> Give me my scallopshell of Quiet,
> My staffe of Faith to walke upon,
> My scrip of Joy, immortal diet,
> My bottle of Salvation,
> My gowne of Glory, Hope's true gage,
> And thus I'll make my pilgrimage.

In the summer of this same year, Clayton suffered another grievous loss. He was home for a few weeks' leave, and visited the R.A.F. at Yatesbury in Wiltshire. There he composed a poem 'one perfect summer twilight in July, 1943'; and on the top of the manuscript appear these words 'I think that Gerald had a hand in it. It was written knowing he was near on July 1st. Tubby'. Gerald Le Mesurier, Peter's brother, had been killed in a flying accident that afternoon at the aerodrome two miles away. Philip Clayton knew nothing of this until he returned to London several days later; but he had had a premonition that something was wrong. 'Midsummer day arrived. I went and lectured; and late that evening felt a strange unrest and wandered out upon the half-seen hills of British Trackways south of Avebury,' he stated afterwards. 'I wrote some verses. I forget the words, but I remember well how the circumambient air of that still night imposed itself on me. I knew someone was dead, someone I valued. . . .' Here are the verses that Philip Clayton wrote:[1]

[1] The original MS. is the property of Mr Peter Le Mesurier, by whose permission it is here printed.

QUIS SEPARABIT?

Why doth He bear our grief and share our sorrow?
Why doth He promise joy to those that mourn?
Why doth He pledge the triumph of tomorrow
To the oppressed, the outcast, the forlorn?
It is because the breath of benediction,
Which overwhelms our frailties and fears,
Is breaking down our sense of dereliction,
Our darkness and our tumults and our tears.

Whence cometh healing for a world heart-broken?
Not from the sword, the sermon, or the pen.
Why are His promises securely spoken?
Why doth His every word bring life to men?
If ye would learn the heart of the Redeemer,
Trust and be true to His indwelling light.
Let workers hope; for dawn will crown the dreamer
Who, step by step, establisheth the right.

At Gibraltar, which he reached on his way home in late October 1944, he received a third shock; for there he was greeted with the news that his lifelong friend and supporter, William Temple, Archbishop of Canterbury, had died suddenly of a heart attack. He was flown home immediately by the R.A.F. in time to attend the Abbey Service.

In the Second World War Poperinghe was over-run by the enemy; and the invaders, having heard something of the Old House and of its Upper Room, climbed up eagerly to see it. But all they found was a loft, empty and desolate; for every piece of furniture, every picture and book, every scrap of paper had been removed by a remarkably well-planned 'operation' of the 'White Brigade', the Resistance Movement of Poperinghe, and stowed in the houses or buried in the gardens of its members. So for some time the faithful Belgian caretakers, René and Olida Bérat, were left in peaceful possession of the place. Then at last in 1941 the enemy requisitioned the Old House at twenty-four hours' notice. The physical requirements of their officers had to be met, and a contingent of their fellow-countrywomen was imported for this purpose. To enquiries about the furniture the Germans received the reply: 'You requisitioned the house, you said nothing about the contents.' So for a time darkness settled on the Old House, an eclipse lighted only by the bravery of members of the White Brigade who ran great risks to demonstrate their affection for Talbot House and its founder.

In September 1944 Poperinghe was liberated by British tanks which were accompanied by Frank Gillard, the B.B.C.'s War correspondent. He had frequently visited the Old House in peacetime: now he was quickly recognized by the townsfolk and given a tumultuous welcome at the door. He wrote:

> At every little house and hamlet on the way, people rushed out into the road to cheer us. The first frontier barrier was swathed in red, white and blue bunting; the second in red, yellow and black. The streets of Poperinghe were full of people, yelling themselves hoarse at each vehicle that passed. So far all the troops passing through had been Poles, of the Polish Armoured Division. We were the first Britishers to show up and – with the letters B.B.C. on our truck giving away our identity – we received an ovation all to ourselves. We pulled up outside the front door of the Old House. A great Union Jack was flying from an upper window. The place badly needed a coat of paint, but otherwise, externally, it was in excellent condition. Not a pane of glass had been broken even. The big front door swung open, and there, in the entrance hall, stood a reception committee – armed members of the Belgian Resistance Movement who were standing guard over this piece of British property.

Gillard made a quick inspection of the whole place. Then he asked about the faithful René and Olida. No information being forthcoming from the Belgian guards, he dashed across the street to the boulangerie, where the good wife, 'after working out her excitement on me', revealed that Monsieur was 'mort' and that Madame Bérat was in the hospital of the Sacré Coeur.

'I forced my way through the crowds in the square,' wrote Gillard shortly afterwards, 'past the lines of collaborators still being marched into the Hotel de Ville by the patriots and walked right in through the front door of the Old Folks'

Building. A Sister led me to the door of Olida's room. She was sitting all alone in a high chair at a little table by the window, eating her midday meal. My hasty entry was a great shock to her. I should have been announced. For a moment she was speechless. Then she was weeping on my shoulder. Her first words were: 'René – he's dead!' Five minutes later she had completely recovered herself, and was her own lively self again, telling how she had protected Talbot House against the Germans. How she had rebuked them when they spilt water on the floors, or left the wash-house dirty. She and René had longed for our return. It became an obsession with René – 'Will they never come?' He had two strokes but recovered. They moved into the Sacré Coeur, where he could have proper care. Then one morning five months ago René had had his third stroke, and in an afternoon it was over. All the more precious belongings of the House, she told me, were in safe keeping. Some were in the care of members of the Association. The Altar Plate was in the vaults of the Bank in the Square. The Germans had removed it to Brussels at one time, but she had forced them, good soul that she is, to bring it back again. Olida now lives for the day when Toc H men and women will return to Poperinghe. . . . She sends her love and 'compliments' to all friends and longs to hear from them. She herself has enough money and is reasonably comfortable and well cared for. When I left her the rain had ceased, and she was putting on her clothes, getting ready to pay her first post-liberation visit to the Old House. With all her widowhood and her seventy years, her loyalty to the family remains as ever. . . .

As soon as permission could be obtained, Major Paul Slessor (from Toc H headquarters), and Barclay Baron flew over, and set about putting the House to rights again. Day after day they welcomed visits from the townsfolk, restoring the belongings of the House, including all the precious contents and fittings of the Upper Room. After a time a British armoured division came in, and its youthful soldiers crowded the House almost to bursting-point. The young women of Poperinghe formed a team which served them in a canteen. In December the founder of Toc H himself came over, and to the delight of all in the revived Upper Room led the celebration of the Movement's Birthday with services and the World Chain of Light.[1]

Here are his first impressions of events written by the Founder Padre to Tom Savage a few days later.

> Last week I studied German rule in Poperinghe, and was sickened by the facts which came to me from folk now grown middle-aged, whom Pettifer and I knew as children. Thirty-five men (I think) and two young boys were shot without the slightest form of trial. About a hundred men were taken from their beds long after midnight and sent into Silesian slavery. Homes have not heard of them since they were seized, and wives were told not to enquire after them.
>
> The Old House was a very drunken billet for German officers who fell down stairs. Our precious relics were fortunately all spirited away by brave townsfolk, buried, preserved and now returned intact. Praise be to God! The House was left in a most swinish state, and only saved by Belgian electricians from being blown up by a scheduled act of demolition on departure.
>
> The Herrenvolk got the wind up after D-Day and scuttled out of Poperinghe one morning, commandeering every cart, bicycle and even pram to carry their loot. So typical of them!
>
> But the Beloved House has shaken off this nightmare of oppression and misuse. It stands almost immune, and much venerated not only by the British Troops in rest, but by the townsfolk. Many generations will owe to the patience, wit and courage of these R.C. homes the restitution of the vestry linen, the Sacramental Plate (all in good order and beautifully cleaned), and above all the Carpenter's Bench itself.
>
> I was not in the house for half an hour before a soldier came out of the night to make his confession. Voluntary Prayers and Preparation for Communion went forward as of old. The Celebrations were (to my faithless surprise) furnished well with joyful guests.[2]

Thus the Old House was reinstated, the Upper Room restored to its former glory to become a shrine to which, year after year, come a steady stream of pilgrims from many lands.

[1] I am much indebted to Mr Frank Gillard and the late Mr Barclay Baron for the information about the recovery of the Old House at Poperinghe.

[2] Clayton to Savage, 21st December, 1944.

20

Phoenix on Tower Hill

'Thus the old Church speaks to you today and sends you blessings from
its tortured walls. Our task then is the same as everywhere. It is our front
which we must undertake all round the world, the building of God's
House. Here are four lines which we may well recall:
> "As we built the house there were scraps of song
> And tatters of laughter and wisps of sighs,
> All tangled up in the binding ties
> Of love and friendliness."[1]

The desecration of the Old House at Poperinghe and the destruction of All Hallows on Tower Hill were perhaps the two events
in the whole war that brought the greatest bitterness to Philip
Clayton. Of the old Church only parts of the outer walls, the north
porch and the shell of the Tower remained; and its contents,
packed in crates after the first bombing, were – before they could
be removed – destroyed by the second. 'Your moving letter much
uplifted me', he told his old friend, General Sir Reginald May,
early in 1941, 'for the new age can scarcely understand the grief in
me, which tends (like selfish sorrow) rather to bitterness, or so I
fear. I hate the enemy this time, with all my heart. . . . About All
Hallows, it is all too sad to be assessed in terms of minor sorrow.
But the old Church has not completely perished and can be
ultimately renewed by God's Good Grace. But not (I feel) by me.
My heart is broken, and I have no desire for all the changes which
slow Committees would decide upon. I simply want the old All
Hallows back. That was the missus and the kids to me. . . .'[2] But
another of the padre's friends and admirers knew that this mood
of despair would pass. 'Perhaps in part this war has been sent so
that not just for John Wesley but for every Christian his parish is

[1] P.B.C., *I bow my knees*, Sermon preached on Sunday, 28th April, 1946. *To
Conquer Hate*, p. 207.
[2] Clayton to May, Plas Warren, Broughton-by-Chester, Flintshire, 8th February,
1941.

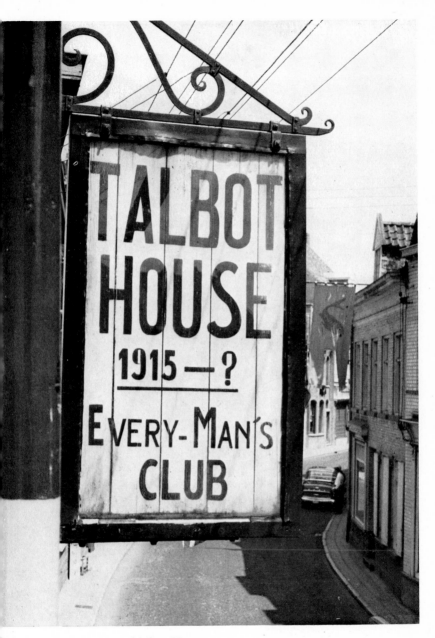

Old sign, still hanging, at Talbot House

Tubby Clayton, 1966

the world,' wrote Lord MacLeod. 'You, more than most men living, have experienced that: the Inner You will not be downcast. Christus Victor.'[1] Indeed MacLeod knew his friend better than that friend knew himself. The heartache in due time passed, and immediately after the war Clayton devoted practically the whole of his energies to the re-building of his ancient Church. 'I long to see the old Church paid for and built prior to my death,' he wrote some four years later, 'that is the last deep purpose of my being.'[2]

To gauge the extent of the task we must recall how inordinately rigorous were the post-war restrictions on building and in what short supply were all essential materials. Yet the vicar of All Hallows refused to be daunted by difficulties, however formidable; and on Saturday, 12th May, 1945 – just three days after V.E. Day – Clayton's old friend, Frederick Baggallay, invited two distinguished architects, the late Lord Mottistone and his partner, Mr Paul Paget, to meet the Vicar at the United Services Club to discuss their possible commission to design and supervise the re-building of All Hallows Church. The meeting took place on the following Wednesday afternoon. The architects, having presumably heard something of their prospective client's foibles, awaited his appearance with some trepidation: but 'as soon as he joined us', wrote Paget nearly twenty years afterwards, 'I realized that here was a client of star quality, full of imagination and quite determined to achieve the results at which he was aiming, no matter what the difficulties and obstacles in his path.'[3]

The weighty Committee that was soon formed to supervise the re-building of All Hallows, first under the Chairmanship of Field-Marshal Sir Claud Jacob, then of Lieutenant-Colonel E. H. Carkeet-James, Resident Governor of the Tower of London, and later of Colonel Frank Follett-Holt, held some memorable meetings, which, according to Paul Paget's humorous comment many years later, 'were an experience never to be forgotten. Tubby was always accompanied by one of his succession of Cairn terriers, which in the puppy stage kept the members wide awake by nibbling

---

[1] MacLeod to Clayton, 4 Park Circus Place, Glasgow, 2nd January, 1941.

[2] Clayton to Ian Collins, London, St. Luke's Day [8th October], 1945.

[3] Paget to the author, 7th December, 1964. I have drawn on his notes for much of what follows on the re-building of All Hallows, and am greatly indebted to my old friend, Mr Paul Paget, F.R.I.B.A. for his assistance.

Q

at their shoes under the Committee Room table. You could never be quite sure whom Tubby might not introduce to the meeting as co-opted members, and the business was sometimes held up by quite extraneous explanations and introductions. Always, however, good humour prevailed, lit up by Tubby's lively comments on whatever was being discussed and by his constant pressure for quicker progress and for some addition to the building such as an extra vestry or living quarters for the resident verger.'

But there were other and more formidable difficulties to be overcome, for the Committee soon found itself short of supplies; in consequence, it was decided that reinforced concrete must be used for the main structure in place of timber, which was almost unobtainable immediately after the war. Thus the core of the internal piers, made of reinforced concrete with a stone casing, would support a reinforced-concrete triforium and clerestory-beams. A roof of the same material followed approximately the form of the old roof with small intermediate beams between the rafters. The incorporation of a triforium with an enriched parapet of fibrous plaster had, as Mr Paget explained, the advantage of providing excellent facilities for both heating at high level (to prevent down draught), and for built-in lighting. It was also decided that – because as much as possible of the ancient stone wall and fabric must be preserved – brick should be used where the stone had been destroyed, in order to reveal in perpetuity the extent of the bomb-damage. The new tower was to terminate with a spire of timber cloaked with copper. Thus the designs for the Church followed what Paget described as the logical development from perpendicular architecture – the latest style of the pre-war Church – employing mid-twentieth century reinforced-concrete techniques.

The bombing had uncovered a portion of the original Saxon church of about A.D. 675 which had been burned and then replaced by a Norman Church in 1087, revealing a Saxon arch with Roman tiles (but with no keystone) dating from between A.D. 640 and 680. From the arcading near by there fell great fragments of stone which proved to be the remains of two Saxon crosses.[1] These crosses were probably originally erected between

[1] Durham, *The Pictorial History of All-Hallows-by-the-Tower*, p. 3.

1016 and 1036. The fragments were eventually removed from the Crypt and can now be seen near the Saxon arch found at a later date. Also revealed were 178 coffins in the south vault, together with the skull and bones of a man buried without a coffin. These were thought to be some of the remains of George Snayth, usher to Archbishop Laud, who was buried in haste about 1657, twelve years after the execution of his master.[1]

As the work of re-building progressed, it was decided that a representation of the Last Supper should be painted on the Reredos, and that this work should be entrusted to Brian Thomas, the gifted mural painter who later designed the windows in the American Memorial Chapel in St Paul's. His is a truly wonderful conception. The painting extends the full width of the chancel, and is of such height that the table in the painting appears to be an extension of the altar, with the figures appearing on each side. When the clergy are celebrating, the whole scene merges into one, with Our Saviour presiding. The apostles wear the dress of various periods to convey the profound truth that the Last Supper is a continuing act through the ages; and the vivid and differing expressions on their faces seem to reflect our own thought and feelings.[2] 'I did not realize the impressive majesty of this conception until I found myself in the front row at a Service,' wrote Cecil Thomas, the well-known sculptor, 'when I seemed to be looking into the Upper Room on that first occasion . . . it is an experience never-to-be-forgotten to attend a celebration of Holy Communion in All Hallows by the Tower and an object lesson to see the great purposes art can serve when it is directed with such imagination and skill.'[3]

In the stone framing of the reredos are nineteen paterae, and the Vicar was anxious that there should be carvings on them of the emblems of the Passion. This work was entrusted to Mr Cecil Thomas who was asked to carve a different emblem on each patera; and to represent the Holy Grail. This precious object,

---

[1] Laud, who was executed on 10th January, 1645, was buried in the Church of All Hallows. His body was removed to the Chapel of St John's College, Oxford, on 24th July, 1663.

[2] Durham, *The Pictorial History of All-Hallows-by-the-Tower*, p. 10.

[3] Thomas, *Memoirs*, 1960. The reredos was the gift of Mrs Garforth-Bles in memory of her husband, and the figure peeping from behind the curtain on the right-hand side is intended to represent her grandson.

Dr Clayton insisted, could be located in the Metropolitan Museum of Art in New York.

On enquiry at the Museum it was learnt that they possessed several early liturgical chalices, of which the Chalice of Antioch, as it was called, was probably the earliest-known surviving Christian Chalice, made especially for use in the Sacrament of the Lord's Supper. It was said to have been discovered, together with other religious objects, in 1910 by Arabs digging a well near Antioch, a prominent early centre of Christendom. This chalice is composed of two cups of which the inner is of plain, unornamented silver; the outer – into which the other is set – being decorated with silver openwork, enriched with gilding, and taking the form of vines in which appear animals, insects and birds. Within the circle of the vines are twelve male figures; ten apostles, and two representations of Christ.

The fact that this chalice consists of two cups, the inner a perfectly plain silver vessel that might, in the early centuries, have been found in any house of good standing, suggested the idea that this ampulla might be the Holy Grail itself, used by our Lord at His Last Supper; and that the elaborately decorated outer vessel was made for its protection when its sacred importance was realized. Unfortunately for Clayton's engaging theory,[1] scholars today consider either that the cup was fashioned during the period known as the Theodosian Revival in the late fourth or early fifth century; or, alternatively, that the chalice is a product of the revival under the Emperor Justinian during the first half of the sixth century.[2] But be that as it may, the last of the emblems on the paterae carved by Cecil Thomas represents the Chalice of Antioch in the Museum in New York.

All this of course was bound to be costly: it was estimated that the total outlay on the restoration would amount to approximately £215,000, of which about £115,000 would be met by the War Damage Commission. Therefore some £100,000 had to be found from other sources. So in October 1947 – at the suggestion of a number of American friends such as Charles Sumner Bird of

---

[1] First expounded in 1916 by Dr Gustavus A. Eisen in an article entitled *Preliminary Report on the Great Chalice of Antioch Containing the Earliest Portraits of Christ and the Apostles* in *American Journal of Archaeology*, XX, pp. 426–37.

[2] *The Chalice of Antioch* booklet published by the Metropolitan Museum of Art, New York.

Boston, William Lusk the Rector of Ridgefield, Connecticut, Barry Cassell of Baltimore, and the Rev. Melville Harcourt – Dr Clayton set out on a tour of Canada and the States in an effort to raise funds for the re-building of the Church. He was accompanied by an A.D.C. of twenty-nine, Andrew Elphinstone, who, however, was to return home in time to attend the wedding in November of his cousin, Princess Elizabeth. 'When Queen Elizabeth comes here in May 1948, as she has kindly promised, to lay the Foundation Stone of the new Nave,' wrote Clayton to his old friend William Lusk, shortly before his departure, 'we want to be quite certain that we can have funds within the Bank to build and furnish. She has most kindly given me the help of the companionship of her nephew, the Hon. Andrew Elphinstone, who, therefore, will be coming out with me for five weeks until the Royal Wedding. . . .'[1] And certainly Elphinstone seems to have been a great asset during the opening weeks of a strenuous tour.

On their arrival they were to stay with Mr and Mrs Barry Cassell in Baltimore, where Cassell had arranged for Clayton to address the Maryland Historical Society and other learned societies in the Eastern States. But the most significant gathering of the whole American tour was held at the India House, New York. This was a luncheon given by General Cornelius W. Wickersham, during the war a distinguished member of General Eisenhower's staff, to meet a number of his influential friends who might wish to help the vicar to restore his Church. As a result of this gathering General Wickersham and his friends organized All Hallows Foundation Inc., to serve as the official recipient of contributions made in the States. The General himself was the first President.

Among those present at the luncheon was John Gilbert Winant, who during the last years of the 1939–1945 war was American Ambassador to the Court of St James's. Clayton and the ex-Ambassador were old friends. Unlike another of America's war-time representatives who, to his eternal shame, did nothing but denigrate Britain's efforts and predict her imminent fall, at the time of the worst fire-raids Winant could be seen night after night in the East End of London, clambering through the smoking ruins and encouraging the brave but helpless families who had lost their

[1] Clayton to Lusk, 11th September 1947.

homes. He had longed to be able to do more to show them his country's sympathy. Here too, whenever he was in England, could be seen on a like mission the Vicar of All Hallows who, during those sad days, had formed a great admiration and regard for the American Ambassador. '. . . John Winant is an angel undisguised,' he told his friend William Lusk during the war. 'I never met a man in politics whom I liked more. Small wonder he is trusted upon both sides of the now shrunken pond . . .'[1] And now in New York five years later Clayton had his opportunity to demonstrate to the great and kindly American how he could help.

During the war years when the Ambassador had taken such a lively and personal interest in the misfortunes of London's East-Enders, he had come to admire their sterling qualities. Now in the years of peace it was imperative that Americans and Englishmen, and especially the young of both nations, should get to know each other; for acquaintanceship could only breed regard, and friendship between the two countries was the very cornerstone to world peace. Would it not be possible to arrange for a group of young American students to visit England each summer and help with the physical work of re-establishing Boys' Clubs and Social Service organizations in the East End of London, and for a like body of British students to visit the States? These young Americans might, suggested Clayton, be called Winant Volunteers. This conception found a ready response in John Winant's heart; he would give it his utmost support, he would do all in his power to make it a success. Thus he assured the padre. Then, a few days later the tragic news broke; his promised aid was no more than a dream, for Winant had died by his own hand.

From New York Clayton and Elphinstone went to Boston whence, as Clayton told General Eddy, Chief of Staff of the United States Army, they were to travel by morning train to Washington to lunch at the Pentagon with General Eisenhower,[2] whom Clayton had not seen since they had first met some years before in Algeria with General Sir Humfrey Gale, then Deputy Chief of Staff under the Supreme Commander. In Washington life was frugal indeed. Lunches for the General and his friends were brought in from the canteen, and took perhaps ten minutes to eat,

[1] Clayton to Lusk, 3rd November, 1942.
[2] Clayton to Eddy, 13th October, 1947.

whilst Eisenhower and Clayton talked of All Hallows, Toc H and the east London Clubs and settlements. Next to the Chief sat Clayton's friend, General Eddy, and he promised to arrange for the padre to see General Omar Bradley, who was destined to succeed him as Chief of Staff of the United States Army. The meeting took place the following Sunday at Bradley's house at Arlington. From there Clayton, armed with a letter of introduction to the Chief Services Chaplain, Luther D. Miller, headed south-westwards, first to Houston and then to San Antonio in Texas. At these and other places he addressed vast audiences of the United States Air Force, giving sometimes as many as three addresses a day. 'They heard me with no small amount of patience and plainly wished to know of London's needs,' he recorded. It was an opportunity of which he could be relied upon to take full advantage.

When Philip Clayton returned to the eastern sea-board, he was feeling none too well and was compelled to enter a Boston nursing-home for an operation; after which he went to the Charles Sumner Birds' home in Massachusetts to recuperate. From there in early April 1948 he travelled to Ottawa to stay at Government House with Field Marshal Lord Alexander and to raise further funds for his great cause.

By now the gifts were coming in thick and fast, not only from the United States and Canada, but shortly also from Australia, New Zealand, Tasmania, India, Rhodesia and Gibraltar. The padre's recent host, Sumner Bird, supplied nineteen tons of steel rods sixty feet long to roof the north aisle; H. R. MacMillan gave twelve standards of constructional timber; J. W. McConnell a carillon of eighteen bells; John Nixon of New York, twenty tons of steel for the south aisle. Three thousand square feet of floor tiles were given by a Montreal building firm: steel came from a firm in Texas, another in New York, and two in Canada. No less a sum than £4,000 was raised by Mrs de Selincourt for equipping the Mariners' Chapel in the south aisle, where a very beautiful ivory crucifix – said to have come from an old Spanish ship of Armada date – provides an appropriate focal point above the semi-circular altar table. General Wickersham raised 150,000 dollars for the new tower and Captain Sir Ion Hamilton Benn, surely the oldest and greatest of Clayton's champions, at the age of ninety made a gift to All Hallows, which enabled the spire, clad in copper from Rhodesia, to surmount the square tower. This, to Benn's intense joy, was completed in his ninety-third year, some six years before his death. One last great donation was made to ensure that there would be no deficit in the restoration of All Hallows; some £33,000 was given to complete the work with the building of the baptistry and the verger's quarters above it. The sole condition attached to this gift was that the donor's name must not be revealed during his lifetime.

Thus, in spite of many difficulties and frustrations, the great work went ahead. No wonder that when Dr Clayton sailed for England in April 1948, his heart was light, for he could feel his work well done.

A few weeks later, on 19th July, 1948, the Queen laid the foundation-stone of the new church with a trowel whose golden handle was presented to her for use as a parasol or umbrella handle. The foundation stone of Cornish granite, the gift of St Ives Toc H, bore an inscription of which the rough translation runs:

Ethelburga founded me in 675,[1]
Samuel Pepys rescued me from the Great Fire 1666,
1940 The Enemy gravely wounded me.
1948 Loving friends restored me.

As Queen Elizabeth left the undercroft at the end of the service a joyful melody from McConnell's eighteen bells pealed for the first time, proclaiming to all the world that God's ancient house was rising, phoenix-like, from the ashes of its former self nearly one thousand three hundred years after its foundation.

Meanwhile, the idea of the Winant Volunteers, suggested by Clayton to the ex-Ambassador at General Wickersham's New York lunch, had caught on. Every year since then a group of young Americans have come to England. At first they visited only

[1] 'The old title of All Hallows-by-the-Tower, that of All Hallows, Barking or Berkynchirche, indicates that the Church was once a dependency of the famous Abbey of Barking in Essex. The Abbey was founded by Erkenwald, son of Anna, seventh King of the East Saxons. Erkenwald was Bishop of London in A.D. 675, and his sister, Ethelburga, became the Convent's first Abbess.' Durham, *Pictorial History of All Hallows-by-the-Tower*, p. 3.

London; but later other bombed cities of Britain, such as Liverpool, Manchester, Birmingham and Glasgow, were included. The League of Winant Volunteers, Inc. soon gained powerful support. Mrs Christopher Soames, Sir Winston Churchill's youngest daughter, became the first President; General Sir Humfrey Gale, Chairman; and the Honorary Chairman was none other than General Eisenhower himself. '. . . it is a personal privilege and distinction to be associated in the magnificent work you are doing,'[1] wrote the President to the padre, and within a few years, so successful was the experiment, that young people from Britain were visiting the States on precisely the same terms. 'The young American men and women who go to England each summer and their counterparts in the United States, the Clayton Volunteers, have done outstanding work on both sides of the Atlantic,' wrote the President long afterwards to the then Chairman, General Wickersham's nephew, Mr Ichabod T. Williams. 'In the non-ending struggle to improve the lot of others, these young people, sincerely motivated and selflessly applied, are indeed ambassadors of goodwill between our two great countries,'[2] wrote the President to Williams; and he paid a well-deserved tribute to the man whose fertile brain had given birth to the whole movement. 'He initiated the concept of the organization of the "Winant Volunteers"', wrote General Eisenhower in 1964, 'and as a result great numbers of young Americans in the post-war years had the privilege of learning more about London and its peoples and contributing some of their knowledge and enthusiastic love of sports to many young Britons who otherwise might never have had the benefit of the outdoor exercise and companionship thus brought about. As a result his influence in developing greater mutual understanding between our two peoples has been marked.

'He is one of the finest characters of our time and is an individual to whom Britons and Americans alike owe a real debt of gratitude.'[3]

[1] Eisenhower to Clayton, The White House, Washington, 31st October, 1956.
[2] Eisenhower to Williams, Palm Desert, 6th April, 1962.
[3] Eisenhower to the author, Gettysburg, Pennsylvania, 3rd September, 1964.

21

End of the Pilgrimage

'Bless'd be the day when moved I was
A pilgrim for to be
And blessed also be the Cause
That thereto moved me.'[1]

'The Passionate Pilgrim will obtain reward.'[2]

The re-building of All Hallows went triumphantly on. By January 1953 the framework of the main body of the church was complete; by the autumn three years later the nave and south Chapel were finished; and on 23rd July, 1957, the whole Church was dedicated by the Bishop of London in the presence of the Queen Mother. Work on the spire, begun in September 1957, was completed in January 1959. In June that year work was started on building the baptistry and verger's flat; and this was completed towards the end of 1960, when the Saxon arch was placed in position. The baptistry, with its beautiful font hewn from Gibraltar rock, with cover carved by Grinling Gibbons, was dedicated on the 11th September, 1960.

All this, of course, had needed money and gifts; and, though the North American tour in 1947 and 1948 had been immensely fruitful, much more was required. Accordingly, in the autumn of 1952 Clayton went on an extensive pilgrimage to raise funds in Australia and New Zealand, spending some two months visiting each Australian state. On departure he was cheered by a letter from the Queen Mother. 'Dear Founder Padre', she wrote, 'I have heard with the deepest interest of the great journey which you are to undertake in September . . . my thoughts and prayers go with you as you set forth on your travels.'[3] From October until December 1956, he was in the United States on a like mission. The

[1] P.B.C., *The Pilgrim's Hymn*.
[2] P.B.C., *A tribute to Neville Talbot,* St Margaret's Westminster, 17th April, 1943.
[3] H.M. Queen Elizabeth the Queen Mother's Clarence House Papers.

success of these tours is shown by the progress made on the new church and its successful completion by the end of 1960. Only Philip Clayton's remarkable tenacity could have overcome the seemingly insuperable difficulties that had faced him and his small band of helpers way back in May 1945; yet in fifteen years they had been surmounted and the new All Hallows had been built and paid for.

In all the circumstances, it is hardly surprising that in the summer of 1954 the Church of England, that had for so long neglected its dynamic parson, should at last make partial retribution by the offer of a Lambeth D.D. 'in recognition of your lifelong work through Toc H and All Hallows Church and for the Glory of God', as his old friend the Archbishop put it.[1] Clayton replied, no doubt with his tongue in his cheek, for he had taken a first in Theology: 'Your Grace overwhelms this village idiot, who took a third in Mods, with the proposal of a Lambeth D.D. With profound thankfulness I here accept. To have it at your hands', he added, 'means much to me.'[2]

But not only had the Church up to this time given Clayton no preferment; its grand Panjandrums – apart from his old friends Davidson, Temple, Fisher and some others – had largely ignored both him and the movement that was so near his heart. Thus, the bishop of a northern diocese, invited to a great Toc H gathering, had replied that in his view Toc H, scouting, and all such things were unnecessary until such time as the Church could be proved to have failed. One result of this stiff-necked attitude was that only two Anglican clergy in the bishop's diocese were supporters of the movement which was in consequence forced to look elsewhere for spiritual sympathy. 'Glory be', wrote Clayton, 'that the Archbishop has so constantly shown his trust towards Toc H, and his determination that this effectual open door towards the fulfilment of the Church's mission among men should not be slammed in their faces. . . .'[3] 'Apart from the Archbishop of York (whose name be ever blessed),' wrote Clayton some months later, 'few bishops have spent any time at all in begging their younger clergy to volunteer for Toc H, and yet Toc H is now responsible for

[1] Fisher to Clayton, Lambeth Palace, S.E.1, 1st June, 1954.
[2] Clayton to Fisher, June 1954.
[3] Clayton to the Rev. Colin Mare, 24th June, 1954.

nearly one whole third of the Church of England ordinals. It is the only movement which fills cathedral after cathedral upon a week-night at the time of its Festivals. It is increasingly in touch with commerce and helps men to serve and worship faithfully.'[1] The Archbishop of York was Clayton's old Chief at Portsea, Cyril Forster Garbett.

Even allowing for some exaggeration in Clayton's proud boast, it is sad that a Church leader could be so pur-blind. True, the offending bishop was hardly an outstanding figure on the bench of bishops of his day and now no one remembers him. But, then, who has ever heard of perhaps eight out of ten of the occupants of the richest sees of the Anglican Church, or the Deans, or the Archdeacons, or any of the prelates holding prebendal stalls in our great Cathedrals? One quality they are sure to have in common: they will one and all be safe, dependable men, men unlikely to give trouble or to raise difficulties. Yet it is just such troublemakers who succeed in stirring the consciences of the multitude, in filling the Churches, and in bringing the religion of Christ into the homes of the people. Philip Clayton was difficult, awkward, unpredictable: so was the apostle Paul whom he much resembled. He might fly off the handle at inconvenient moments: so might St Paul. True, he was famous in many lands; true, he was a saintly priest universally revered for his unique work for mankind. But he was, again like St Paul, a tiresome saint, and the Church has small use for tiresome saints. Safe men who can always be relied upon to say and to do the predictable thing are much more to her taste. So the Philip Claytons of the world get small preferment. The State made Clayton a Companion of Honour in 1933; the Church bestowed upon him a Doctorate of Divinity in 1954!

With the building and dedication of the new All Hallows, Clayton's work was largely done. Nevertheless, he continued to travel far and wide on behalf of Toc H, and to call on all and sundry from whom he could expect support. Indeed, he was a great caller, as one American friend humorously put it. 'Dear Tubby,' he wrote, 'Professor Horace M. Kallen, who was George Santayana's Assistant at Harvard, once said of him: "Santayana is like the Pope; he does not return calls." But you, Tubby, do

[1] Clayton to the Rev. Hugh Lister, 23rd April, 1954.

return calls. You returned the calls we made on you in August 1962. And in doing so you gave us very great solace. You are not like the Pope. You are not like George Santayana. You are not like anyone else in the whole wide world. You are unique. You will ever remain so in our hearts. Thank you for returning our call.'[1] 'You will be very much in our hearts during this Christmas Season,' wrote Mr Robert Anderson, the Secretary of the Treasury, from Washington in December, 1958, 'and as we add up all the other things for which we are thankful, we shall be thankful as well for the life and contribution of Tubby Clayton to this old world.' Early in 1969, commenting on the fact that the padre had signed himself 'your debtor', Anderson wrote: 'I often think of the fact that all of us have a great number of unpaid debts, some of which we can never repay. They are the obligations that we owe to our family, our friends, and, above all else, to those who carry on the work of the Master. Because we owe so much to you, it makes me exceeding humble to receive a letter with such a signature.'[2]

There must be a great number of people who, like these two Americans, received solace from Philip Clayton's calls, regarded him as unique, and were grateful for the debt tehy owed him for his life's service and for his contribution to 'this old world'. Why is that so?

First and foremost, perhaps, it was his nearness to God that seemed to mark him out from other men. He was convinced, and he conveyed to others his conviction, of the reality of God at work in human hearts. 'He brought our Lord's Presence into the room where we sat,' recollected Dr Paul Moore, Coadjutor Bishop of New York, of a meeting in 1964. 'This, the power to evoke the Presence, is, it seems to me, his greatest gift.'[3] Like St Paul, he was absolutely certain that he was chosen by God to do His work; and that, being chosen, he would be given the needed strength to accomplish the task. Like St Paul again, he knew that God's work was for all mankind – not just the Jews, but for Jews and Gentiles alike. He had a fearless approach to God. He was not inhibited by

---

[1] F. Raymond Dyer to Clayton, 418 Olive Street, St Louis, Mo., 10th March, 1964.
[2] Anderson to Clayton, The Secretary of the Treasury, Washington, 9th December, 1958, 19th February, 1960.
[3] Bishop Moore to the Author, 27th December, 1964.

hesitancy or reserve. As Father Graham has pointed out, it was perfectly natural to him to see God at work wherever men were living; and, seeing, he would regard it as perfectly natural to speak with God, as a man might converse with a friend. Mr Vincent Massey has recorded how he once went to All Hallows to see what had been accomplished there under Clayton's leadership, and was taken by the Vicar into the small chapel in the crypt: '. . . and before I knew it, I was kneeling at the altar with him (no one else was in the Chapel but ourselves). He started to pray, in almost conversational tones, without any self-consciousness whatever, talking about what was happening, with a combination of intimacy and reverence. It was very moving.'[1]

Indeed it was by prayer that Clayton kept his contact with God: and to illustrate this he would tell a story of his childhood at a farmhouse in Somerset near his mother's home. Mrs Clayton would read to her sons of an evening, then lead them up to bed. On one dark and stormy night she led the three boys up the stairs; she held Jack's hand, who in turn held Hugh's, who in turn held little Philip's. As they walked thus in single file down the dark and draughty hall and up the stairs, lit only by one candle, the smallest boy, aged five, felt through Hugh's hand a warm and secure contact with his mother. But on the stairs Philip lost his brother's hand, and panic closed in on him. He had lost his mother. With fear clutching at him he ran forward until he had caught his brother's hand and was safe again in his contact with his mother. He used to compare this childish experience to contact with God, likening his mother's hand to prayer. 'Prayer', he would say, 'is the helping hand needed by us all to maintain our contact with God.'[2]

Being thus convinced of the immense importance of prayer, Clayton would frequently compose intercession for special occasions. Thus when in 1960 that intrepid yachtsman, Francis Chichester, a Vice President of Toc H, set forth in Gypsy Moth III on the first single-handed trans-Atlantic yacht race, the padre christened the craft in Beaulieu River and said a special prayer for his friend the night before the start.

[1] Massey to the Author, Batterwood House, Port Hope, Ontario, 26th November, 1964.
[2] I am grateful to Mr John R. Severance of the United States of America for telling me of this story.

May God preserve Her Majesty The Queen and every loyal servant of her Realm, especially tonight our mutual friend named Francis Chichester of Gypsy Moth III, proceeding on the morrow to the Main. May God speed the bonnie boat like a bird on the wing and over the sea to her appointed haven. The sailors here cry 'Onward in God's name'.

Father, be with us in this gallant friendship. Give Francis guidance from Thy Holy Spirit. We ask this through thy Name above all names. Amen.

And when six years later Chichester set out on his even more daring exploit in Gypsy Moth IV, he and his wife came to Tower Pier where his friend conducted a service of blessing upon the enterprise. And when the wonderful feat of a solo voyage round the world was successfully accomplished, Dr Clayton paid tribute to Sir Francis Chichester in lines from the poet Clough, only a few of which can be quoted here:

Go from the east to the west, as the sun and the stars direct thee.
Go, with the girdle of man, go and encompass the earth.
Not for the gain of the gold; for the getting, the hoarding, the having,
But for the joy of the deed; but for the duty to do.
Go with the spiritual life, the higher volition and action,
With the great girdle of God, go and encompass the earth.

It would be hard to find words to pay a more eloquent tribute to the spirit of this gallant enterprise than Clough's noble poem from which these few lines are taken.

Just because the priest was so near to God, so completely sure of God, he could venture to take the same sort of liberties in speaking to or of Him as we associate with St Teresa. And if he could take liberties with God, he could surely also take them with men. Thus he ruthlessly pressed people into his service demanding their complete allegiance, for his work was God's work, and God's work must be done. Father Graham once told of an occasion when Clayton, armed with a letter of introduction to some stiff, courteous, but bored pro-consul, proceeded unabashed to propose to this icy front a plan for him to preside at a Toc H meeting the next evening. Little by little, a grudging consent was obtained, and the faultlessly-attired magnifico duly did as he was asked. In his opening remarks he quoted from *Alice Through The Looking Glass*: 'I always thought Padre Clayton was some sort of fabulous monster,' he declared; 'but now I find myself driven to say, as the Unicorn said to Alice, 'Now we have seen each other, if you'll believe in me, I'll believe in you".'

Dr Paul Moore had a similar experience when he first met the padre in 1944. They were lunching together at the Century Club in New York when Clayton told him of the tragic plight of the slum priests who had had no holiday since the war. 'Wouldn't it be grand if some fine young Americans could relieve these men for the Lord's business?' Moore replied that that sounded like a fine idea; then the two men went on to talk of other matters. The next day Clayton begged Moore to call on him. 'Sit down, old man, glad to see you, glad to see you. See here, I have put you in charge of recruiting sixty or seventy fine young Americans from all over the country to go to London on the business of the Lord we discussed last night. You can book their passages, supervise the whole thing, and get them home again. I know so and so at the Cunard Company – there will be no problem – just call him and say Tubby needs the space. . . . Paul, old man, I can't tell you how grateful I am for all this. Now we will have a prayer.' The prayer ended, the victim spluttered forth his regrets that he was unqualified, busy, that the scheme was impracticable, ill thought-out, unreasonable. But remonstrance was useless; the work was the Lord's and therefore must be done; and Paul Moore must do it. And Paul Moore did it!

Father Richard Barnes of the House of the Resurrection, Mirfield, has recorded another incident of the same kind. In November 1937, he wrote to John Graham, who had recently 'had the very rare experience of accompanying a mystic in the dark night of the soul'. Unlike Graham, Barnes knew Clayton only slightly and had not heard from him for some time. Then, out of the blue, had come a brief note, 'a scrawl from a battleship' – H.M.S. *Codrington*, of which he had been made chaplain at the invitation of the Commander-in-Chief of the Mediterranean Fleet, Admiral Fisher – asking him to write a service for the Toc H coming-of-age festivities, and referring him to Pat Leonard. Barnes demurred: in the first place he was too high church; and then he disagreed with the whole plan. Toc H should, in his view, forget about its festivities and 'first think in greater terms of dedication'. He voiced his doubts to Leonard, who replied: 'Tubby has written to ask you to do it; and he is *generally right.*' Whereupon both men accepted at once and without further hesitation, and Barnes proceeded without more ado to sketch out the theological implications and outlined the service. And he added: 'I have several times been told of its appropriateness and use.' 'He is a man', Barnes wrote to Graham, 'who moves on a plane of activity of quite a different character to that of most of us. He is the genuine poet and his poesy's insight expresses itself in swift and effective action and occasionally in words. – His urge to action is that of the Spirit, the image, or the prophets. "Thus said the Lord."'[1]

Then again, Mr Vincent Massey has recalled how, when Clayton stayed at Government House during his Governor-Generalship, many people, including his secretaries, were commandeered to help the padre in his mission; and they were still immersed in the tasks that had been assigned to them long after he had left Ottawa. But, as Massey is careful to add, you could be quite sure that everyone who was enlisted to help him was happy to be associated with his affairs. Such was the magnetism of the man. Another distinguished Canadian, the man who followed Massey at Government House, Ottawa, had similar memories of Clayton: 'It is not easy to write about Tubby Clayton the apostle – he is unique. There will not be another,' wrote Major-General Vanier, the former A.D.C. to Lord Byng, more than forty years later. 'A happy disciple, I have followed his work with affectionate admiration during the half century that the lamp of Toc H has been burning. God has been good to him – he has been a reaper as well as a sower. The little tree of Poperinghe has become the great cedar of Lebanon. It was planted, pruned and watered by him. Christ said: "Ye shall know them by the fruit they yield." The tree has thrown out branches which have reached beyond the seas bearing the good fruit in Commonwealth lands of Her Majesty: it will not wither, it will not be cut down.'[2]

[1] Barnes to Graham, House of the Resurrection, Mirfield, Yorkshire, November 4th, 1937.
[2] Vanier to the author, Government House, Ottawa, July 1965.

R

One great asset was his remarkable sense of humour, for he had an engaging and amusing way with him that enlivened all he said and did. Stories of his Puckish humour are legion, for he would poke fun at the over-solemn, prick the bubble of pomposity (especially in a fellow-cleric), illumine the most serious discussions with mirth, and drag forth into the light of day realities that were becoming tangled and choked in the undergrowth of theory. He, more perhaps than anyone of recent times, did indeed walk with God yet retain the common touch. 'One of the most shattering statements made about Jesus', Father Graham wrote, 'is contained in the six words "He knew what was in men·"' At an infinitely far remove, these words, with tremendous modifications, spring to the mind in thinking of Tubby Clayton. In so far as they could be applied at all, they are true because he was first and foremost a disciple of His Master.'[1]

His positive genius for friendship, too, must not be overlooked, for he brought it into literally thousands of homes. 'I am sure', writes Mr Coleman Jennings, the distinguished American banker, 'that if the fortunate legion who were the recipients of this particular gift were asked what they regarded as his most impressive attribute, they would say that it was his genius for friendship. His keen mind, his restless imagination, his qualities of leadership, his mastery of the written word, his relentless selfspending of all his powers, were all dedicated to and channelled through those who had become his friends.'[2] And those friends were in every walk of life. Jennings recalls how he once introduced to the padre the lift-man in a London hotel where he was staying. During their brief ascent, Clayton engaged the man in a protracted conversation which went on long after they had reached their destination – regardless of the persistent rings from those kept waiting for the lift – with the result that such a bond was established between them that, for ever after, this porter would ask Mr Jennings about 'the most remarkable man he had ever met'.

At the same time he was a very humble man, frequently choleric, but always anxious to do penance the instant the mood was past. Mr Jennings gives a remarkable example of this, told to him by his friend, the saintly Brother Douglas of the Society of St Francis of

[1] Graham to the author, December, 1964.
[2] Jennings to the author, 29th January, 1965.

Assisi. Once when he was passing through London, Brother Douglas decided that he would drop in on his old friend on Tower Hill. Clayton's secretary, asked by this honoured and familiar person in his Franciscan garb whether the Vicar was at home, said that he was, and bade the visitor go straight up to his study. A morose 'come in' greeted the knock on the door; and when Brother Douglas entered he was met with a tirade: 'How did you get up here? I gave strict instructions to my secretary that I could see nobody while I was working on an article that positively must be completed this evening. I have no time for talking.' The humble Brother Douglas made his apologies and turned away; but before he could close the door behind him, he was summoned back into the room. 'Please forgive me, dear Brother Douglas,' he begged; 'I'm not worthy to have a friend like you.' Then, kneeling before his visitor, he implored him to place his hand on his head, forgive him and give him his blessing. 'That was our Tubby,' commented Jennings: 'inconsiderate, impetuous, arrogant perhaps, irascible, but at the same time on his knees, as humble as a penitent little child.' Mandell Creighton once defined life as an opportunity for loving, and Clayton's life was spent precisely in living out that opportunity at every level. Hundreds of bereaved parents and wives found in him a creative urge to cherish the nobility of men's souls, and transmit that nobility to future generations in practical service. Hundreds of Christians, making their progress from this world to that which is to come, found in him a Great-heart to conduct them on their pilgrimage. 'By the end of the 1914 war everyone in Britain thought Tubby Clayton was a great man,' wrote Sir Francis Chichester, 'now we know he is not only that but also generous, compassionate, and piercingly perceptive of the human soul. And with all this a charming companion.'[1]

Yet Clayton had one great drawback. He was not successful with women. Though we have seen how he was loved and admired by the Alexander sisters, how he loved them with a pure platonic affection, it cannot be gainsaid that with the opposite sex he lacked the common touch. The Alexanders were members of a rich and influential family. He was at home with the wealthy, the noble, and particularly with royalty. Thus he wold fre-

---

[1] Chichester to the author, 9th January, 1968.

quently tell the author that the two most remarkable women
he had ever met were the late Queen Mary, and Queen Elizabeth
the Queen Mother. The former, he was fond of saying, showed a
would-be martinet how to become a democratic sovereign beloved
by his people; and the latter aided her reluctant, retiring and
constitutionally weak husband to shoulder the burden so unexpectedly left him by his elder brother. As all impartial witnesses
will admit, both wives were remarkably successful. But on women
of less exalted station he made small impact; indeed, many found
him difficult and tiresome in the home, inconsiderate about such
mundane matters as meal times, and thoughtless on what he
doubtless regarded as the trivial matters of the home. It is perhaps
strange that a man who could have so vast an influence on all
strata of male society, should prove so inadequate with all women
save those of the highest standing.

Of his impact on men there can be no question.

'I will always admire, love and treasure the memory of Tubby
Clayton,' wrote Dr Thomas H. Wright, Bishop of East Carolina;
'one of God's great troubadours – a gallant disciple of Jesus
Christ.'[1]

As his seventy-fourth birthday approached in the autumn of
1962 Clayton retired from All Hallows, to be succeeded by Canon
Colin Cuttell. He had been Vicar for forty years. On hearing this
rather sad news, the Queen Mother sent him a message of warm
good wishes, adding how much she was – even at that early date –
looking forward to the Jubilee Year Toc H Celebrations in 1965.[2]
This was tactful, for she knew very well, as did all his closest
friends, that Philip Clayton was living for the occasion when, with
suitable pageantry, they would commemorate the fiftieth anniversary of that notable day in 1915 when he opened the Old House
in Poperinge.[3]

The eagerly-awaited Jubilee Celebrations were held at
Poperinge during the week-end of 18th June. On Saturday there
were receptions, first at the beautifully decorated Town Hall,
Festzaal, when the Burgomaster of Poperinghe made Clayton a

---

[1] Wright to the author, 23rd February, 1965.

[2] Gilliat to Clayton, Clarence House, 3rd November, 1962. H.M. Queen Elizabeth,
the Queen Mother's Clarence House Papers.

[3] Now spelt without the h.

Freeman of the town – the first person to be so honoured for forty years; and then at Ypres when the Burgomaster presented him with the town's highest award, the 'Medal of Honour'. Wreaths were laid at the Belgian war memorials in both towns, and a special Jubilee Toc H Lamp was presented to the town of Poperinge. The Lamp already owned by Ypres was used for the Ceremony of Light in the Cloth Hall. A great garden-party was held in Talbot House, when the guests were entertained by St Stanislas' College Youth Band, some eighty strong, gaily clad in their green hats and ties, white shirts and black shorts. Tea was served by a team of volunteer Belgian ladies; and the *pièce de résistance* was a giant four-tiered sugar-coated cake.

The visitors attended the usual ceremony at Menin Gate, simple but most impressive. The procession of some three hundred was headed by the Ypres Town Band, a wreath was laid on behalf of Toc H, and four bugles sounded the Last Post. Afterwards, Dr Clayton addressed the company from the ramparts above the town; this was followed by prayers and the Nunc Dimittis in St George's Church, crowded to the doors.

On Sunday a procession was formed from Poperinge Town Hall to the new *Toc H Straat* – it leads from a cemetery into Future Lane! – headed by the Band of the Royal Fusiliers followed by the Padre in an open car, and a vast crowd of visitors and locals to witness the unveiling of the small plaque at the road-side which records that the street was opened by the Reverend Philip Clayton on 20th June, 1965.

In the evening a solemn Te Deum was sung in the Church of St Bertin before a congregation of over a thousand. The Bishop of Bruges with attendant priests, gorgeously attired in golden vestments, Clayton resplendent in his scarlet robes as Doctor of Divinity, and attended by Canon Cuttell his successor at All Hallows, other Anglican priests in cottas and cassocks, and two English Free Church ministers in their black Geneva gowns, went in procession to the brilliantly-lighted High Altar. Before the Te Deum, a psalm was sung – 'Praise the Lord'; and a hymn specially written for the occasion – 'O Mary, our town will in loud Magnificats always praise Thy high protection'. Finally, 'Abide with me' was sung jointly in Flemish and English by the whole congregation.

When the Bishop addressed the company from the Sanctuary, he dwelt on Poperinge's pride at being the birth-place of the Movement that, from small beginnings, had in half a century grown so that it reached all over the world. He spoke movingly of the work of the movement and of its founder whose eightieth birthday was only a few weeks away. He spoke too of the unifying effect that it had on men of goodwill the world over. 'In Toc H', he said, 'there are members of the Roman Catholic Church. In Toc H there are members of other Christian churches and Communities. In Toc H there are members of non-Christian religions and many men of goodwill: to all of them Toc H says – Let all this that is best in you grow and increase.' And he commented on the great gathering in St Bertin's Church that evening. 'The leaders of Toc H have asked the head of the Catholic Church in this town, the cradle of their movement, to accompany them in thanksgiving to God on the fiftieth anniversary of the foundation of the movement. They have asked the Bishop of this See to pray with you and with them to God for His grace . . . My brothers, let us with one heart raise our song of thanks. Let us pray that for all victims of both wars the vision of the prophet of the Apocalypse may be true: "And lo, a Lamb stood upon the Mount Sion, and with Him an hundred and forty four thousand, having His name and the name of His Father written on their foreheads."'

Edmund Blunden, who was present, in the stanzas he wrote shortly afterwards felicitously commemorated this meeting of churches in honour of the Founder Padre:

> Shall we not also join the friends
> Of Clayton (Rev. of Reverends)
> And see how far his sway extends?
>
> For there are Doings: Jubilee
> Of what this Padre longed to see
> In old War One grow like a tree
>
> Out of the fearful crash of fates,
> – The grim gun-quarrel at the gates
> Of gentlest towns; and now those hates

Have sunk from sight. Here, here we stare
Across the old loved perilous square,
And (eighty) Dr Clayton's there.

Poperinge and leper both acclaim
Clayton and all who with him came,
And feast us in the halls of fame.

Behold the man; he robed is set
In great St Bertin's grandeur yet,
And Church with Church for him has met.

On Monday morning, before returning to England, the party
visited Kemmel, with brief stops at Tyne Cot and St Julien, and
prayers were said at Gilbert Talbot's grave in Sanctuary Wood.
Thus ended a memorable week-end commemorating a notable
anniversary. 'What a heritage we have received!' commented one
of those present: 'What a heritage we are handing on!'[1]

Less than a year later, on May 13th, 1966, the Queen, accompanied by the Duke of Edinburgh and King Baudouin of the
Belgians, visited Talbot House. They were greeted at the Birth-
place of Toc H by its Vice-Patron the Hon. Angus Ogilvy, by
Jack Trefusis, Sylvain Lahaye (President and Secretary of the
Talbot House Association), and by Burgomaster De Sagher, who
conducted them to the Upper Room. There they were received by
Dr Clayton – 'frail but indomitable', as *The Times* put it, following
a spell in hospital – who told his guests the story of the beloved
Chapel. A Garden Party followed, at which many of those
invited, both Belgian and British, were presented. Then the royal
guests signed the Visitors' Book, and the Queen presented Talbot
House with a signed photograph of herself and Prince Philip.
That done, she went on to Ypres to hear the Last Post at the Menin
Gate.

Thus ended a happy and memorable day in the eventful life
of the Movement that had had its birth fifty years previously in
that 'home for Jesus Christ in Flanders'.[2]

It can also be said to have completed the great work of the
Founder of that Movement. It is a noble and a fitting memorial to

[1] Jackson, *Poperingem Jubilee Celebrations,* Toc H Journal, September 1965.
[2] Toc H Journal, March 1958.

him, a memorial to keep his memory green for many years to come. His Epitaph, written by himself, may close this account of his earthly pilgrimage.

> Lord Jesu, Redeemer,
> Wilt wake an old dreamer?
> Of workers the weakest,
> Of liegemen the least,
> Of faint-hearts most faithless,
> Of Saints' scars too scatheless –
> Wilt robe in Redemption, a fool for thy Feast?

Index